IRISH FAIRY STORIES FOR CHILDREN

if can not
return to people
call this number
343-0454
or bring to
this house
431 Fiar Ave.
N.W. 4th stre
et

Irish Fairy Stories for Children

EDMUND LEAMY

ILLUSTRATED BY

FRANK & GAIL DOWLING

Calliannie Dixon
2-A1
Calliannie D
2-A1

THE MERCIER PRESS

The Mercier Press
P.O. Box 5, 5 French Church Street, Cork
24 Lower Abbey Street Dublin 1

This selection © The Mercier Press, 1979
Second edition, reset, 1983
This edition 1992

ISBN 1 85635 008 8

Printed in Ireland by Colour Books Ltd.

Contents

The Fairy Minstrel of Glenmalure

I

The Little Minstrel

Kathleen and Eamonn were under the beech tree that stood in the hollow down near the stream. Kathleen sat against the tree trunk, stitching the sleeve of her dolly's dress. Eamonn was lying on his back, his hands under his head, his cap down on his forehead, and his eyes closed.

'Eamonn, do you believe,' asked Kathleen, 'that there are any real live fairies now?'

'I don't know,' said Eamonn, scarcely moving his lips.

Just then a beech nut fell and hit him on the nose. He opened his eyes, started up, looked above him, and saw, sitting on the fork of the tree, a little man, about twice the size of your finger. He wore a little, three-cornered black

hat with a red plume in it, a little black coat and a red waistcoat, a little yellow knee-breeches and white stockings, and little black shoes with gold buckles.

'Oh! you don't, don't you?' said the little man. And, without another word, he took a little reed out of his pocket and began to blow from it bubble after bubble as beautiful as the wing of a dragonfly in the sunlight.

'Are they soap bubbles, Eamonn?' asked Kathleen.

'Soap bubbles!' returned Eamonn. 'How could they be soap bubbles, you goosie? Sure, he has no soap, and he has no water.'

Then the little man blew another bubble, still more beautiful, which was about half as big as himself. He hopped on to this, and the bubble floated away with him over the meadow and across the stream and up into the wood.

'Well, in all my born days, I never saw the like of that before,' said a magpie that had flown down close to where the children were. But they had not seen him, so engaged were they in watching the little fairy man sailing way.

'Oh, Eamonn,' said Kathleen, 'look! There is a single magpie.'

'There are some little girls that I know,' said

another voice, 'who are in a very great hurry to speak sometimes.'

And Mrs Magpie hopped down beside Mr Mag.

'There are two magpies now,' said Eamonn, 'and two are for luck.'

'True for you,' said Mr Mag, 'and both of you are in luck today.'

'Who was that little man?' said Eamonn to the Mag.

'He is Fardarrig, the fairy minstrel of Glenmalure,' said the Mag.

'And what tune was he playing?' asked Kathleen.

'He was playing *The Wind in the Reeds*,' answered Mrs Mag. 'It is a very sweet tune, but it is very sad, and it always makes me cry,' said she, while a tear dropped from her eye. 'Dear me,' she went on, 'I am sorry I left my little lace handkerchief at home,' and she put her head under her wing to dry her tears.

Mr Mag chuckled, and got a fit of coughing that almost choked him. When he recovered, he said:

'It is a sad tune, indeed. But, oh! if you could hear him playing *The Bees among the Blossoms* you would never tire of listening to it.'

'Where could we hear him playing that?' asked Eamonn.

'If you go round there to the sunny side of the wood,' said the Mag, 'and go in through the first mossy pathway you meet, maybe you won't be long till you find him.'

'Oh, come on, Eamonn!' said Kathleen.

And the children ran off, hand-in-hand, as fast as they could.

When they were gone, Mrs Mag began to peck and peep around the foot of the beech tree.

'Dear me!' said she, 'how forgetful some children are, to be sure.'

'Why, what have you got there?' said Mr Mag.

'Kathleen's silver thimble, which she left after her.'

'Well, there is no use in leaving it there after you,' said he.

'No,' said Mrs Mag, 'and you would never know when it would come in useful.'

Snatching up the thimble, she and Mr Mag, like the pair of thieves that they were, flew off to their nest.

In the meantime, the children had got round to the sunny side of the wood, and they soon came to a pathway that was all aglow in the sunshine. They ran up this till a little rabbit ran across their way.

'Oh, let us catch the rabbit, Kathleen!' cried Eamonn.

And the two rushed after the rabbit, when, all of a sudden, they heard a voice saying:

'Oh, botheration to you, for a little rabbit, you nearly knocked me down.' And who was it that spoke but one of the nicest little old Grannies you could see in a day's walk. She had a little three-legged stool in her right hand.

'Dearie me,' said she, addressing the children. ''Tis I am glad to see you, darlings, and now will you come and help me find my little Kerry cow with the black silk coat and the silver horns?'

'Oh! we will indeed,' said the children, and the three tripped away together.

'I hear someone whispering over there,' said Kathleen.

'That is the stream whispering to the brambles,' said Eamonn.

'I hear a little weeny bell,' said Kathleen.

'That's the Kerry,' said the little woman. And they had not gone far when they saw the little cow.

'Oh, Eamonn! Eamonn! did you ever see

such a little moo cow? She would almost fit in my Noah's Ark,' said Kathleen; and no wonder she said it, for the cow was only a little bigger than their black pussy-cat at home, and each of her silver horns was nearly as long as herself.

When the Kerry saw them, she trotted up.

'Well! Well! What a lot of trouble you have given me,' said the little woman. 'Go straight home before me now.' And the little cow went on crying 'moo, moo-oo', while her little bell kept tinkling.

'Is she saying "I'm sorry"?' asked Kathleen.

'Oh, she is very ready to say that,' said the little woman.

'And does she really be sorry?' returned Kathleen.

'Not always, I'm afraid,' said Granny.

'That's the way with a little girl I know,' said Eamonn.

'I hope he does not mean you, Kathleen,' said the little woman.

'No; it's another little girl that we play with sometimes,' said Kathleen.

By this time, they had come up near Granny's cottage, and the little cow stopped in front of the lovely little summerhouse, covered all over with creepers and beautiful blue and white and golden-coloured flowers. Then the little woman put down the stool and the little milking-pail.

'Now, Miss Kathleen,' said she, 'would you like to milk my little Kerry cow?'

'Will you show me how?' asked Kathleen.

The little woman did, and then Kathleen began to milk; and the little cow was so pleased that she never switched her tail – although the midges were tormenting her – lest she might frighten Kathleen.

Suddenly they heard the sound of music. Eamonn looked to see where it came from, and what should he see but the little fairy minstrel of Glenmalure sitting on a ferny bank playing on his little reed.

'Oh, what is he playing now?' asked Eamonn.

'He is playing *Cailín deas cruidhte na mbó* "The pretty girl milking the cows".'

'I never heard that before,' said Eamonn.

'Of course you never did,' said Granny, 'nor did anyone else. He is making it up now in honour of Miss Kathleen; but it will be sung everywhere yet all over Erin by the milkmaids in the sunset on the summer eves.'

Well, when the cow was milked –

'Come with me now into the summerhouse,' said the little woman. 'I have the nicest griddle-bread you ever tasted, and the biggest and the sweetest blackberries, and you never drank any cream that is half so rich as this milk.'

'Could the little minstrel man come with us?' asked Eamonn.

'My darling boy,' cried the little woman, 'that's the very thing I would like, for I never let a minstrel pass my door, and have never sent one empty-handed away.'

'Can we both go and bring him in?' asked Kathleen.

'Of course, dearest,' said the little woman, kissing Kathleen, 'and I'll go and get ready the griddle-bread.'

The two children ran towards the little minstrel, who popped down from the bank and doffed his little plumed cap.

'Will you come and lunch with ourselves and Granny?' said Kathleen.

'I shall be delighted, my lady,' said the little man, bowing almost to the ground. He walked between the two children, who kept well out from him lest they might tread on him; for he was hardly as high as the top of Eamonn's boot.

As they entered the summerhouse, the little

woman cried: 'Welcome, and welcome again, Fardarrig!'

Then the whole four of them sat down at the table; but two chairs had to be set for the little man, one on top of the other, so as to bring him above the level of the table.

The children said they had never tasted such griddle-bread in their lives, and as to the blackberries, they were as big as plums and melted in the mouth. The cream, too, was simply delicious, and when they had partaken of these, the little woman said:

'Dearie me! there is something I forgot. Could you guess, Kathleen, what it is?'

'I don't know,' said Kathleen, 'unless it is honey.'

'The very thing,' said Granny, 'and I am so sorry.'

'I know what I would like,' said Eamonn, looking shyly at the little minstrel.

'And what is it?' asked Granny.

'I would like to hear another tune from the little minstrel.'

'Oh, you would, would you?' said Fardarrig, blushing, and quite pleased. 'What would you like?'

'Will you play *The Bees among the*

Blossoms?' asked Eamonn.

'With the greatest pleasure,' said the little minstrel, and he took out the little reed from his pocket.

At first, the children could scarcely hear any sound, but the most wonderful perfume filled the summerhouse as of numberless sweet-scented flowers. But soon they began to hear a faint drowsy hum, something like that which they were wont to hear up in the top boughs of the sweet-blossomed lime tree that grew near their house. As they listened, the sound seemed to come nearer and nearer, and to shape itself into the most exquisite melody. As it sank into their ears and into their hearts, the children stood as if they were fascinated, their eyes wide open watching the little man. They hardly dared to breathe lest they might miss a note of the bewitching music. And they would have so stood for ever, if the little man had not finished playing and put the reed in his pocket.

Then he popped off the chair, and he said:

'I must be going. I see a crow out there from Glenmalure. I know he is from Glenmalure by the twist of his tail, and if I catch him in time he will give me a lift home. So goodbye to you all now, and may good luck attend you and bles-

sings shower down on you, but don't come further with me than the door, lest the crow would hear you, and take himself off.'

When they came to the door, the little minstrel doffed his plumed cap and kissed goodbye to Kathleen. Then he trod lightly on the tops of the blades of grass until he came to where the crow was pecking away. Before the crow knew where he was, my bold little minstrel hopped up, stretched himself flat on his back, and put his head on the crow's poll, which made him a very comfortable pillow.

'Caw! caw! caw!' said the crow. And up he flew to where a long line of other crows were sailing away between the south and the west, and he followed after them. As he went up, the little man once more took the reed from his pocket and began to play, and the fairy music floated down to the children.

'He is playing again,' said Kathleen.

'He is,' said Eamonn, 'and I know what he is playing.'

'What is it?' asked the little woman.

'*Over the Hills and Far Away*,' said Eamonn. And it was.

II

The Little Outlaws

Then Granny and the children went back again into the summerhouse.

'Oh, my!' said Kathleen, as she saw the table.

'Honey, Eamonn! Honey! Where do you think it came from?'

'Where do *you* think it came from?' asked the little woman.

'I don't know,' replied Kathleen.

'Neither do I,' said Eamonn, 'unless it was the bees amongst the blossoms that we heard in the little man's music that brought it to us.'

'You have guessed right, Eamonn, asthore,' said she.

'But why did we not see the bees?' asked Kathleen.

'Because you could not take your eyes off the fairy minstrel's face,' said the little woman.

'That's really true,' said Kathleen. 'I thought my eyes were fastened to his.'

'I thought so, too,' said Eamonn.

Well, then, they had the honey, and such

honey! No mortal children had ever tasted its like before.

When they had eaten it, the children whispered to each other, and Granny noticed them:

'What is it?' she asked, 'speak out and don't be afraid.'

The children looked at each other shyly, and then Eamonn said with a smile:

'We would like to take some of it home to little mother.'

'We would,' said Kathleen. 'We always like to bring her home flowers and sweets, and everything that's nice.'

'You shall bring her home the honey too,' said Granny.

And from a little cupboard in the corner she took two dainty little baskets, woven of green fragrant rushes. She packed the honeycombs in every so neatly.

'Now,' said she, 'I am sure you would like to get home to your little mother.'

'We would,' said Kathleen, 'and we thank you for a very happy day.'

'I can only go a little bit of the way with you,' said Granny, 'for I want to take some milk to a poor lone widow who lives on the side of the mountain; but I will put you on the right track, and when you are once on it, don't stop to look at anything, or maybe you'd get into trouble.'

The three started off from the summerhouse, but soon they heard 'Moo! moo!' behind them, and who came trotting up but the little Kerry cow.

'She wants to come with us,' said Kathleen. 'May she?'

'She wants to do more, I think,' said Granny. 'I know her.'

'What is it?' asked Kathleen.

Before Granny could answer, the little Kerry had put one of her silver horns under the handle of Kathleen's basket, and the other under Eamonn's.

'That's what she wants – to carry the baskets for you,' said the little woman. The Kerry, as proud as possible, marched along between the two children, her little bell tinkling musically all the time. When it came to the turn where they had to part, Granny put them on the right track. She kissed them and blessed them before she said goodbye. They kissed her, and they patted and thanked the little Kerry for carrying the baskets. Then catching each other's hands, the two of them sped away.

They had not gone very far when Kathleen

saw hanging from the branch of a tree something like a long pocket or stocking.

'Oh, Eamonn, Eamonn,' she cried, pulling him by the hand, and checking him. 'What is that growing on the tree?'

'Come on, come one, did not the little woman tell you not to stop?'

'Yes; but what is it?' said Kathleen.

'I think it is a wasp's nest,' said Eamonn.

It was, but what was worse still, the wasps had caught the delicious scent of the honey, and they swarmed out of the nest in thousands round the children, and their angry buzzing said: 'We'll sting you to death! we'll sting you to death!'

Eamonn put his arm round Kathleen's neck, and pulled her to him to try and shield her from the wasps who kept on buzzing: 'We'll sting you to death! we'll sting you to death!'

The children thought they almost felt the stings, when they heard a voice crying:

'Will you sting them to death? Charge, my gallant knights, and don't leave a wasp alive!'

Like the rush of leaves speeding before the blast, hundreds of little horsemen in silver armour, with little green silk cloaks fluttering on their shoulders, some armed with little

swords and some with lances half as long as knitting-needles, charged on the wasps, and cut and slashed and thrust at them. In a few seconds, hundreds and thousands of wasps were lying dead and dying on the ground. The little woman, hearing the noise of battle and suspecting danger to the children, rushed back and pulled them out of the thick of the fight, and told them to remember the sting of a dying wasp was worse than the sting of a live one.

When the wasps were all killed or put to flight, the little horsemen formed their ranks; and with their captain, little Prince Golden Hair, at their head, they marched towards the little woman and the children.

'Welcome, Prince Golden Hair! Welcome, my bonny outlaws of the woods of Glenmalure!' said the little woman. 'Now, after your hard fight and great victory, I am sure you all want a drink of milk, so come along and take it.'

So eager were they to get it, that they galloped right up against the little pail, and three of them fell over their horses' heads into the milk, and they would have been drowned if Granny had not been there to pull them out by the heels. Their captain, the Prince, was very much annoyed at this. He told them they should march round the pail in regular order, and as each passed by he was to dip his drinking horn into the milk.

Then each of the outlaws, taking a little silver horn from his belt, dipped it into the milk and drank it off. When all had finished, there was not a drop of milk less in the pail!

Then the little Prince spoke to Eamonn and Kathleen, and said he was glad he was in time to save their lives, and he was very sorry he could not send an escort home with them. But he could not do so, as he and his outlaws were bound to be back in Glenmalure before sunset.

'It is nearly that now,' said the little Prince, and he begged permission to kiss Kathleen's hand. Then shaking hands with Eamonn and with Granny, he ordered his trumpeters to play up a march. And to the music of their little trumpets, the fairy outlaws of Glenmalure marched up through the heather and over the hill, their little helmets glowing like rosy jewels in the light of the setting sun.

III

The Three Riddles

'Now, children,' said Granny, 'I wish I could go with you. But run as fast as ever you can, and don't look to the right or to the left until you get out of this enchanted wood. Blessings on you again, Eamonn, asthore, and on you, Kathleen, aroon,' and having hugged and kissed the two of them, she pushed them away from her, saying – 'Run for your bare lives.'

The children ran as hard as ever they could. One little turn more and they would be out of the wood. But just when they were close to this, and could see through the opening the fields and hills that they knew were near their own home, they heard a voice as of thunder and the crash of falling timber. With their hearts in their mouths they ran faster and faster, thinking it was a thunderstorm. A big tree crashed down on the pathway before them, followed by another sound as of thunder, and then a giant, almost as high as a tree, stepped out crashing and slashing the trees as he passed. It was his voice they mistook for the thunder. He had a huge club, all studded with iron bolts, and it was with this he was knocking down the trees, as a boy might knock down with his cane the weeds and thistles that came in his way. He had a huge paunch, and around it was a broad belt, and fastened to this was a wallet in which you could stow away a cow. A dead sheep was slung over his shoulders, her legs tied under his chin. He had only one eye, a horrible eye in the centre of his forehead; his nose was large, flat and broad, his nostrils as big as chimney tops, and his mouth as broad as a trap-door. Every one of his teeth was as long and as sharp as a scythe.

The children were nearly frightened to death when they saw the monster.

'Ho! ho! who have we here?' he shouted; and his voice rolled through the wood, and the trees trembled.

'Two children,' said Eamonn, 'who are going home to their little mother.'

'Home!' said the monster – 'home was never like this place!' and with one hand he grasped the two children, lifted them up, and dropped them down into his deep wallet.

When they were down in the bottom, the top

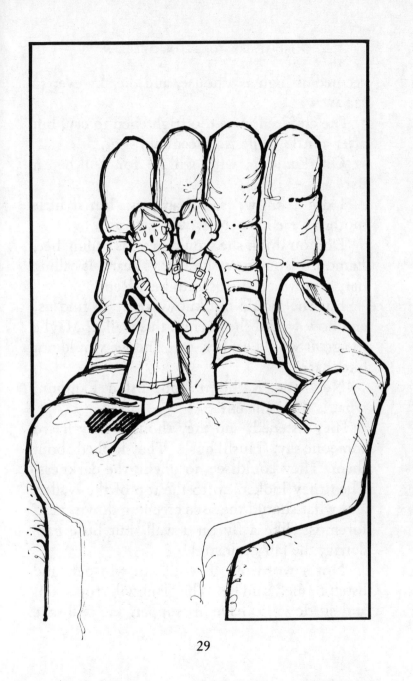

seemed as high as a house, and the sky ever so far away.

The children were too frightened to cry, but after a little while Kathleen said –

'Oh, Eamonn, what will he do? Will he eat us?'

'I don't know,' said Eamonn, 'but if little mother were here she would save us.'

'Do you think she would hear us calling her, Eamonn? You know she always heard us calling her, even when she used to be asleep.'

'But she would not know where to find us, and how would she get into this wallet? Maybe the giant would eat her, too, and we would not like that?'

'No,' said Kathleen, 'but listen Eamonn, what is that? Listen!'

They listened, and they thought they heard someone say, 'Hush! hush.' They looked about them. They could see no one in the darkness. Then they looked up to the top of the wallet, and what should they see creeping down, head foremost, like a fly on a wall, but little Fardarrig, the fairy minstrel.

'Not a word out of you; but whisper, and listen to me,' said he. 'The giant will stop soon, and sit down to have his supper. He will take the two of you out of this, and he will give you a chance for your lives. For he does that to all his prisoners. He will ask you, Eamonn, three riddles, and if you can answer all three right, he will let you go. If you can't, it will be all up with you,' said the little man, sadly.

'What are they?' said Eamonn.

'I am sorry to say,' answered the little man, 'I only know two he is sure to ask you. You must try to answer the third for yourself.'

'What are the two?' said Eamonn.

'The first is, "What is whiter than the snow of one night?" and the second is, "What is blacker than the blackest night?"'

'What are the answers to them?' asked Eamonn.

'I beg your pardon, Miss Kathleen,' said the little man, 'for whispering in the presence of a lady, but I am under a bond never to tell these answers to more than one person at the same time, and that person is under a bond never to tell them to anyone until he is asked the riddles by the giant. For if he should tell them, the giant would ask him other riddles which he could not answer, and he would be put to death.'

He whispered the two answers into

Eamonn's ear. Then he said aloud: 'I'm sorry, my poor Eamonn, I can't tell you the third answer, but if all goes to all, and you can't think of it, try and remember what children see in their dreams in the darkness. And now,' said he, 'I must go, for if the giant discovered me here, he would make me a prisoner for life. But keep up your hearts, and may blessings attend the two of you.'

The little man climbed up the wallet, and got away without the giant seeing him.

It happened as he had said. The giant stopped, and sitting down on a bank to prepare for supper, he plucked the dead sheep off his shoulder and cast it on the ground. Then he put his hand down in the wallet, brought up the children, and set them on the grass before him. Kathleen was very frightened, but Eamonn was trying to remember the answers to the riddles.

'Come now,' said the giant, 'before I cut you up for my supper, I will give you three chances for your lives. Do you know what a riddle is?' he said to Eamonn.

'I do,' said Eamonn.

'Well, I will ask you three riddles, and if you answer the three right, this club which I have stuck here in the ground will fall by itself without anyone touching it, and the moment it falls you must fly for your lives, or I might be tempted to forego my word. Are you ready?'

'Yes,' said Eamonn.

'First riddle, then,' said the giant. 'What is whiter than the snow of one night?'

'A soul without sin,' said Eamonn, repeating what the little minstrel had told him.

The giant's face became black.

'Second riddle,' he cried, in the angriest tone.

'What is blacker than the blackest night?'

'A heart without gratitude,' said Eamonn. The giant's face became blacker and blacker still.

'The third riddle,' said he, bellowing like a bull, 'and remember,' he roared, as if he wanted to frighten the wits out of poor Eamonn, 'on your answer depend your lives. What is brighter than the stars of night?'

Poor Eamonn was dumbfounded; he tried to think and to think.

'I'll give you two minutes to answer,' said the giant, and he pulled out from his pocket a watch that was as large as a frying-pan, and the face of it was as black as coal, and the hands of it were made from dead men's bones, and so also were the figures.

Kathleen nestled up to Eamonn, and the tears were stealing down her cheeks, and Eamonn was trying to think and think.

'One minute gone,' said the giant, and his voice sounded like a death-bell.

Eamonn began to think, and he thought of diamonds that he had seen sparkling; and he re-membered that he thought at the time they were brighter than stars, and he was going to say diamonds, but the diamonds don't shine in the darkness, and the stars do, and make it bright. So he did not say diamonds. Then he tried to think again.

'A minute and a half gone,' said the giant, and his face grew brighter and brighter, while poor Eamonn became more downcast, and his head drooped, and his heart sank, and Kathleen leaned against him like one bruised reed against another.

'A minute and three-quarters gone,' growled the giant, and his face became brighter and brighter.

Suddenly Eamonn pushed Kathleen back from him, while still holding her hand. He drew himself up till he was as straight as an uplifted lance, and he looked the giant defiantly in the face.

'I know it,' he said, and his little voice rang clear as a silver bell. For he had thought of what the little minstrel had told him – to try and remember what children see in their dreams in the darkness.

'What is it?' groaned the giant, and his face became black again, fearing that his prey was about to be lost to him. 'What are brighter than the stars of night?'

'A mother's eyes!' said Eamonn.

The club fell of itself, and groaned as if it were alive. The roar of the disappointed giant made the wood tremble. But Eamonn, dragging Kathleen along with him, rushed like the wind. They had scarcely got outside the enchanted wood, when they heard:

'Kathleen! Kathleen! Eamonn! Eamonn! where are you?'

'Eamonn! Eamonn! that is mother!' cried Kathleen.

'Hurrah, hurrah!' shouted Eamonn, and at the sound of the dear, sweet voice, their fears and terrors left them as the nightmare leaves the sleeper, awakening to the songs of the birds and the light of the rosy morning.

'Where, where have you been, my darlings?'

'Oh, mother, mother,' said Kathleen, as the

two children were crushed together within their little mother's arms, 'Eamonn told the giant that a mother's eyes are brighter than the stars of night, and now we know – don't we, Eamonn, that her voice is sweeter than the music of the Fairy Minstrel of Glenmalure?'

The Little Red Juggler

A long, long time ago a little thatched cottage stood on the side of a steep hill and looked down through a pleasant valley. Never anywhere did the bloom of the furze take on such a deep, rich golden hue; never anywhere were the purple of the heather and the green of the bracken so restful a sight for tired eyes, and never was a valley in all the world half so fair. Down the hill a little stream danced trippingly in and out through the pebbles, and sometimes over them, flashing as brightly all the time as a merry little maiden's eyes.

Sometimes you would think it was talking to the pebbles, and sometimes you would think it was whispering to itself, but you would never tire of listening to the music of its voice. When it came down and passed through the pleasant valley, it moved so gently that you would hardly notice its motion, and its voice sank so low you would have to strain your ears to catch its tone. But you knew it was moving because of the faint rustle amongst the rushes that here and there skirted its banks.

The little hut on the side of the hill looked like a bunch of roses flung on the mingled gold of the gorse and the purple of the heather, for roses grew all over it, and when the wind of the morning stirred them they tapped at the little window that lit the room where two wee girls were sleeping in the daintiest little white cot that ever was seen. The names of the two little girls were Gladys and Monona, and they lived there all the year round with their mother, whom they loved with all their heart.

But that didn't hinder them getting fond of the furze and the heather, and of the bees and the birds and the green waving woods that clothed both sides of the valley; above all, they were fondest of the bright little stream that danced away down the hill. They had no little playmate save it. It called to them first thing in the morning; they heard it babbling away when they got into their little nest at night, and it sang them to sleep with a drowsy tune. But they were very much troubled that they could not make out what it was saying to them, for they did not doubt it was trying to talk to them, as they used to talk to it, sometimes 'hushing' it, and telling it not to be so noisy, sometimes flinging a sprig of heather or a leaf upon it, and asking how far it would carry it.

One day, when it was babbling very loudly, Gladys said:

'I wish you'd tell us what you want to say?'

'Run down there below where it dips between the boulders, and you'll learn what it is saying.'

The children looked round to see who had spoken, but they saw nothing save a yellow-hammer flying off. But they went down all the same, and sure enough when they came to where the stream bustled through the boulders they heard it saying: 'Follow me! Follow me!'

'Oh, let us follow it, Gladys,' said Monona, and away they trotted after the stream. They followed it along its banks till they were stopped by a high grey rock up which the ivy had begun to trail, but they found their way around and up through the crevices, and after a little struggle they climbed to the top of the rock, and sat down there. A thick branch of a noble elm rested on the edge of the rock, as you might rest your arm on an armchair. Another branch, nearly as thick and round, stretched out free towards the wood.

The children had hardly seated themselves

when they heard a voice saying: 'One, two, three! Here goes to Fairyland!' and they looked, and on the other branch what should they see skipping along but a little brown squirrel. When he came to the tree, he took a hazel nut that was not quite ripe out of his pocket, and he knocked three times at the tree.

'Who is there?'

The children heard a little weeny, weeny voice from inside the elm tree.

'It's Brown Coat,' said the squirrel, 'and I'm off to Fairyland!'

Then a little door, like the door of a doll's house, opened in the tree, and the little brown squirrel popped in, and the door closed after him.

Well, the two children had their mouths open all the time wondering what was to happen next, when they heard again: 'One, two, three! Here's off to Fairyland!' and what should they see but a little grey squirrel; and what did he do but go up to the tree and take a nut out of his pocket, and knock – 'Rap! rap! rap!' until the little door was opened for him, and in he popped.

'I wonder where that little fellow went to?' said Gladys.

'Of course he's gone to Fairyland,' said Monona. 'Didn't he tell us he was going there.'

'One, two, three! Here's off to Fairyland!' and the children looked round again, and there was a little white squirrel with pink eyes tapping away at the tree. In answer to the little man inside, he said he was 'White Coat', and wanted to go to Fairyland, and, when the little door was opened, in he popped.

But the door was not closed after him as it had been after the others, and the children heard the little old man inside the tree say:

'Well, well, a great many people are coming here today, and I think I might as well keep the door open and look out.'

He stepped out from the tree on to the branch.

Such a funny little old man he was! He was hardly twice as big as your thumb. He was dressed all in green velvet, save his little white stockings and his black shoes, with little silver buckles. His cap was shaped like the fingers of the fox-glove, and at the peak of it there was a peal of little fairy bells, that sounded like faintly-heard far-off music.

When he stepped on the branch, he jerked his little head this way and then that, like a perky robineen. Then he put up his hand to his eyes to shade them from the sun, which pierced through the branches of the elm, and flashed straight towards the little door in front of which he was standing. In a second he saw the children, and as soon as he did he whipped off his little cap, and the music of the bells dropped round them like a shower.

'Why, you must be two little duchesses,' he said, as he bowed almost to the ground.

'We are not duchesses, Mr Man,' said Gladys. She was going to say 'little man', but she thought he mightn't like it.

'Well, then, you must be countesses, at least.'

'We are not countesses,' said Gladys.

'Well, who in the world are you?' said the little fellow, 'for the sun is in my eyes, your ladyships.'

'We're mammy's little children,' said Monona, who plucked up courage enough to speak when she saw what a civil little man he was, but all the same she nestled under Gladys' arm.

'Well, bless my soul!' said the little fellow, 'how silly I'm getting! Of course, you are mammy's little children. Who else could you be? Didn't I often see you playing up on the

43

hills amid the heather!' said he.

'Did you?' said Gladys. 'We never saw you.'

'Oh, that was because I wore the four-leaved shamrock,' said he, 'and that made me invisible.'

'Why did you do that?' asked Gladys.

'Because I was afraid of the bees,' said the little man, and he winked at Monona, 'and now I fear I am staying too long out here, and I must go back, but wouldn't you like to come to Fairyland for a little while?'

'Oh, we would,' cried the children together, 'but we wouldn't like to go without telling mother.'

'Can you write?' asked the little man.

'We can,' they replied.

'It's well for you,' said the little man, shaking his head very solemnly. 'I can't, for I neglected my schooling when I was young,' he said. 'I used to play truant, and instead of minding my lessons I used to go roaming through the woods and the gardens and over the moors, stealing the fruit from the beak of the blackbird, and the honey bags from the bees.'

'Is that the reason you are afraid of the bees?' said Monona.

''Tis,' said the little man, and he winked again

at Monona, and I am afraid Monona winked at him, 'but now here's notepaper for you.' He took out of his waistcoat pocket the daintiest little pocket-book ever you saw, and from this he brought out a little sheet of notepaper, no bigger than a postage stamp. He handed it to Gladys:

'Write, my lady, and tell your mother to wait for you here till you come back,' said he.

'Oh, you funny little man,' said Gladys, laughing, 'I always begin my letters, "My darling mammy", and the first letter, "M", would fill up the whole page.'

'Oh, but you never wrote with a pen like this,' said the little man, and he handed her a weeny pen with a crystal handle and a point of gold. 'Try now, my lady,' he said, and Gladys took the little pen in her hand and she tried to write a big 'M', but the little pen wouldn't do it; instead it wrote in golden ink the tiniest little letter 'M' you could see, and so on with all the other letters; and when she had finished –

'Now,' said the little man, smiling, 'you see you didn't fill up the page after all.'

'Then put in another basketful of kisses to mother,' said Monona – 'half for me and half for you.'

Gladys did, and then the little man gave her a tiny envelope.

'But how are we to send the letter?' asked Monona.

The little man, instead of answering her, cocked up his eye, and said:

'I saw you all the time, my gay buccaneer,' said he, 'with your head on one side, and you listening to every word the young ladies and myself have been saying.'

The children looked up, and what should they see on a branch over their heads but a robineen, and he looked as bold as you please.

'Take this,' said the little man, handing up the envelope to him, 'and be off with you!'

The robineen caught it in his beak, and away he flew.

'But how will he know where to go?' asked Gladys.

'He knows the place as well as yourself, my lady,' said the little man. 'Don't you remember putting the crumbs on the window-sill in the winter,' said he, 'and the robineen that used to pop on to it and peck away as if he hadn't a bit to eat for a twelvemonth?'

'And was that he?' said Monona.

'The very same,' said the little man, 'but he's

got so stout now that you'd hardly know him. Now if you're coming with me, let us go,' said the little man, and the three of them stepped along the branch until they came to the little door in the tree.

'All you have to do is to slidder down,' said the little man, and down they all slid together, and when they got out below, what was there waiting for the girleens but two little horses not much bigger than greyhounds? One was as black as the wing of a raven, and one was as white as driven snow, and the black one had golden shoes, and the white silver ones. Gladys jumped up on the white and Monona on the black.

'That's right,' said the little man, 'I wish I could go with you, but you know I must stay here to mind the door. All you have to do is to sit still, and the little horses will take you to the Fairy Queen's Palace; but don't stop them a second, for if you do you'll never get there.'

And kissing hands to the little man, off the children galloped, and they thought the little steeds were treading on air, and no wonder, for the blades of grass didn't give way under the little hooves. It was not long till they were galloping over a mossy pathway through a great forest, when, lo! in a little glade what should the children see but a little red man!

He was all in red, from the top of his head to the shoes on his feet. His head was red, and his eyebrows were red, and the little buttons on his jacket and the little buckles on his shoes were all of red gold. What was he doing but standing on his head and tossing up in the air with the soles of his feet ten little golden balls that, as they rose and fell, struck against each other, making the most musical sound that ever you heard. So wonderfully sweet was it that you felt you could stay listening to it all the day long; and the children, forgetting the advice of the little door-keeper, stopped their little horses to look and listen, till their hearts were filled with wonder and delight. Suddenly they were startled by a frightful barking and miowing, and what should sweep past them like the wind but the two hunters of the Woods of Darkness. One of them was a dog by day and a cat by night, and the other was a cat by day and a dog by night.

The little steeds were so frightened that they reared, and the children slipped off them, and away the little horses went through the wood. The little man had vanished like a spark of fire, and when the children recovered from their

49

fright, they did not know what to do or where to go.

But just then Gladys saw that the little red juggler had dropped three of the little gold balls, and these were hopping along of themselves and striking against each other, giving out the same delightful sounds as before, and the children were so taken with the music that they forgot their plight, and they followed on after the balls, and these hopped, and hopped, and hopped, until they came to a little cottage all covered with ivy, and its door was open, and in through the door the balls bounded.

The children stood as if they didn't like to follow them into the house; but in a second, out came a little woman no higher than your knee. She wore a little white cap, and a little black dress, and she had little gold spectacles on her nose, and she had so sweet-looking a face that anyone would trust her. She bade the children a hundred thousand welcomes, and she brought them inside, and she gave them such cakes and such fruit as were not found anywhere out of Fairyland.

While Gladys was biting into a delicious peach, she happened to look up towards the roof of the cottage, and whom should she see sitting on a beam near the rafters but the Little Red Juggler. She was going to call out, but the little man put his hand on his lip and shook his head solemnly, and she knew he did not wish her to speak.

The little woman kept on pressing the children to eat.

'Eat, my little dears, 'twill do you both good, and that delicious fruit will improve your flavour.'

'Our complexion, you mean. Mother says fruit does that,' said Gladys.

'Oh, of course, your complexion, that's what I meant,' said the little woman, but she reddened up to the two eyes; and Gladys happened again to catch the eye of the Little Red Juggler, and again he shook his head very solemnly.

Well, the children had to stop eating at last, and then Monona said she'd like to go home to Mammy.

'Go home to Mammy! Ho! ho!' laughed the little woman, 'of course you would, and so you will too, ho! ho!' and the little woman kept on laughing as if it were the funniest thing in the world. The children laughed too, though they didn't know why, and then the little woman caught Monona and tickled her until she got a fit of the giggles.

'But now, my dears,' said the little woman, 'stay here and wait till I come back; I'm going out into the forest to get wood for the fire for my son's supper.'

Before they could answer, she had passed out and locked the door behind her. The children began to get frightened, when down jumped the Little Red Juggler to the floor.

'My poor little children,' he said, 'you don't know where you are at all, at all. That little woman, for all that she looks so sweet, is a cruel Witch, and she means to give the both of you to her son tonight for his supper. One of you will be roasted, and one boiled,' said the Little Juggler.

When they heard this, the children threw themselves into each other's arms and began to cry.

'Crying is no use, my dears,' said the Little Red Juggler, 'and 'twill spoil your eyes,' said he, 'but if you will be said by me I'll save the two of you.'

'We'll do anything you tell us,' said the children.

'Well, then,' said he, 'one of you must go into the next room and get the black-hafted knife that is on the window-sill. I dare not go into the room, for I'm under bonds to the Giant – that is the Witch's son – not to do it, and what's more, if I did go in, my feet would stick to the ground, for the Witch has put enchantments on it.'

'Maybe I'd stick there too,' said Gladys.

'Oh no,' said the little man, 'I wouldn't send you in if you would, for how could you bring me out the knife if you got stuck?'

'That's true,' said Gladys, and without another word she darted into the room, and brought back the knife.

'Now,' said the Little Juggler, 'I'll put my head on the table, and you must cut the head off me.'

But Gladys dropped the knife on the table, and said she couldn't, and she wouldn't, and she wouldn't.

'Well, you'll do it, womaneen,' said the Juggler, turning towards Monona, but Monona backed away from him and began to cry.

'Oh, stop crying, or I'll cry myself,' said the Little Juggler. 'If you don't cut my head off, maybe you'd cut off my finger.

But the children wouldn't.

'Ah, I was only trying you all the time,' said the little man. 'But one of you must give me a little cut with the knife on the finger and get one drop of blood. That will be enough to free me from the enchantments that are over me.'

'Why don't you do it yourself?' asked Gladys.

''Twouldn't do,' said he. 'It can only be done by a good little maiden that never told a fib.'

'Very well, I'll do it,' said Monona.

'Oh, Monona!' exclaimed Gladys, 'how could you?'

But Monona made a little cut in the Little Red Juggler's finger, and a tiny drop of blood came out, and in a minute the Little Juggler was a fine, tall, handsome young Prince.

'Now, my little darlings,' he said, folding the children in his arms, 'I shall be able to save you from the horrible Giant.'

He had hardly said this when there was a loud knocking at the door.

'Run in there and wait for me,' said the Prince, and the children ran into the next room.

The knocking at the door became louder.

'Open, open, or I'll break it in!' shouted the Giant, for it was he, and wasn't he astonished when the door was opened, and he saw the Prince standing before him?

The howl of rage that he uttered nearly

frightened the children to death, but he never uttered another word, for the Prince had drawn his sword, and though the Giant had a club as big as a small tree, the Prince attacked him, and with one blow swept the head from his shoulders. When he fell, the children heard a horrible screech outside in the forest, and they peeped out of the window and they saw the Hounds of the Woods of Darkness gobbling up the Witch.

Then the Prince came in to them, and he told them that the Giant was killed, and they asked him would he take them home.

'Mammy won't know what's become of us,' said Gladys. 'We told her to wait for us at the tree through which we came to Fairyland.'

'I will, of course,' said the Prince, 'but it is getting too dark to go through the forest tonight, and if you lie down and go to sleep, I'll take you with me in the first light of the morning, and if you are asleep then, I won't waken you,' said he, 'but I'll carry you to mother.'

The children were so tired that they fell sound asleep, and never wakened when the Prince took them up the next morning and carried them through the forest.

He went up through the tree down which they had come, and there outside the little door

Mammy was waiting. He put the children down beside her, and when they woke up they saw their mother bending over them.

'Shaun of the Leaf'

Once upon a time there lived in a house near a great forest, two little children named Donal and Eily. They had been very, very happy until a stepmother came over them, who could not bear to have them in her sight. She hunted them out of the house during the day, and packed them off to bed as early as possible and often without their supper, and they were no longer allowed to sit up to hear the songs of the wandering harpers or the stories of the bright beautiful fairyland over the sea, where all were young and ever free from sorrow. Their dear old nurse, who loved them better than she loved herself, was sent away, and their father took hardly any notice of them, and the servants treated them almost as badly as the stepmother did herself.

They had only one friend in the world, and this was the dog 'Bran', a big, shaggy wolf-dog, that always slept beside their bed at night, and, when he had time, used to go with them, and show them the way into the wood when they desired to play there.

One day, when the stepmother was very, very cruel to them, they went to the wood and sat down under a large tree and began to cry. Bran looked at them very sorrowfully for a while, and then put his face up to theirs and whined as if he were crying too.

'Poor Bran,' said Eily. 'What would we do without you?'

Bran shook his head three times, as much as to say, what would he do without them, and then he pulled Donal by the sleeve and ran away four or five steps, and came back again and gave Donal another pull.

'He wants us to go with him,' said Eily.

Bran wagged his tail and barked three times, as much as to say 'you are right'. Then the children rose, and Bran ran on before them, but he turned round every minute to see if they were following him. He went on and on, and Donal and Eily after him, until they came to a grassy, open place in the wood.

In the middle of this, lying on the ground, was a big tree blown down by a storm, and sitting on the tree, was a little man in a frieze coat, with tails that came down to his heels and knee-breeches with brass buttons, and he had

an ivy-leaf up to his lips, and on it he was play-
ing very sweetly, but in so low a note, that he
could scarcely be heard. Bran and Donal and
Eily were very close to him before he saw them.
When he did, he stopped playing, and, jumping
down from the tree and pushing his spectacles
up on his forehead, he cried out:

'How are you, Eily and Bran and Donal? 'Tis
I that am glad to see you, and many's the time I
saw ye when ye weren't thinking of me.'

When Bran heard his name he barked and
danced for joy, and he would have jumped up
on the little man only he was afraid of knocking
him down. Eily and Donal did not know what
to make of it all, and they couldn't guess how
the little man knew their names. But all the
same, they said:

'Very well, thank you sir.'

'I see you don't know who I am, Donal and
Eily,' said the little man; 'but Bran remembers
me, don't you, Bran?' said he, winking at the
dog in a way that would do your heart good to
see.

Bran was so delighted that he stood straight
up on his hind legs, but overbalancing himself
he fell on the broad of his back, and the little
man and Donal and Eily shook their sides

laughing at him.

'But I must tell you who I am,' said the little man to Donal and Eily. 'Don't you remember "Shaun of the Leaf" as they used to call him, that often and often sat by the fire in your house, and played many a tune for you, and told you many a story?'

'That used to tell us the stories of the bright fairyland, where everyone is happy,' said Eily, looking sharply at the little man.

'Yes,' said the little man.

'Of course, we remember him; we never forgot him,' said Eily.

'Well, then, I am he,' said the little man, 'I am he – I am "Shaun of the Leaf", and I have just come from the land I used to tell you about,' said Shaun, taking out a tortoise-shell snuff-box and treating himself to a pinch.

'But, I thought it was only the fairies lived there,' said Eily.

'Well, it is only fairies live there, except myself, and for that matter I'm nearly a fairy myself now,' said Shaun. 'I was playing here one summer's evening in this very spot, trying to take off the notes of the thrush and the blackbird, when who should come by but the King and Queen of the Fairies, and a lot of the quality attending them, and they took such a fancy to the music that the queen asked the king to invite me down to their palace under the sea; and they made such fine promises – and I was willing to do anything to oblige a lady, not to say the Queen of the Fairies herself – I consented, and I am as happy as the day is long.'

'But sure you were a great big man when you used to come to our house,' said Donal.

'I was six feet high in my stockings then,' said Shaun, and he drew himself up very proudly, and he took another pinch of snuff, 'but you know I had to become small, or I couldn't go into the Fairy King's Palace.'

'Was it the fairies made you small?' asked Eily.

'It was,' said Shaun.

'And how did they do it? said Donal.

'Boiled me – boiled me down,' said Shaun.

'Boiled you!' exclaimed Eily, and her eyes got nearly as big as saucers.

'They put me to simmer for two hours over a slow fire,' said Shaun, solemnly.

'In a pot?' said Eily.

'Well, they said it was a cauldron,' said Shaun, 'but between you and me, Miss Eily, not to tell anything but the truth, I think it was a pot.'

'Did they put herbs into it?' asked Donal.

'They did,' said Shaun.

'Then I know what it was, it was a "magic cauldron",' said Donal.

'Maybe so, Donal asthore, but having spent two hours in it, you wouldn't much mind whether they called it a pot or a cauldron,' said Shaun. 'But it's nearly time for me to go home, and I am afraid I did very little practice today.'

'What kind of practice?' said Donal.

'Music,' said Shaun. 'Didn't ye hear me playing when ye came up?'

'We did,' said Eily, 'and we thought it very, very sweet.'

'Oh, then, ye can hear music sweeter this minute,' said he, 'and that is the song of the birds. There are no birds down in the land I told you about, and I have to come up here every fine day when the birds are singing, to try and learn their notes for the king and queen. There's one black bird that sings in the tree near the stream there that almost breaks my heart. But my time is up, and I must go,' said the little man.

'We wish we could go with you,' said Donal, 'for when we go home our cruel stepmother will beat us.'

'Wirrastrue,' said Shaun, 'is that the way at home now? Leave it to me,' said he, 'and I'll tell the Queen of the Fairies, and you may be sure she will take care of you when she learns from me how good your poor mother was to "Shaun of the Leaf". This is Monday, and I can't be back here again until Thursday, as there is a great wedding tomorrow, and the dancing will be kept up for two days and two nights. So come here again on Thursday,' said he, 'and now run home as fast as ye can.'

When he had said this, little 'Shaun of the Leaf' disappeared through the trees. Bran gave a couple of barks to say goodbye, and then started home with Donal and Eily.

When they arrived home the stepmother was trying to light the fire, which had gone out. When she saw Donal and Eily she screamed at them and abused them, and said they were good-for-nothing idlers, roaming about the country instead of staying at home to mind the fire.

'As for you,' said she, throwing a burnt stick at Bran, 'you're not worth the bit you eat.'

Bran snarled and showed his teeth, but Donal and Eily crept into a corner, and said nothing.

That night when they went to bed, they talked about the little man, and were longing for Thursday to come. The next day passed, and the next, and the stepmother's temper was worse than ever. She slapped Eily because she gave a sup of milk to Bran, and boxed Donal's ears and took up the broomstick to beat him because he kissed Eily and asked her not to cry. That night she sent them to bed without their supper – but they did not mind, they knew the next day was Thursday, and talked themselves to sleep, and dreamed all night of 'Shaun of the Leaf', and of the fairy queen they were going to see. When they awoke in the morning the sun was dancing in the room, and one would think all the birds in the air were singing outside the window. They could hear Bran, too, barking away down in the fields.

'Bran is chasing the larks,' said Donal.

'Oh, Donal,' said Eily, 'did you ever hear the birds singing like that before?' They listened and listened, and the birds kept singing, and what they sang was – *Come with me to Tir-na-nÓg* – that is the fairyland where all are young; and the children felt very happy when, after breakfast, the stepmother turned the two of them out. Bran was outside, and when he saw them he gave them a look as much as to say 'follow me', and they set off to the wood. It wasn't long till they came to the place where they were to meet 'Shaun of the Leaf'.

But they could see no sign of him, and Eily and Donal began to feel very sad. However, Bran looked at them and wagged his tail as much as to say 'It's all right.' Sure enough it was not long until they heard Shaun playing on the ivy leaf, and soon they saw him pushing his way through the ferns.

'I'm sorry for keeping you, Eily and Donal and Bran,' said he, 'but I have good news for you. The Queen of the Fairies sent me up to tell you that she's dying to see the two of you, and she wants you to come to her this very day.'

When Bran heard this, his head hung down to the ground; but when Eily saw Bran, she took pity on him and said:

'Can't Bran come too?'

'Well,' said the little man, 'I didn't get an invitation for Bran, because I thought he wouldn't care to come, for there are no birds to hunt there, you know.'

Bran straightened himself up and gave a low growl, as much as to say: 'As if I wouldn't rather be near Eily then have all the birds in the world.'

'But I'll put in a good word for Bran,' said he, 'with the Queen of the Fairies, and I'm sure she'll let him come to the palace; but at present he must stop at the house of the friend where my horse is stabled.'

Eily and Donal agreed to this, and so, too, you may be sure, did Bran, who began to bark and jump about like mad.

'Stop, now, for a minute or two,' said the little man, 'till I take off that blackbird's note, and I'll be ready to go with you.'

Shaun sat down on the tree, and, closing his eyes, his head rested on his left shoulder, and he played so softly on the leaf that Eily could hardly hear him.

'I have it at last,' said the little man, starting up, his face beaming with delight. 'And now come with me to Tir-na-nÓg.'

He sang the very song the birds had been singing that morning when the children were listening to them!

'Shaun of the Leaf' went before them, pushing aside the ferns. Eily and Donal followed. Soon they passed through the wood. A broad plain was before them, and beyond the plain the sea shining like silver. When Shaun passed out of the wood, he began the play upon the leaf, and so sweet was the music that Eily thought it was only a minute until they came to the sea.

As soon as they came to the strand, what did they see coming around the rocks and swimming gracefully along but a beautiful snow-white swan, with a gold bridle and a saddle of purple and gold.

'Is this your horse?' said Donal, his eyes opening wide in wonder.

'He is,' said Shaun, 'my sea-horse you know,' said he, winking at Eily. And in a second after, they saw a tiny boat with six little sailors and little red tassels in their caps coming in to the strand.

'Oh, what is this for? cried Donal.

'That is to take you and Eily to the little green isle in the sea, where the pleasant land of youth is,' said Shaun.

'But that tiny little boat won't hold us,' said Eily.

'Oh, wait till you see,' said Shaun, and when the little boat slid in on the strand, the little sailors with little red tassels in their caps, asked the children to get in.

When Donal and Eily got in, they had plenty of room, although the boat didn't get a bit

bigger; and then the little sailors got in, and 'Shaun of the Leaf' got up in the saddle of the swan and gave the word to start.

'Bow, wow, wow, wow!' cried Bran, when he saw the boat and the swan leaving him.

'Oh, stop, dear sailors, and take in Bran,' said the children.

'He'd sink the boat,' they said. 'We cannot take a four-footed animal into a fairy boat.'

'But Bran can walk on his two hind legs,' said Eily.

'But he has four legs all the same, and he would drown us,' said the little sailors.

'Bow, wow, wow, wow, wow!' barked Bran.

'Oh, we must go back,' said Eily. 'We can't leave poor Bran behind, for mother told us never to go out without him'; and Eily began to cry, and she was sobbing until she heard a voice calling: 'Bran, you goose, swim out and catch the swan's tail.' Then Eily looked, and what did she see but a mermaid sitting on the rocks plaiting her golden tresses.

Bran, barking joyously, plunged into the sea, and tried to catch the swan's tail. The swan got such a fright that she opened her wings, and then she threw Shaun head over heels into the water, and he would certainly have been drowned, if Bran hadn't caught him by his little frieze coat.

'Well, it is not you are to blame, Bran, if I was nearly drowned,' said Shaun, 'and I must admit that you have saved my life, and so if you promise not to touch the swan, you can swim quietly after us, and I'll make it all right for you with the Fairy Queen.'

The swan had come back and let Shaun get up again, and then said Shaun, turning round and shaking his fist at the mermaid: 'I'll pay you off for this yet.' But she only answered with a laugh, and blowing a kiss from the tips of her white fingers, dived into the sea.

And were not the children delighted watching the beautiful swan and Bran swimming close beside them, and the little fairy sailors rowing away with their tiny oars!

But after a while they began to look out for the little green isle in the sea, and they could not catch a glimpse of it anywhere.

'Oh, look, look, Donal! What is that?' shouted Eily, her face aglow, as she stood up in the boat and pointed in the direction to which it was going.

''Tis, 'tis – oh, I really think it must be a

bundle of sunbeams,' said Donal, 'that has fallen on the waters.'

''Tis the true word you spoke, Master Donal,' said 'Shaun of the Leaf', 'a bundle of sunbeams it is, for it is the head of herself, and no mistake,' said he.

'Who is herself?' asked Eily.

'Who would it be, but that deludherin mermaid that you saw on the rocks beyond,' said Shaun.

And sure enough it was the mermaid!

When she lifted her head above the waters, her tossing golden tresses brightened them like dancing sunbeams, and never was sea foam half so white as her white shoulders, and her round white arms.

Higher still she raised herself, until the children saw that she had in her hands a little harp of gold, and as they watched her with all their eyes, they saw her stringing it with strings woven with her own shining tresses.

Then she began to play, and oh! for the music that came out of that little harp of gold.

It stole across the waters to the ears of the children, and crept down into their little hearts; and they hardly noticed the movement of the oars as the little sailors rowed on and on in search of the little green isle in the sea. They barely saw the sea itself, for they could do nothing but listen and listen, and they thought that never had sweeter sounds been heard anywhere in the world.

'Wait till you hear her sing,' whispered 'Shaun of the Leaf', who was able to guess what the children were thinking of. 'Wait till you hear her sing.'

He had no sooner said the word, than the mermaid began to sing.

The little sailors had kept time softly with their oars, to the music of the little harp of gold, but when the first notes of the strange sweet voice fell on their ears, they ceased rowing as if some spell of enchantment had fallen on them. The little boat stood, and the waters became motionless.

The children thought it was all a lovely dream, from which they were awakened by a long deep-drawn sigh from 'Shaun of the Leaf'.

'What are you sighing for?' asked Eily.

'Musha, then, it is no wonder I'd sigh, for sure I never hear her voice that it does not coax the heart out of me, and I'm not worth a pin for a month of Sundays after, and she does not care a thraneen about me,' said he, with another sigh that would almost bring the tears to your eyes.

A merry laugh rippled along the waters, and the children saw the mermaid waving her white arm to them, and then she sank beneath the sea; but for a while there lingered on its surface the glistening of her golden hair, as the golden light of the sun that has set often lingers in the evening skies.

Then all at once the little sailors began to ply their oars, and soon the little boat was sliding over the circles in the water which told where the mermaid had gone down. They had no sooner passed beyond the circles than the children saw before them the little green isle in the sea.

Well, it was not long till the boat ran in on the brown sand, and the little sailors jumped ashore and handed out the children.

'I was here as soon as yourself,' said the little man, jumping off his feather sea-horse, which had just stepped on the strand.

'Oh, Bran, mind what you are doing, you naughty dog!' cried out Eily.

For there was Master Bran, shaking himself for the bare life; and he had very nearly made a mess over Eily, owing to the showers of water he flung on her.

'I knew it was not right to bring dogs here,' said the little man. He whisked out his snuff-box and took two pinches.

'Bow, wow, wow, wow, wow!' barked Bran.

'Who is that barking?' said the Fairy Queen, who had just come down a pathway all covered with bluebells that made a carpet under her tiny feet.

When Bran heard her he hung down his head and looked very sorrowful, as if he was thinking of saying: 'I beg pardon, your majesty,' and he got behind the children to hide himself.

When Donal and Eily saw the Queen, they were so dazzled with her beauty that they could not speak for wonder. But the Fairy Queen came over and put her arms round Eily, and kissed her and hugged her, and then kissed and hugged Donal, and said: 'A hundred thousand welcomes to Tir-na-nÓg.' Then she brought them into the palace, and all the little fairies came thronging around them, and made them welcome. Then there was a grand feast, and after that there were games of all kinds and dancing, and no two children were ever so happy as Donal and Eily.

But in the middle of the dance the little

trumpeters on the battlements of the palace sounded a note of warning, and the music ceased, and the dancers stayed their steps.

A little herald, dressed in brown silk, entered the ballroom.

'What message do you bring, O Herald?' said the Fairy Queen.

'The Fairies of the Sea, your Majesty,' said the herald, bowing almost to the ground, 'challenge the Land Fairies to battle.'

'Bid the trumpets blow,' said the Queen to her attendants, 'to announce that we accept their challenge, and you, my gallant knights, get you ready for the fray.'

The ballroom was emptied in the twinkling of an eye.

'Come down with me to the strand,' said 'Shaun of the Leaf' to the children, 'and we'll see the fight.'

The children went down with him to the strand, and they looked out upon the sea; but they had at once to put their hands to their eyes to shade them from the dazzling light that flashed from its countless ripples, for every ripple bore along a glancing Sea Fairy, whose little coat was studded all over with shining pearls.

'Look behind you,' said 'Shaun of the Leaf' to the children, 'and rest your eyes.' Donal and Eily looked behind them, and saw descending the grassy slopes that bent towards the strand the fairest sight that ever mortal eyes beheld.

Regiment after regiment of little Land Fairies were marching down, and they looked like a garden of moving flowers.

The first carried in their hands poppies nearly as red as the heart of the rose, the second bore bunches of cowslips nearly as golden as the heart of the sun, and after them came the wild roses of the hedges, white and red, and as lovely as the cheeks of little girls, and the bluebells from the woods came after, and nearly every flower that grows all through the year followed. For this is the way the battles were carried on between the Land Fairies and the Sea Fairies.

The Land Fairies fought with flowers and the Sea Fairies with pearls. The Land Fairies rushed out towards the incoming wave, and flung their flowers against the Sea Fairies, but woe betide them, if while doing so, the tips of their toes went into the water, for if they did, they became prisoners and servants of the Sea Fairies, for a year and a day.

The Sea Fairies, casting their pearls, skimmed along the wave, until they came to the very edge of the strand, but woe betide them if the tips of their toes touched the dry sand, for if they did, they became prisoners and servants of the Land Fairies for a year and a day.

Well, the battle had hardly begun, when the edge of the sea was a mass of fragrant flowers, and the edge of the strand was white with shining pearls, and the shouts of the little combatants filled the air, and many prisoners were taken on both sides.

'Donal,' said Eily, 'wouldn't you like to play?' – for the children thought it was all play.

'I would,' said Donal, and before little 'Shaun of the Leaf' could say a word the children had their boots and stockings off, and they were out in the water, and they thought they never had such fun.

They used to catch up a whole armful of the Sea Fairies, but the merry little fellows slipped out from under the children's arms as water slips throught the fingers, and they pelted them with pearls, and Donal, and Eily followed them out till the water got deeper and deeper.

'Come back! Come back!' cried 'Shaun of the Leaf', but the children did not hear, or, if they did, they did not heed him. But at last Eily found she was going out too far, and she wanted to turn back, but she couldn't, for the little Sea Fairies had fastened round her a rope of pearls and they were drawing her along.

'Oh, Donal! Save me!' she cried, but Donal was a prisoner himself and could do nothing; the Sea Fairies were also drawing him far out from the little green isle in the sea, and goodness knows what would have happened to the children, if the Fairy Queen had not come down to the strand in time to see their plight.

'Shaun, Shaun!' she cried, 'go out after the children and bring them back.'

'I dare not do it, your Majesty,' said Shaun, 'for I can't swim. The last time the Sea Fairies caught a hold of me they nearly drowned me, and sure 'twould be no use for me to get drowned, though I'd give my life to save Eily's little finger.'

'I know that, Shaun,' said the Queen.

Then the Fairy Queen ordered the little sailors to go out and save the children, and they pushed out their little boat. They rowed and they rowed, and it was not long until they came close to the children, and some of them stretched out their hands to take Donal and Eily in when a crowd of little Sea Fairies climbed up the sides of the boat and tumbled into it, and at last so many came in that they swamped it, and all that the Fairy Queen could see of her little sailors was their little red caps floating on the top of the water.

'Oh, what will I do at all, at all,' said the Fairy Queen, 'if the children are carried away.'

She wrung her hands, and never before was she so sorry, for she loved the children for themselves as well as for their sweet mother's sake.

'I know what we'll do,' said little 'Shaun of the Leaf', for he, too, had been very miserable.

'What is it?' said the Queen.

'Let us call Bran,' said he, and he whistled, and down came Bran with a bound. He had been sitting up on a sand hill all the time longing to join Donal and Eily, but he was afraid of the Fairy Queen.

Shaun pointed to the children. 'Bring them back, Bran,' he said, and out went Bran. He plunged into the waves, and, resting his chin on the waters, he swam, and he swam, until he came up to Eily. The little Sea Fairies scattered before him as the minnows scatter before a pike, but one of the Fairies, bolder than the others, tried to fling a rope of pearls around Bran's neck, but Bran showed his white teeth – whiter than the pearls – snapped at the Fairy, and nearly gobbled him up. This so frightened all the rest of the Fairies, that they dived under the sea.

Bran was just in time to catch Eily, and Donal was close enough to fling his arm over Bran's neck and grasp his shaggy hair, and the gallant wolf-dog brought the children safely back to the strand.

'Oh, Bran, Bran!' said the Fairy Queen, when he had brought her back the children safe and sound, 'you may bark as much as ever you like now.'

And didn't Bran bark! And didn't he caper, and didn't he shake himself, and fling showers about him on every side!

Then the Queen hurried the children to the palace, for they were wet through, and her little maids of honour attended to Eily, and they took off her clothes, and gave her a lovely bath, and they wiped her dry in gossamer, and they laid her down on the daintiest little bed that ever was. It was as soft as air, and as sweet as roses. The gentlemen of the Fairy King's bed-chamber (the King himself was away on a visit to the High King of Erin, at Tara) attended to Donal. Then what did the Queen do, lest the children might feel lonely or frightened if they woke in the dark, but send one of her little fairies up to the sky for a little green star, and she hung this for a night-light on the wall of their dainty bedroom. But the children were no sooner in bed than they fell fast asleep, and did not wake till morning.

Then the Fairy Queen went herself and helped them to get up and dress, and she hugged them, and hugged them, and said she wished she could keep them to herself. But she had promised their mother that she would look after them at home, and she had brought them to Tir-na-nÓg only that she might give them, with her own hands, a little present that would rid them of all their troubles and sorrows.

She took out of her pocket a little crystal flask, and in this was a red-coloured fluid. She held it up to the light, and it shone like a ruby, and she told Donal, as she handed it to him, to throw some of it over his stepmother the next time she attempted to strike him. Then she gave the children a fairy breakfast, and such a breakfast, but there is no use in trying to tell what it was like to anyone who was never in Fairyland.

After this, the Queen, attended by all her maids of honour, accompanied the children down to the strand. Here she bade them a fond goodbye, and Shaun and the little boat and the sailors were on the shore waiting for them; and Donal and Eily were very sorry when they got into the boat and turned their backs on Fairyland, and very frightened they were when they came near to their father's house, for they knew their stepmother would beat them. And so it happened. The moment she caught sight of them she rushed out with the broomstick and made a blow at Donal, shrieking:

'Where have you been, you villians?'

But Donal avoided the blow, and taking off the gold top of the flask, he flung the red fluid on her. He had no sooner done so that she uttered a horrible screech, and on the spot she was changed into a witch-wolf. And all the dogs, with Bran at their head, rushed at her as she sprang out of the farmyard and fled off howling towards the forest.

She was a witch, and she had put a spell on their father. But, after he had found this out, he was never unkind to the children any more, and although they often thought of Fairyland, they lived very happily ever after. And you may be sure they never forgot their dear old Bran.

Irish Folk Stories for Children

T. Crofton Croker

These exciting and spell-binding stories are full of magical people and enchanted places which will delight and entertain children of all ages. *Irish Folk Stories for Children* are tales of past centuries when magic and mystery were part of everyone's life. They include such well loved stories as 'The Giant's Stairs', 'The Legend of Bottle-Hill' and 'The Soul Cages'.

Irish Legends for Children

Lady Gregory

Irish Legends for Children is a heart-warming collection of exciting stories which will give all children hours of pleasure as they catch the flavour and atmosphere of ancient times.

These traditional legends, which have been handed down through countless generations, are written in a direct and simple style and include such well-loved tales as 'The Children of Lir', 'The Coming of Finn', 'Finn's Household' and 'The Best Men of the Fianna'.

Irish Fairy Tales

Edmund Leamy

In writing these fascinating stories Edmund Leamy turned to our Gaelic past to give the Irish people something which would implant in them a love for the beauty and dignity of their country's traditions.

'Princess Finola and the Dwarf' is a tale so filled with simple beauty and tenderness and there is so much genuine word-magic in it that one is carried away under its spell. All of the stories reveal the poetry of the author's style and show how charged they are with qualities which are peculiar to the Gaelic temperament. At times there is a simple, sweet beauty of language and some passages — especially in 'The Huntsman's Son' – of true prose poetry.

The other spell-binding tales in this book are 'The Fairy Tree of Dooros', 'The House in the Lake', 'The Little White Cat', 'The Golden Spears' and 'The Enchanted Cave'.

No one can read these pages without feeling the charm of a fine delicate fancy, a rare power of poetic expression and a truly Irish instinct.

LUCIFER'S PROMISE

What the critics are saying about Alan Thompson's _Lucifer's Promise_:

"Thompson's new novel is equal parts legal thriller, medical ethics conundrum and old-fashioned murder mystery. Decades after Harry and Alex Monmouth made their debuts in Thompson's previous novel, **Gods and Lesser Men** (2014, etc.), they're once again caught up in controversy and conspiracy. Harry's hometown of New Hope is in the midst of football fever as a new quarterback shatters records and promises great things for the college's future. But there are troubling rumors about the team's academic performance, and the dean calls on Harry to investigate. At the same time, Alex is losing her battle with leukemia . . . Harry soon meets Dr. Franklin Steiner and realizes there might just be a miracle in store for his wife. Meanwhile, when the people who've helped him with the football case start turning up dead, he realizes that New Hope conceals more mysteries than he'd bargained for . . . Fortunately, while Harry tries to understand how these people and cases are connected, the novel's prose is startlingly detailed, allowing readers to understand the disparate realms of genetics and college athletics while also painting a vibrant picture of the town and college . . . A complex, thought-provoking story that defies genre conventions to remind us of difficult questions and tangled answers." _Kirkus Reviews_

"With a keen eye to detail, Alan Thompson has written not only a murder mystery, but also an exposé of disturbing trends in American society. *Lucifer's Promise* takes us into the world of lawyer Harry Monmouth as he grapples with his alma mater's exploitation of ill-prepared athletes, its unquestioning support of genetic research, and his own culpability. A smart, tightly-woven page turner." Sharon L. Dean, author, *Tour de Trace*

"One of the delights of *Lucifer's Promise* is that it begins like a Big Bang of intrigue, opening with the singular challenge of a couple facing a possibly-fatal illness but rapidly expanding outward to embrace an equally deadly force that could affect mankind itself . . . And because [his wife's] survival depends in part on genetic engineering, this fine line between good and evil is not a clear call for [the hero] to make. This is one of the devices that gives *Lucifer's Promise* such an intriguing twist: the protagonist/hero himself relies on the very thing that could save or destroy lives - and so there are no clear answers, no clear evils, and no singular path towards redemption . . .

Lucifer's Promise isn't a mystery or detective story per se, though plenty of elements of the thriller genre are embedded in the plot and fans of genetic or medical mystery reads, in particular, will be delighted with the way this investigation goes . . . Fans of Robin Cook, Michael Crichton, and the like will thus find plenty to admire in **Lucifer's Promise**, which successfully crosses genres. Adventure, mystery, and higher-level thinking: it doesn't get better than this, for a reader who looks for more than mere entertainment." D. Donovan, Senior eBook Reviewer, *Midwest Book Review*

"Harry Monmouth, Thompson's quasi-hero, is slowly drawn into a world of strange science and exotic promises while he attempts to determine why three women had to die. Beset by his own desires, Harry is faced with choices that will affect not only him but his loved ones as well as his friends and acquaintances. One choice could lead to an unimaginable life, while the other could result in his own death . . . **Lucifer's Promise**: a gift from God or a bane from Satan, is a quest that leads Harry to an astounding conclusion. A totally captivating story that will hold the reader in thrall until the last mesmerizing word . . ." Jonathan Penroc, author of *War of the Gods* series

Amanda,

One of the settings in this novel is a little town — called Twin Rivers. I think you'll recognize it —

LUCIFER'S PROMISE

ALAN THOMPSON

Alan Thompson

W & B Publishers
USA

W & B Publishers

For information:
W & B Publishers
Post Office Box 193
Colfax, NC 27235
www.a-argusbooks.com

ISBN: 978-0-6923712-3-7
ISBN: 0-6923712-3-0

Book Cover designed by Dubya

Printed in the United States of America

For my grandchildren, who confront a future I can barely imagine

Town

2 - Post Office
3 - Old N-H Cementery
4 - Franky's
5 - Old Stucco Bungalow
10 - Academy Inn
11 - The High
13 - West End Mosque
14 - Courthouse
18 - Harry + Alex
19 - College Coffee Shop
20 - The Chronicle

Gown

1 - Castle Hall
6 - Chancellor's House

7. Amphitheater
8 - Bell Tower
9 - Steiner's Temple
12 - The Circus
15 - South Bldg.
16 - Human Enrichment
17 - The Bower

NEW HOPE

N

WEST END

MILLTOWN

Michael
Chapel
⑬
W. Second ⑪
W. High
⑳
Bishop
College
⑩
Hill
Weaver Mill

1

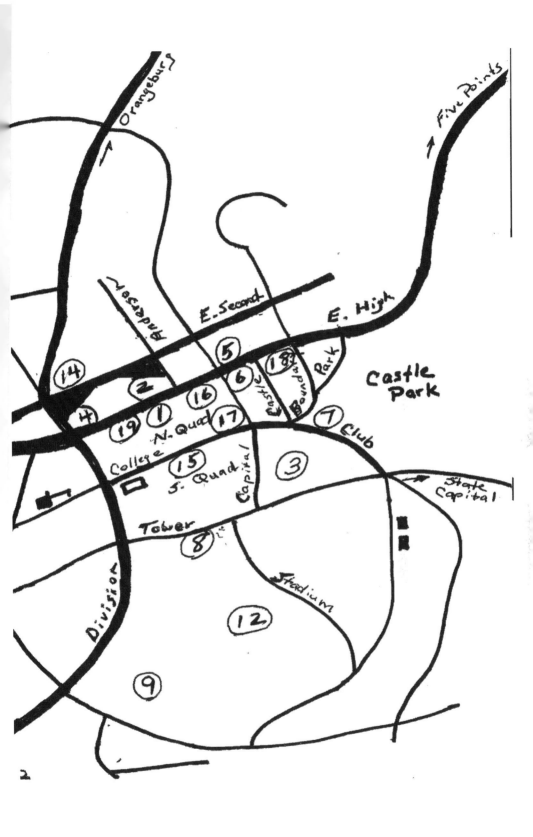

LUCIFER'S PROMISE

MOONLIGHT STREAMED through the windows into the darkened room, pale illumination that contrasted with the bright, dense glow of the fire. The only sound was the crackle of the flames, the only scent the burning oak. Despite the fire, the carefully prepared chamber was cold. The clock chimed 10 times.

The woman stumbled to the window, and closed the drapes. Behind her, a million miles away, she heard the door open and close. Tears, unnoticed before, wet her face. The love was almost hate, but nirvana – fleeting, urgent – was close at hand. She drew a box from the bedside table, and found the instruments of her salvation.

The needle pierced the bulging blue vein. In seconds that seemed like hours, the poison made its way across the blood-brain barrier, and the pain began to recede. The hurtful words and scalding emotions faded, replaced by the false serenity she needed so badly. Her lids grew heavy and her head nodded. Somewhere in the distance, she heard footsteps. She tried to open her eyes . . .

BOOK ONE

A sound magician is a mighty god – Christopher Marlowe

ONE

THE GREAT stadium, impatient, waited as the bearers lifted the motionless boy onto the mechanized litter and turned toward the gaping black tunnel at the east end of the amphitheater. The vast array of lamps, all aimed at the pitch enclosed by the oval arena, made the manicured grass look artificial. A full moon, pale next to the lights, looked on. The boys who remained forgot their fallen comrade, and returned to the business at hand.

"I hope he's not really hurt," said Alex.

I shared her sentiment but, schooled in the same perspective as the boys on the field, suppressed it. "It's part of the game."

"I hate it."

"I know." She had refused to attend the games our sons played, and this was the first time she had accompanied me to the College stadium in years. Curiosity had overcome her aversion. The old stadium was refurbished and enlarged, and dozens of air-conditioned "suites" wrapped in glass now looked over the remainder of the seats – still subject to the sweltering humidity of late August – at the field below.

We were seated in the largest such enclosure and most of the people around us, if they were watching the game at all, looked at one of the televisions arranged along the walls. It was called the "College Club," and it was reserved for the school's royalty – department chairs, deans, and the new

princes, the professors and administrators respon-
sible for the fabulous influx of cash into the Col-
lege's coffers. The stadium itself was a small, but
not insignificant, manifestation of the new money.
Alex and I had received a last-minute invitation
from the Chancellor she was unable to resist.

A white-coated waiter extended his tray.
Alex lifted the scotch and handed it to me, then
raised a glass of wine to her lips. Her hand shook.
"It seems funny to just have a drink at a football
game," she said. "Is it legal now?"

"No." I gestured. "Those folks out there still
have to hide their booze. I'll need my flask again
next time."

She smiled. "I think I liked it better that
way."

Our host sat down in one of the plush seats
behind us. Winfred Honeyman had been Chancel-
lor of the College for more than 30 years. A former
Professor of Philosophy, he had continued teaching
a class or two every semester, a practice only re-
cently abandoned. He was a widower without chil-
dren and the College was his family, and the recent
troubles had taken their toll. Only a few months
short of a retirement he had resisted, he wanted
things to be better. "What do you think?" he said.

"The accommodations?" I said. He nodded.
"Very nice. You don't even need the football game."

He lifted his head to gauge the hum of voices
around him. "Most of these people haven't been to
a game in years." He looked at Alex. "How are you
feeling, my dear?"

"I'm fine, Win. Thanks for asking."

He considered another question, but thought better of it. Instead, he leaned close to my ear and said, "I need to speak to you. In private. Can–?"

"Winfred?" A tall, bulky man with a florid complexion loomed over us. Completely bald, he wore a white suit, black shirt and white bowtie, and he held a bottle of champagne in one hand and a flute in the other. A pair of wire-rimmed glasses, identical to mine, sat on his nose.

A diminutive blonde, whose breasts seemed to begin at her neck and end at her waist, stood beside him. Her clothing matched his, New Year's Eve instead of the College's first football game, ensembles that set them apart from everyone else in the room. One or both of them were bathed in a cologne that smelled like wood. "You remember my wife, Susan?" The accent suggested he was not one of us.

The Chancellor rose and took the proffered hand. "Of course." He looked at us. "Do you know the Monmouths?" The man shook his head. "Harry and Alex Monmouth, this is Doctor Franklin Steiner and his wife, Susan. Frank's the Director of our School of Applied Genetics."

I shook his hand. The grip was painful. "You're in the new building at the Medical Center, aren't you?" I said.

"Yes."

"It's very impressive."

The strong white teeth inside the smile gleamed. "Thank you. Come see us. I'll give you the tour."

"Frank's a Harvard man," said the Chancellor. I grinned. The reflexive obeisance to antiquity and pedigree, whatever the achievements of the College's own faculty, always amused me. The hierarchy the professors railed against was alive and well on campus. You could never have too many Harvard men.

"Do you teach here?" Steiner said to me.

"No. I'm just a citizen."

"Harry's our most respected attorney," the Chancellor said. "His family's been here for centuries." He paused. "One of his people used to have my job."

I laughed. "It's only two centuries, and he was only acting Chancellor. It was during the Civil War. No one else would take the job."

Steiner re-filled his glass, and emptied the bottle into hers. "You must have good genes to maintain that sort of longevity," he said. "We might be able to use you over at the lab."

I laughed again, and put an arm around Alex. "You should recruit my bride. She's the heavy hitter in that category."

He shifted his eyes to her, brows raised. "I'm afraid my genes aren't what they used to be, Doctor Steiner," she said. "Sorry."

He gazed at her carefully for a moment. "What sort of law do you do, Mr. Monmouth?"

"Harry. I'm a jack-of-all-trades, master of none. Whatever comes up."

"You spend a lot of time at the courthouse? With the judges and the other lawyers?"

"Not as much as I used to."

"But you are well-known? Distinguished?"

"Well —"

"Don't let him kid you, Frank," said the Chancellor. "Harry's the best damn lawyer in the state."

Steiner hesitated, then looked at Honeyman. "Have you heard from Ender?"

"Yes. I'm meeting with him on Monday."

"Good."

Steiner nodded at us, and they moved away. "So that's the famous Doctor Steiner," said Alex. "Is he German?"

"Swiss," said the Chancellor. "We lured him down here about eight years ago. Very big in the commercial genetics field."

"He's in charge of the sickle cell program, isn't he?" I said.

"Yes."

"What's commercial genetics?" said Alex.

"He runs our fertility clinic, and sells genetic screening at $2500 a pop."

"To who?"

"Whoever wants it. He brings in more money than the Athletic Department."

I smiled. "I thought you were a non-profit institution."

"It depends on how you define profit, Harry. Our academic brethren are losing money hand over fist."

"What does his screening do?" Alex said.

"It reveals, um, tendencies. Someone's susceptibility to disease. Or some physical trait like obesity or baldness. There's a whole list of things they look for."

"They can't fix those things, can they?" I said.

"Not yet."

"Then why would anyone want it? Who wants to know he's going to get fat if there's nothing he can do about it?" I sipped my drink. "What do you do if you *might* get breast cancer? Become a patient?"

"That's the serious part of his work, Harry. They're treating sickle cell anemia now. Half the building's doing research on gene therapy for other things like heart disease and – and leukemia. Probably obesity and baldness, too." He laid a hand on my arm. "Can you stop by my office tomorrow? Around one o'clock?"

"On Sunday?"

"Yes. No one will be around. We can talk without interruptions."

"All right."

A few minutes later Alex said, "I'm tired. Can we go home?"

"Sure." We took the elevator to the concourse level, and stepped through a door tended by two armed state patrolmen. The new plaza was paved with gray stones. Marble fountains and concrete benches and statues – one a larger than life image of the man responsible for the expansion of the stadium and its new amenities – were situated at strategic intervals.

The original donor, dead for 75 years, had been cast aside, and the new man – an admirer of antiquity – wanted a classical allusion attached to his name. In the event, his name had too many syllables, and was quickly forgotten – the product of his largesse was universally known as "the Circus." The scent of pine was gone, as was the forest that once rose over the concrete bowl, and the cricket serenade was muted.

We turned north toward the campanile and the road. As we reached the sidewalk, the tower's carillon played the fight song and rang the hour –

8:00 P.M. "How about supper?" I said. "At the Inn? We'll have the place to ourselves." She hesitated. "If you don't feel like it –"

"No, no. I'd like that."

We walked west on Tower Road. The land-scape – once a soothing refuge of green grass and orange bricks – rose over us. Angular, dispropor-tionate structures encroached on the walkway and the lawn and the road, obscuring the moon and casting our path in darkness unrelieved by the streetlamps that illumined only themselves.

I took her hand as we navigated the saw-horses and construction equipment that marked more of the self-mutilation on which the College was embarked. We climbed the hill at Division Street and, moments later, sat at a table for two in the dining room at the Academy Inn. The elegant space and its attendants were already primed for the onslaught of post-game diners but, since it was only half-time, Alex and I were the lone patrons. The light was dim and she'd forgotten her glasses, so I read the brief menu to her.

We ate in silence. Married couples of our vintage often have few words at solitary meals, es-pecially after their children are gone, but our reti-cence was the result of having too much to say, not too little. I yearned to tell her the things I had ne-glected to say, or said poorly because emotion was hard, but I couldn't – the specter that hung over us wouldn't permit it. Out of the ordinary words would invite the shadow to the table, and we were exhausted by the time already spent in its compa-ny.

She tried to dredge up a few topics of conver-sation, and failed. A new chance – miniscule, problematic, remote – had materialized, but the length of the odds made me wait for her to bring it up. She had always been our optimist.

"Do you think this gene therapy thing could help me?"

WE CROSSED College Avenue at the light. "Let's walk through town," Alex said. Instead of cutting across the North Quadrangle – the quickest way home – we continued north on Division. The fraternity parties on the other side of the street were in full swing despite the fact that the game still wasn't over. Of the 75,000 people in the stands, no more than three or four thousand were students. The College allotted them fewer and fewer tickets each year, all situated in the second deck on the sun side looking down at the end zone. The alumnae, and the wannabe alumnae, were happy to purchase the tickets the students didn't claim.

High Street was crowded, too. Years before, New Hope's old commercial district was all but deserted when the College was playing at home, but now the restaurants and bars and other attractions were jammed. Undergraduates, tourists and cops – interspersed with bumptious panhandlers – loitered.

Everyone, even the beggars, talked on cell phones, oblivious of their fellow pedestrians, and automobiles that barely moved on both sides of the street broadcast whatever was playing on their music boxes. Three buses – one for each of the drunken, unshaven men asleep in the plastic shelter – spewed their noxious waste while lined up in front of the Methodist Church, bound for who knows where among the far-flung, clotted clusters that New Hope was now.

We sat down on a bench in front of Castle Hall, an ancient brick dormitory with bay windows and diamond-shaped panes. Across the street was the old Post Office building, abandoned now for more than a year, and beyond us stretched the North Quadrangle, mostly unchanged since the first structures were erected at the southern end 200 years before.

Change, however, was coming. Bulldozers and backhoes were assembled on the grass. A week earlier, two statues – one dedicated to the College's Civil War dead, the other to the slaves whose labor had made the school a reality – had been spirited away, and construction of yet another misplaced building dedicated to some ephemeral enterprise was slated to begin on Monday. Its back to High Street, it would rise four stories from the ground and enclose an open space left virtually untouched for two centuries.

Alex returned to our earlier conversation. "I've seen some newspaper articles about genetic engineering. I'm not sure it's a good thing."

"Why not?"

"Well – it seems like these scientists are trying to play God."

God had assumed a darker mien over the past few months. "So?"

"You know. Interfering with nature."

"Who cares? If it helps you get better, that's all that matters."

"I don't know. Some things –" She was interrupted by the sound of fireworks coming from the direction of the stadium. Another recent addition to the spectacle, they signaled a College victory. A loss was followed by an ethereal rendering of the alma mater, enticing the faithful to return next week.

I looked around. Whorls and eddies of people, all dressed in the school colors, streamed toward us. A few were students, but the bulk of them had graduated long ago or never matriculated at all. Some of the men carried banners or waved flags, others – their faces painted blue – clutched cans and bottles and cups overlooked on football Saturdays. The women, youthful from a distance, grew older as they approached. "Some things are better left alone," Alex said.

I turned back to her. Her hair, once a thick, auburn mane, was thinner now and shot through with gray. Her body was diminished, too, and the sharp features of her face were without flesh. Light still shone from the china blue eyes, but it seemed to grow dimmer every day. A familiar, unwelcome moisture washed my own eyes. "Alex, what are you talking about? All we do is interfere with nature." I paused. "We'd still be living in caves if we didn't."

"But – this involves human beings. Changing our – our chemistry."

The pent-up rage – at the world, at God, even at her – broke loose. "Goddamn it, Alex. Listen to me. I don't care about all that bullshit. All the treatments, the medications, everything you've gone through, *changed* your chemistry. That's what medicine does." I felt the tears begin, and ignored them. "But that was yesterday's medicine. If this gene business will save your life, we'll do it. Somebody has to play God because He's not doing a very good job."

The crowd had reached us now, and I became aware of the glances cast my way. I wanted to yell at them, too – thoughtless cartoons undeserving of the vitality they enjoyed – and decided against it. I swiped at the tears and stood up. "Let's go home."

She rose and took my arm. "I'll be fine, Harry," she said in the voice she had used to soothe me for 30 years. "Don't worry."

TWO

BECAUSE I would leave no stone unturned, and wasn't willing to omit any ritual that might make things better, I had started going to church again. It didn't help. I wasn't expecting miracles, but I *was* looking for an explanation. Sure, other people got sick and died, but that didn't help, either. What had she – we – done to deserve this?

The fire and brimstone of my youth were gone, replaced by the "I'm okay, you're okay" ethos of modern Christianity. It was numbing. Why try to live right if it didn't make any difference? I was no saint and I could understand retribution, but the idea that it was just the luck of the draw was infuriating. Tired of the worn platitudes of the Church of my ancestors, I decided to seek consolation in a newer place.

Stepping outside our gray Federalist "farmhouse," the oldest dwelling-place in New Hope, I pulled the door closed quietly. Alex was still asleep. At the end of the brick path, I turned left, walked down the hill past the Chancellor's House, and crossed the street at the light. My church destination was only a few blocks away, so I had time to kill. I pushed through the heavy door of the old stucco bungalow that had served as an office for generations of Monmouths and Randalls, and crossed the reception area to my office.

There was a note from my secretary on the desk:

Dear Mr. Monmouth,

We've <u>finally</u> managed to make an appoint-ment at the fertility clinic. Someone died or got sick or something, and they called us. It's for 9 A.M. Monday morning. I don't know how long it will take, but I'll call you if I can't come in at all (I'll take a vacation day). Thanks for understanding.

Abby

I smiled. Abigail Sloan was a lovely young woman with minimal secretarial skills that matched my negligible need for a secretary. It was unlikely she even had a vacation day to trade. She and her husband, a tired, henpecked fellow who worked for her father in the insurance business, had been trying to "get pregnant" ever since they were married, without success. She evidently expected to conceive on her wedding night three years earlier and, as each succeeding night passed without sperm meeting egg, she grew more and more impatient.

There were doctor's visits – alone at first, accompanied later by her husband – books, pills, old wives' nostrums and, recently, dark allusions to his fertility. Steiner's clinic had been pronounced the solution over a year ago but, despite pledging a robust add-on – financed by her father – to the already considerable fee, she had to wait in line like everyone else. My occasional witticisms about the joys of delaying children, which I had not experienced, found a deaf ear.

On my way out, I paused at the framed caricature that Alex had drawn before we were married. I hadn't changed very much, I decided. There was some gray in the thick yellow hair, shorter now. The features – the wide mouth, the small nose and ears – were the same, and the blue eyes were almost purple. The puckish attitude, however, was gone.

A survey of the rest of me forced an acknowledgment of the added pounds and lack of tone. I decided to resume the weight-lifting regimen interrupted by Alex's illness. The idea made me uneasy for some reason, but I brushed the worry aside.

Outside on High Street, I turned right. Sunday morning was the only time I recognized the little village where I grew up, though its structure was unchanged. The few people about were going to church. Nothing was open, not because the law or religious belief required it, but because the students weren't up yet.

The local preservation society had attached "memorials" to the buildings, sturdy bronze plaques that recalled a time when they had served the small population of New Hope that was distinct from the College. Some of those people were still here, living in the old neighborhoods bordering the school, but they didn't shop on High Street anymore because there was nothing there they wanted to buy.

New Hope, unable to manage the change, was overwhelmed. As the new people and the new money poured in, the villagers whose families had been there for decades left. High Street became an arcade devoted to the amusement of the new people, and the new money dictated that New Hope be dispersed.

West End, the businesses and neighborhoods that flanked High Street on the western side of Division, had been ravaged as well. Initially, there was much self-congratulation among the political class over its gentrification. The poor people who had lived and worked there for generations were forced out by high taxes and high real estate prices, and more of those who catered to the College moved in.

Those few square blocks, once overwhelmingly black, were now mostly white and, predictably, the people responsible for the apartheid were now demanding "diversity" and "affordable housing." Even Milltown, the once-rural community on New Hope's western border, had been infested by the newcomers.

My destination, the West End Mosque, was situated on the corner of Michael and West Second Street, only two blocks from the long-established New Hope AME from which it was spawned. It was a low brick building that once housed a combination pool room and pawn shop. Services were held on Sunday to accommodate the parishioners. Prayers had already begun when I sat down on a wooden bench along the back wall.

A few white faces, some of whom I recognized, mixed with the black and brown. I was surprised at the crowd, mostly young families with children, given the brevity of the mosque's existence. Its founder, who was also its imam, had grown tired of the "culture" engrained in the old church, and decided to preach a new religion. Controversy a few months later had given him an issue that drew some of the old congregants to him, and enticed a few heretofore churchless people along with them. His vision was apocalyptic, and his words enjoined the people to return to the God of their forebears.

Head bowed, he sat in a chair at the front of the room, a massive man in a black suit, white shirt and black bowtie. His gleaming brown pate reminded me of Frank Steiner. He had "converted" to Islam and taken a new name, though he didn't insist on it with friends. In fact, his conversion was more for show than anything else. He believed the Muslim faith, despite its excesses, was what religion should be, but tenets of the black church he had absorbed as a boy were just below the surface. He had not left the church of his fathers – it had abandoned him.

Confronted with the barbarity of his fellow Islamists – mass executions, beheadings, suicide bombers – he shrugged it off. "Religious fanatics are nothing new," he said. "And life's not all it's cracked up to be anyway."

When the last prayer was said, the people sat back to listen. The preacher remained motionless for a full minute before crossing the room to a makeshift lectern elevated by a platform of raw white pine. Drawing a pair of horn-rimmed glasses from his pocket, he settled them on his nose, lifted his head and surveyed the crowd.

We leaned forward. "There's a war going on," he said, "and the objective is our destruction. You and me. Too many of us don't know about it, or have enlisted on the other side, and time is short. Our enemy has perfected his weapon, and the slaughter has begun."

It was quiet as death. Even the children, who moments before babbled and cried, were silent. He continued: "I see a few more white faces today."

He looked at me and smiled. "It's not just a war between black and white. It's not just a war between rich and poor. It's also a war between the eternal meddlers and those of us who just want to be left alone. It's been going on since we were cast out of the Garden, but all of the battles up to now were skirmishes. The weapons turned on us were insufficient, but now the means is at hand. If we do nothing, we will be obliterated."

He spent the next half hour explaining how the "meddlers" and their science, in full view of the world and perhaps – by their lights – with the best intentions, would rain down Armageddon on those they considered inferior. "If you do not think as they do, or look or speak like them," he thundered, "they will cure those deficiencies. And the cure is annihilation."

No one moved. He took a sheet of paper from his pocket and spread it on the lectern. "According to the College's website, Project Sickle Cell has treated 220 adults and 105 children in this community since it began four months ago. It says, 'barring unforeseen circumstances,' they plan to make the science available to the rest of the country, the world, within a few months. What do you think those unforeseen circumstances might be?"

He pounded the lectern with his fist. "Their science violates the order of Allah and nature. Mutants will be brought forth." He paused. "And they're not content with 'curing' disease. Soon they will tamper with our children, born and unborn. And that will be the end of days." He stopped again. "We must resist. We have no choice." The people, rigid for almost 45 minutes, relaxed as he returned to his chair, but only a little. After another prayer, they began to file out, silently.

Moments later, the building was empty except for us. He gripped my hand. "It's good to see you, Harry."

"Thanks, Wes. Same here." Wesley Vaughn and I had known each other for almost 40 years, and we'd been friends for most of that time. The beginning was not auspicious. We played on the last football team the old high school had fielded, me because I wanted to, him because the politics of the time dictated that he leave his friends at Booker T. Washington High School and play with the white boys at New Hope.

We won a lot more than we lost that season, largely because of him, and the pain and the elation and – finally – the awful disappointment we shared had obscured the skin we wore. He was an All-State linebacker that year and I was just another quarterback, but the crucible of the game we played ensured affection and respect and loyalty that eventually became friendship. "You're kind of hard on the folks over at the College, aren't you?" I said.

"I meant every word of it. Set aside the morality of what they're doing, it's not ready. Even Steiner said it was years away before the politicians and the race crowd convinced him otherwise." He grimaced. "They're experimenting on us."

"I hear everything's fine. People are actually being cured of sickle cell anemia."

"That's not necessarily so. You have to listen carefully. What they're saying is they've altered the cells and the disease is in remission. They don't know if it'll come back or not." He paused. "They also don't know how this treatment might affect other cells. Or babies born to the people they're treating."

"But it's a terrible disease. Why not try to fix it?"

"It needs to be fixed right. It's not a political football or – or just another way to cash in." He stopped. "All these scientists claim to believe in evolution. Darwin is – was – their god. Everything in nature is supposedly the result of microscopic events occurring over millions of years." He leaned forward. "Man emerged from the ooze in teeny, tiny steps and yet, when there's money to be made or people to be manipulated, they abandon Darwin. 'Let's fix it all today, evolution be damned.'"

I smiled. "You sound like quite the expert."

"Hey. I'm a college graduate now."

"Since when?"

"Central started a program a few years ago, trying to get the guys who didn't graduate – football and basketball players, mostly – to come back to school. I got my diploma last month."

"Congratulations. What did you study? Genetics?"

He laughed. "History." He hesitated. "When they started pushing the sickle cell project, I read up on it. Genes control our cells. Mutant genes cause disease or deformity. They eliminate the bad gene, or change it, and the problem goes away."

"What's wrong with that?"

"I'll spare you the theology. Look ahead a few years. Gene therapy isn't used just to treat sick people. It's used to *change* people, and not just the people here now. Babies will be engineered for everything from genetic disease to the color of their

hair." He paused. "It'll be irresistible and expen-
sive. Those who have will have more, those who
don't will have less. The gap will grow." He
stopped again. "Nobody owns the gene pool. It be-
longs to everybody. It shouldn't be tampered with
unless everybody agrees."

We sat without speaking. "Well," I said fi-
nally, "I only care about one sick person."

He stared at me for a moment. "How's she
doing?"

"Not good. The bone marrow transplant
didn't take, and they're afraid the cancer has
spread. She has a tumor in her head. We're wait-
ing for the tests."

"I'm sorry."

"No prayers?"

"Prayers are for those who believe in them."

"I'm going to see Steiner." He nodded. "I
don't give a damn about the rest of it. I just want
Alex to get well." The tears that came so frequently
now tried to form in my eyes, but I beat them back.
"I'll be one of the people you disapprove of."

He shook his head. "You're just a human be-
ing, Harry. That's the problem."

Outside, I retraced my steps. There were
people on the sidewalks now. The long block of
High Street between Division and Anderson had
been "preserved," but the preservation was only
skin deep. The two-story Georgian buildings, brick
with plate-glass storefronts, still stood, but the
bakeries, bookstores and gift shops were gone. One
of the theaters remained, and a drugstore, and
Becker's College Shop displayed the high fashion of
the day, but the rest of it was a midway, an ap-

pendage to the colossal carnival the College had become.

THE CHANCELLOR looked up from his book. Winfred Honeyman was a tall, gawky man with a full shock of white hair and rheumy blue eyes under heavy brows. He was never without a tie and, except for formal affairs – of which there were now quite a few – he was always dressed in tweeds and desert boots, the recommended costume for a professor in his day and one he had never relinquished.

I was unsure if it was comfort or affectation. Like me, he refused to carry a cell phone, and the only computer in his office was on his secretary's desk. This, of course, led to charges of old fogeyism, which he acknowledged cheerfully. "Harry. Thanks for coming."

"What are you reading?"

He picked the book up, and thrust the spine at me. "Aristotle. I sometimes need to be reminded to think instead of just reacting." He stood up. "It's nice outside. Let's sit on the porch."

I followed him through the door. The "porch" at South Building was actually an Ionic temple that had been added to the Palladian structure a hundred years after the building itself was constructed. It stood on high ground – two levels of steps descended to the South Quadrangle where brick walks on either side of the quad led to the Main Library a hundred yards away. Additional paths crisscrossed the yard, and ancient oaks and poplars provided shade. It was a vista that recalled the warmth and beauty of a place I still loved.

The teak benches on the porch clashed with its architecture, and I had never seen either of them occupied before. I sat down beside him and stared through the trees at the library. The cone atop the bell tower, behind the building and across Tower Road, looked like a dunce cap perched on the library's dome. "It was good to see Alex yesterday," he said. "How's she –?"

"She's lousy, Win. She's sick of it and so am I. Why did you want to see me?"

He bit his lip. "Sorry." He began again. "The Organization's investigation is finished. I expect the final report by the end of this week."

"What are they going to do?"

"Probation, a few scholarships, no bowl games for a while. We'll lose some wins. Maybe a fine."

"When does it take effect?"

He smiled. "Next year. It took so long to finish, we're into another season. And this team's clean." He turned his head. "This could be a good year."

I nodded. The football team had been ranked 10th in the nation a few days earlier, and yesterday's blow-out insured the rank would improve. "What did they find?"

"The usual. Agents, money, cars. Parties at South Beach."

"How many players were involved?"

"Ten. They're long gone. And the coaches. We're starting this season with a clean slate."

"What did the coaches do?"

"Nothing. They're scapegoats." He looked at his hands. "I'm not proud of it, but it was – necessary."

"Why did it take so long?"

He shook his head. "They have to do one of these every now and then to keep everybody else in line. It's cumbersome, and it's supposed to be." He stopped. "The Organization wants to pretend the College – not the Athletic Department or the alumnae or the networks – is actually running the football program. They make deans and professors and chancellors participate." He sighed. "I'm the worst guy in the world for something like this."

"Why don't they just do it themselves?"

"They don't have the resources. What they have is a rule book thicker than the New York telephone directory. It forces us to investigate ourselves and punishes us if we don't, even if we had nothing to do with whatever they're investigating. Any failure to admit something is wrong invites further punishment. It's Kafkaesque." He reached into his coat pocket and withdrew a letter. "This is from the Chairman. Read the last paragraph."

I unfolded the sheet of paper: "We agree that the College neither knew nor should have known of the violations at the time they occurred." I handed the letter back. "So why are you being punished?"

"Because the rules of the Organization say we're responsible for all of it, whether we knew about it or not."

"And the College has agreed to those rules?"

"Yes. Otherwise we have no football team. Or any other team."

I smiled. "Is that so bad?"

"Come on, Harry. I'd be strung up tomorrow, and not in effigy, if I even suggested such a thing."

"Why do you do it, Win?"

"Football?" I nodded. "I don't care about football. I like the pageantry. We leave the cloister on Saturday afternoons – or whenever the networks tell us to – and mingle with the outside world. Our students compete." He stopped. "And it's good for business. The football and basketball teams are the most potent advertising we have."

"Has this investigation hurt that?"

He shook his head. "Not at all. I just got the final numbers for last year. Applications are up 30 per cent. We've raised over $291 million, our best year ever, and we've moved from 17th to 10th in the amount of federal money received. More than $554 million." He laughed. "It looks like the notoriety's been good for us." He stopped. "But we don't need any more."

We sat without speaking. The Chancellor was conflicted, and he didn't even know it. On the one hand, he viewed the College as a "cloister" where the inmates emerged occasionally to greet the outside world. On the other, he acknowledged – boasted – of its success in drawing the attention and the money of business and government. One of those perceptions was wishful thinking.

The town and the College had been laid out on the same day in the last decade of the 18th century. They had co-existed easily for most of the following 200 years but, by the first decade of the 21st century, the school had changed radically, and its mutation had infected New Hope. An institution created to teach, the College was now a conglomerate dedicated to the bottom line.

Tuition was raised every year, the acquisition of grants from governments and foundations had its own building, and corporate funding – and the strings that came with it – was importuned by a cadre of "administrators" from the Chancellor on down. Financial considerations and business concerns and research intended to benefit its private benefactors had replaced the traditional mission of scholarship and learning. Students, "customers" whose grades and test scores added to the "brand" and provided cover for the greed, were recruited with fancy dorm rooms and gourmet food, but their educations were subservient to the commerce. Everyone pretended nothing had changed.

"So," I said, "what can I do for you?"

He leaned toward me. "We have a mandatory tutoring program for our athletes. It costs millions of dollars a year to operate. The School of Arts and Sciences administers it, and the Dean told me Friday she thinks one of the tutors is – involved with one of the players."

"So?"

"Anything out of the usual at the intersection of athletics and academics is troublesome."

"For God's sake, Win, do they have a rule against that, too?"

"Probably. Or they can stretch another one to cover it."

I took a deep breath and let the air out slowly. "What do you want me to do?"

"Ask a few questions. If it's just sex, we'll ignore it. Let the bureaucrats in Kansas City interfere with young love without our help. If it has anything to do with his academic performance, though, we may have to do something else."

"Why me?"

"I wasn't kidding when I described your pedigree to Steiner last night. You are the most respected member of this community, town and gown. You are of the College, but not in it. You know the people who might know what's going on – the Dean, the Athletic Director, probably others – and you're discreet. Whatever you find out, I won't be reading about it in the papers or on the Internet."

I rose. "Okay. I'll look into it. I'll start with Helen."

"Thanks. Her office is right upstairs."

I turned for the steps and looked back. "Speaking of Steiner, who is he besides head of the very profitable Genetics Department?"

He looked at me appraisingly. "He's an overbearing boor, but he knows his stuff. He's one of the world's leading gene therapists. We're lucky to have him, but it wasn't cheap. The building alone cost over $100 million."

"He looks pretty fit. How old is he?"

"He must be in his late sixties, at least. He got his last degree in 1973."

"Did he object to Project Sickle Cell?"

He hesitated. "Not exactly. He wanted to run a clinical trial before treating the general public."

"How long would that take?"

"Several years, apparently. When the governor came out for it, and the legislature passed the bill, he agreed to go ahead."

"How does it work?"

The Chancellor shook his head. "I have no idea. You'll have to ask him."

THREE

THE TELEPHONE in the reception area rang. I debated whether to pick it up in the absence of my secretary, then lifted the receiver. "Harry Monmouth."

"Mr. Monmouth, it's Abby." The excitement in her voice was palpable. "I'm going to have a baby. Twins."

"Already? I thought it —"

"I haven't started yet. I'm staying at the clinic overnight and tomorrow they'll harvest my eggs. Then David will make his contribution, and by the middle of next week I'll be pregnant. Isn't that amazing?"

"Yes. Yes, it certainly is." I pictured her husband, doing whatever was necessary to "make his contribution," and pitied him again. "I thought it took a lot longer than that."

"Doctor Steiner says it used to, but they have new techniques now. We could've done it all today, but the egg has to sit in some kind of dish for a week."

The gratification wasn't quite instant, but the romance was certainly gone. "What made you decide to have twins?"

"It was Doctor Steiner's idea. It doesn't cost any more."

A two-for-one deal. I shook my head as I recalled the early years of our marriage when Alex and I had four young children under foot. We had

to hire a nanny. "You know, looking after two in-
fants at the same time is a lot of work. Twice as
much, in fact. Maybe more."

"Oh, we'll be okay. David's going to help."

I stifled a laugh. Her husband's already har-
ried existence was about to get a lot harder. "Well,
congratulations. Any idea when I might see you
around here again?"

"I'll be in after lunch tomorrow."

"Great. See you then."

"Thanks, Mr. Monmouth. See you tomor-
row."

I leaned back in the chair. Abby was only 24
years old. Blonde and pretty, she'd been Homecom-
ing Queen at one of the local high schools, and a
cheerleader at the College. She had at least a dec-
ade to make a baby in the ordinary way, and yet
she wanted one now, damn the expense and poten-
tial emotional trauma. A baby was something to
consume or acquire, like groceries or furniture.
The process at the fertility clinic was supposedly
developed for people at the end of their child-
bearing rope, but now it was just another product
to be bought and sold, flogged in the newspapers
and on television.

I picked up the phone again. "This is Harry
Monmouth. Let me speak to Doctor Steiner,
please."

He came on the line. "Steiner."

"Harry Monmouth, Doctor Steiner. How are
you?"

"Couldn't be better, Harry. And call me
Frank."

"Thanks. I'd like to take you up on your invitation. When would it be convenient for me to drop by and tour the facility?"

There was a pause at the end of the line. "How about tomorrow? Say, one thirty."

"That's fine. I'm looking forward to it."

I laid the phone down and sat still for a minute, then withdrew a bottle of scotch from the drawer. Rising, I found a glass and ice, and sat down in a black leather chair by the window. Lifting my feet to the ottoman, I poured the scotch and stared out at the parking lot. I couldn't shake the feeling that Steiner knew exactly why I was coming to see him, and it wasn't for a tour.

ALEX WAS asleep on the chaise in our bedroom. She didn't stir when I kissed her on the forehead, so I tiptoed from the dark room and went back downstairs. In the kitchen, I checked the leftovers in the refrigerator — spaghetti, vegetable soup, chili made from chicken and white beans — and decided to let her decide.

Our meals now were habits. My "cooking" was perfunctory, as were our appetites. The occasional offering from friends provided an excuse for anticipation that lasted only a couple of bites. Unread issues of the local newspaper, the *New Hope Chronicle*, lay on the counter. I poured a glass of brandy.

She appeared in the doorway. Alexis Bradford Monmouth was a Yankee whose relatives arrived on the *Mayflower*. She descended several notches to marry me, though my ancestors were supposedly at the pinnacle in New Hope. Our lives together had begun in chaos almost 30 years earlier, but we had righted ourselves and enjoyed a life that perhaps we didn't deserve. She stood beside me, and braved the revelations regarding my people without flinching.

I had finally brushed the troubles aside, but Alex was never able to forget them. Proud of the genes she had inherited, it was her birthright that threatened us now. "How was your day?" she said.

She received news of the world outside our house from me. No detail was too small – the weather, birds, people I'd seen on the street – and I had begun making notes so as not to forget anything. Abby's news was the highlight. It provided an excuse to reminisce about the boys, a topic she returned to again and again as her illness wore on. They were far-flung, and not very good at staying in touch until she fell ill. Now each of them called her every day.

I omitted the conversation with Steiner, and concluded my summary: "I'm going to see Helen Tanner in the morning." She smiled. I could see the wheels turning, and tried to stop them. "Win asked me to."

"Why?"

"One of the football players is apparently involved with his tutor. She's part of Helen's department. He wants me to look into it."

"What for? What business is it of his?"

"It seems that when you agree to play football for the College, your life is no longer your own. It's a return to the plantation. Anything that might affect your ability to play is open to question."

"I don't understand."

"The tutor's job is to make sure the player is doing well enough in school to play football. If his grades fall below a certain level, he can't play. If she's doing more than the rules allow, the program might get in trouble."

She frowned. "So the tutoring has nothing to do with getting an education?"

"Well – I suppose the player might pick up something. But, yes, the tutor's there to keep him eligible." I paused. "It's not just the College. Everyone has a plantation."

"Why do they do it?"

"Who? The College?"

"And the players."

"The College does it because they've always done it. It's part of the 'experience' for everybody, not just players."

"You mean the other students?"

"It's not really for the students anymore. It's for the alumnae. And fans and media. They obsess over the team. Hundreds of little industries – talk shows, blogs, memorabilia – exist only because of the College's football team. The better the team, the higher the profits." I leaned back. "And then there's television. College football generates billions of advertising dollars for TV. The College gets a pretty good chunk of it."

"What does any of that have to do with a college education?"

I smiled. "Nothing. The players used to be real students, amateurs more or less. People thought amateurism was a good thing. We're way past that now."

"Why not just hire the players, then?"

"Because amateurism tied to an academic tradition is what sells. The public wants it. Fans can wax nostalgic about their days at the College, and imagine that the players are really just like they used to be. A little bigger and faster, maybe, but still just students at the dear old alma mater, going to class and pep rallies." I stopped. "If you pay them, it's just another small-time game like — like minor league baseball."

"Your cynicism is showing."

"It's hard not to be cynical about college football."

"What's in it for the players? Pro football?"

I shook my head. "The percentage of college players who play professional football is tiny."

"Then why?"

I considered. My own experience had ended when I was a senior in high school, and yet, all these years later, those games were still vivid. It wasn't the individual contests or my few personal highlights — the lowlights were much easier to recall — but the sheer physical brutality of knocking another guy down or taking a blow myself, over and over, to impose my will and that of my clan on the other.

The violence came easily to some — Wes Vaughn was one of those — but others, like me, had to learn it. Victory was an elixir that healed the wounds, defeat a hemlock that caused them to endure until the next opportunity. Our last loss, in the College stadium on Thanksgiving Day so many years before, was my last game, and the pain lingered. "Have you ever seen a video of bighorn sheep going after each other?"

"Yes."

"That's one reason guys play football."

"It's barbaric."

I laughed. "Barbarism's in our genes. Football and war are all we have left, and war seems a little squishy these days."

"That's not why our boys played."

"Maybe not. Some just want to test themselves, or maybe their fathers insisted." She smiled. "Some drop out along the way. Others keep playing at whatever level they can." I paused. "Every now and then, a chosen one appears. Our current quarterback, for example. He dominates his team, his conference, maybe the whole state in high school. He's in the papers and on TV, a commodity to be auctioned to the highest bidder."

"By who?"

"His coaches. His parents. Someone he trusts."

"They don't really bid, do they?"

"Oh, yes, but not with money. With dreams."

"Meaning what?"

"Pro football and all that comes with it. Celebrity, money, fancy cars."

"But so few –"

"Everybody knows most of them won't make it, probably even them. But the College promises great training and coaching and television exposure. It has a pro day and an agent day and so forth. If they do what they're told, they have a chance."

"But the odds are so long."

"These kids have been special since they were 12 years old. They're already celebrities in the little world they know. A lot of them have overcome terrible environments to succeed. A kid like that's not going to believe he might fail." I stopped. "Sometimes it's all they know."

We sat for a while without speaking. The sun poured through the windows on either side of the fireplace, and glanced off the old brick floor. Alex was bathed in the brightness, but she didn't turn away. I imagined for a moment it consumed her, converting her into swirling motes absorbed by the rays. When I blinked, though, she was still there. "Give my best to Helen," she said.

HELEN TANNER was standing at the window when I entered her office. The years had been kind. Tall and slim, vermilion hair framed her face. The fair complexion was unblemished, and wide-set, almond-shaped eyes the color of caramel turned toward me. She extended her hand and I took it. The fingers were cool. "Hello, Harry."

"Hi, Helen. How are you?"

"I'm good. Thanks."

"Your folks?"

"They're fine." She gestured to a pair of armchairs beside her. "Sit down."

We sat facing each other. Despite my once overblown reputation, I had slept with only a few women in my life, and she was one of them. She had surrendered something that was important to her, and now – more than three decades later – I felt moved to tell her why it was accepted so casually.

It was nonsense, of course. We were other people in another time and it would only embarrass her, and I had no explanation anyway beyond a sense of entitlement and a callow immortality.

Still, the words were forming when she recalled me. "How's your wife?"

I had forgotten Alex for a moment, and I was stunned at the resentment and the guilt. Why should my life, still robust, be burdened always by hers? Disgusted by the thought and the thinker, I was ashamed. What was wrong with me?

"She's doing okay, I guess. She's weak, and endless doctors and hospitals don't help. There's a – a new treatment we might try." The "new treatment" was not really ours to try yet, but my unpardonable failure of loyalty forced me to mention it.

She gazed at me for a few seconds. "When you called, I wondered why you were coming to see me after all this time."

"Well, I –"

"But I ran into the Chancellor a few minutes ago. You're taking on Teddy Black and his girlfriend."

"Teddy Black?" She nodded. Teddy Black was the football team's quarterback and, before that, the object of a nationwide contest for his considerable services. Only 19, he was nevertheless a man among boys. Almost six and a half feet tall, he ran 40 yards in 4.3 seconds despite his 240-pound frame, and he could heave a football the length of the field. The various rushing and passing records he claimed were eclipsed each time he took the field.

As he neared the end of his senior year in high school, the competition grew more intense. He was drafted as a pitcher in the first round of the baseball draft, and the National Basketball Association changed its rules so he could play right out of high school. His decision to play football at the College, the flagship school in his home state, had been greeted with delirious predictions of a national championship "before he turned pro." His performance in the first game had met every expectation, and the College was already mounting a campaign for the Heisman Trophy.

He was also an enigma. No one had ever heard him speak in public, and his teammates said that his words on the field were limited to whatever was necessary to play the game. He shunned all interviews and was silent in the classroom, and the people on campus – awed or indulgent – left him to himself as best they could.

Indeed, in the short time he'd been there, the College had wrapped him in a cocoon designed to thwart outsiders from disturbing his peace. In an age of blanket celebrity, where Warhol's 15 minutes were now interminable, the public's unwavering ardor was so far unrequited. "And his girlfriend?" I said.

"Yes. She's his tutor, too."

"What's the problem? Is she sleeping with him?"

"I don't know. He has a dorm room at Spencer Hall and so does she. Same dorm, different floors." She smiled. "Not that that's any barrier to whatever they want to do."

"So what's wrong?"

"The girl – her name's Cat Edwards – has never been part of the tutoring program before. She's the only freshman we've ever had. She was added to the roster by the Athletic Department and assigned to Teddy, all without consulting the people in charge."

"You?"

"I'm *not* in charge, thank God. I'm a figure-head. We provide a sheen of academic oversight. The Athletic Department pays them. If something blows up, of course, it'll be my head." She paused. "The program's run out of that monstrosity they built next to the stadium. They have Directors, Associate Directors, academic counselors and learning specialists. And dozens of tutors and learning assistants. I've managed to sneak a couple of my people in, and one of them came by last Thursday." She stopped again. "Anything unusual in a player's academic profile raises red flags. You wouldn't believe the hoops we go through to make sure we follow the rules. It's a nightmare."

"How do you know they're, uh – friends? Maybe she's really just a tutor."

"As far as we can tell, she never leaves his side except when he's sleeping, if then. I'm not sure what she is, but she's more than a tutor. And they're from the same hometown." Helen rose and walked to her desk. "This," she said, handing me a manila folder, "is all the paperwork we have on her. I asked for his records, too, and was politely refused. That's another red flag."

I was reluctant to leave. Alex was now more intimate with her doctors than with me, and the menace of death hovered over us always. Helen and I were just old friends. "Are you happy here?" I said.

She considered. "As much as anyplace, I guess."

"What's wrong?"

"I came here as a girl because I wanted to learn. I had teachers who wanted to teach. It's not like that anymore." I nodded. "All these kids want today is a credential, and they want to have a good time while they're getting it. The grades and test scores go up every year, but the lack of preparation before they get here is shocking." She paused. "It's not just the football team."

"Don't the professors –?"

"The professors are worse. They don't teach. Ideology and tenure are all that matter. The few good teachers are forced out by the students, and the bad ones fill up the space."

"Can't you do something about it?"

"Not me. I'd be crushed if I tried."

"But how do they get the – credential if nobody learns anything?"

"They buy their diplomas. No one really flunks out. Students are put in remedial classes, or just passed along, until they run out of money. That's the definition of academic failure now. When it finally happens the student leaves and another, with money in the bank, takes his place."

"Win Honeyman's a good man. Why does he let it go on?"

"It's all he can do to put out the little fires. I see it every day. This place is a runaway train, and Win's in the caboose."

At the door, I looked back. "Who's Tanner?"

A range of expressions crossed her face before it settled on amused. "He was a man who didn't work out."

I walked down the stairs and leaned into the Chancellor's office. His secretary looked up. "I'm Harry Monmouth. Is he here?"

"I'm sorry, Mr. Monmouth. He's meeting with the Director of the School of Human Enrichment. At the building site."

"The School of Human Enrichment?"

"Yes, sir."

For the second time in three days, I perched on one of the benches on the porch at South Building. The bell tower began to chime eleven o'clock, and the students on the walkways scurried inside the buildings.

When I first met Helen Tanner, she was Helen Cheek. She had come to the College my junior year from the Woman's School in Whitesboro. In those days, females weren't permitted to attend the College until they were juniors unless they were nursing students or residents of New Hope who could live at home. The paucity of women on campus led to all sorts of frenzied behavior, especially on weekends. The relentless inversion of the student body now, where women far outnumbered men, had merely given the frenzy a feminine cast.

Helen and I had been close, so close, in fact, there were murmurs of marriage. I met her parents, she spent time with my mother, and we practiced the little things that married people do. Raised in a devout Catholic household, she rejected the conventions of her family and tried to adopt those of her peers, but the conversion was awkward for her and painful for her parents. A portrait of Helen in her confirmation dress hung over the mantel – her mother, clutching a rosary, wept when I asked about it.

It was early days in Helen's liberation – sex was *de rigueur*, but she was reluctant. I foolishly prodded her into it and, though she never said so, that was the beginning of the end. The relationship continued for a while, but the friendship was over. The tentative plans we'd made were forgotten, and we drifted from each other's lives. A committed scholar, she went to graduate school up east, and eventually landed on the faculty at Barnard. Thirty years later, she had returned to the College as the Dean of the School of Arts and Sciences.

We had been invited to a reception welcoming her back to the College, an unusual circumstance that required me to explain who she was, and Alex had been suspicious of her ever since, or pretended to be. I found out later Helen herself was responsible for the invitation, a bit of news I kept to myself. She lived only a few blocks away, and we ran into each other periodically, but that was all. She had learned of Alex's illness, and sent me a note.

Still shocked at my betrayal, I tried to push it out of my mind. The task the Chancellor had set me was impossible. Any hint that I was tampering with Teddy Black would probably get me shot. And what the hell was the School of Human Enrichment?

I walked around the building and crossed College Avenue. The North Quadrangle stretched before me. Construction equipment was in motion at the far end, and a significant gash in the ground was already evident. I considered seeking the Chancellor out in order to hand back the Teddy Black project, but decided to wait. Maybe I could speak to the girl. After that, I would return my commission.

I turned east. At the end of the sidewalk, I descended steep concrete steps and passed into the Bower, a garden with lawns and shrubs and trees and flowers, and sandy paths lined with stones that wound among them. Once a trysting place, it was now largely deserted – even at night – because the students no longer required seclusion to carry on their affairs.

The bench I was looking for, the one Helen and I once claimed as ours, was shaded by a blue Chinese fir tree. I sat down and tried again to force her image from my head. I loved my wife, and would do anything to make her well, but Alex was an inevitable reminder of my own mortality. Helen was a symbol of what I had lost, what we all lose if we live long enough. Disturbed by the turn of events in my head, I opened the folder and began to read.

FOUR

THE SHELL was a replica of the ancient Greek temple dedicated to Zeus. The original structure, located a few hundred yards from the Acropolis in Athens, took six centuries to build. This one required only six years. Situated on the College's highest ground, it stood where the Medical Center's first hospital – a modest, three-story building made of orange brick – once stood.

Over the years, the old building had survived while others around it were demolished and replaced by new ones made of concrete and glass, structures designed in the heat of the architectural moment whose moment was now long past. They resembled nothing so much as a child's building blocks, assembled erratically and left lying in the yard at odd angles. When Frank Steiner agreed to bring his genetics operation to the College, he demanded a structure and site of his choosing, and the fate of the old hospital was sealed at last.

Erected on a massive limestone platform, the exterior of the structure was marble. The building itself was surrounded by Corinthian columns – triple rows of 8 supporting pediments front and back, double rows of 14 under galleries along each side – 55 feet high and 6 feet around. The classical motif extended to the façade, but once inside it was a conventional, though still well-appointed, medical clinic.

The design had drawn derision from the local architectural clique, not for its own charms but for its obvious contrast to the buildings around it, leading some to suggest that the existing eyesores be torn down. Others made snide remarks about the grandiosity of the clinic's proprietor. Steiner had no comment.

He met me in the lobby. "Is there anything in particular you'd like to see?" he said.

"No. I'm curious about the whole thing."

We passed through doors and walked corridors on the first floor dedicated to the fertility clinic. "My secretary is one of your patients. Abigail Sloan. She was here last night, I think."

His eyes widened slightly, and the detached, tour guide demeanor left his face. "Yes. A delightful young person. Very enthusiastic."

"That's an understatement." He laughed. The rear of the ground floor included patient and consulting rooms, and the entire second floor was devoted to the laboratories that supported all of the programs – *in vitro* fertilization, gene therapy, genetic screening and Project Sickle Cell. "Do you know my friend Wesley Vaughn? He has another name now – Mahmoud Mohammad."

He smiled. "I know of him. He's a friend of yours?"

"We go back a long way."

"He's very – tenacious. He and his friends harass me sometimes." I lifted my brows. "They occupy the plaza out front. Try to turn my patients away."

"Successfully?"

"Not very. Someone cancels occasionally." Then, dismissively: "It's only the sickle cell patients. We've had to call the authorities a couple of times."

We stepped onto the elevator. The third floor was a maze of offices utilized by him and his staff. As we pushed through a door into his office, the phone rang. "Excuse me," he said. I wandered around the large room while a lengthy technical conversation ensued.

The usual accouterments for a professional's office – diplomas, citations, other evidence of achievement and excellence – were missing. Instead, there were books, hundreds of them. I examined the titles. Most were written in English, but there were many in German and a few in French, Italian and Greek.

An oversized volume – too large for the shelves – lay on a table next to the window. I picked it up. The title was in German, but I recognized the last word – "Hygiene." Written by a man named Fritz Astel, it was published in Munich in 1930. There was an inscription by the author on the flyleaf, addressed to someone named Wilhelm Egger, that I couldn't translate.

The door in the wall behind Steiner was open. I leaned into the room. It was another lab, smaller than the others but jammed with the same cabinets and equipment I'd seen on the floor below. When I turned back, he was staring at me, the receiver in its cradle once more. He gestured to an armchair on the other side of his desk. After I was seated, he looked at me over his glasses and said, "Now, Mr. – Harry, what can I *really* do for you."

Unable to come to the point, I dissembled. "Wes told me you thought Project Sickle Cell was premature. So did the Chancellor." He nodded. "Why did you go ahead with it?"

He leaned back in his chair. "I'm sure you're aware of the – campaign."

The last word was an epithet. "Yes."

"I was threatened. The politicians and the College and the – the others, made it clear they would sabotage my work if I didn't." His laugh was without mirth. "So I gave them what they wanted."

The contempt was patent. Shortly after Steiner moved into his new temple, he announced that he had devised a genetic cure for sickle cell anemia. The black community – from which all his patients would be drawn – greeted the news with jubilation, and the College, for different reasons, did likewise.

The story, replete with histories of the scourge that affected only blacks, and interviews with obviously sick children who had inherited the disease from their parents, was all over the networks and newspapers. The clinic was bombarded with demands from "advocates" of one stripe or another that certain segments of the black community receive the first treatment.

Steiner, alarmed that his public relations effort had been oversold, tried to walk the revelation back, but it was too late. A suggestion that the treatment was still years from actual implementation led to charges that he was a charlatan or a racist or both. He was pilloried by the press, the black pulpits and, most especially, by his colleagues on campus.

Sickle cell was a "race disease" that had been part of the country's politics for half a century. It was an obscure, painful illness unknown to the white community, and the medical establishment had ignored it until forced to take notice. Politicians, pandering for votes and the money that came with "curing" selected ailments, elevated sickle cell to a cause.

For a few years the disease was in the spotlight. Doctors, hospitals and government spent billions of dollars on research and treatment with indifferent success before moving on to something else. Sickle cell languished, stoking fears that it – and the people who suffered from it – would be forgotten again. Steiner's announcement had made it an issue once more and, when he hesitated, a familiar coalition of demagogues forced him to begin the program. "Is there really any danger?" I said.

"Certainly. These *people* –" he was almost sneering "– will get what they deserve."

"But the patients aren't the problem." He didn't respond. "I mean – they weren't responsible for the campaign." He remained silent. "You can't blame a sick man for trying to get well." He stared at me.

I was beginning to regret my mission. Steiner's bedside manner was lacking, to say the least, and trusting Alex to his ministrations seemed problematic even if he agreed to help her. Still, he was all I had left. I temporized further while trying to make up my mind. "Why didn't you leave?"

"I finally have what I need. I refuse to be driven out."

I hesitated. "How does it work?"

"The sickle cell therapy?"

"Yes."

The rancor diminished as he spoke. "DNA is what makes living organisms what they are. Human DNA is contained in 23 pairs of chromosomes. There are approximately 19,000 genes within the chromosomes. We've discovered several thousand genetic mutations related to human disease." He paused. "Sickle cell results from a flawed gene in the red blood cells. That mutation makes the cells change shape and impede the flow of blood. Normal cells are round and pliable. Sickle cells are rigid and shaped like the blade of a sickle."

He made a quick sketch on a scrap of paper and pushed it across the desk. "That leads to various chronic conditions, some of which are fatal. Science has made some strides over the past 50 years, but life expectancy for those who have it is still three decades short of the general population."

"How do you fix it?"

"We used to treat it with blood transfusions and bone marrow transplants. The accepted genetic treatment now is to use stem cells from the patient's bone marrow. Anti-sickle cells are introduced which create a continuous source of normal red blood cells that outlast the sickle cells."

"And that cures it?"

He shook his head. "It improves the patient's condition but it doesn't cure the disease." He paused. "*My* treatment cures sickle cell anemia."

"How?"

"I transplant donor stem cells into the patient. Cells without the gene mutation."

"Donor?"

"Not the patient's. It's been done experimentally before, but the cells were always rejected by the patient's body."

"Why?"

"The patient's immune system fights the foreign stem cells. The problems vary from patient to patient – gastro issues, liver disease, organ damage – and the transplant may simply be refused. The cure is worse than the disease."

"And you've fixed that?"

"I – yes."

"But you wanted a clinical trial?"

"That's correct. The reality is that Project Sickle Cell is one big, unregulated clinical trial. There've been no problems so far, but it's not – scientific."

I took a deep breath. It was time. My wife –"

"Is very ill. I could see that. What is it? Cancer?"

I nodded. "Leukemia." He waited. "The Chancellor says you're doing research on leukemia."

"Yes."

"Is it pretty far along?"

He gazed at me. "It's very experimental."

"Can you – can you help her?"

He stared at me, longer this time. His face was blank except for the large black eyes – they blinked rapidly and at odd intervals as if transmitting a message in code. "Who's her doctor?" he said at last. I told him. He made a note, and flipped through an appointment book on the desk. "I want to see her. Bring her in Thursday at –" he looked at the book again "– five thirty. That's day after tomorrow."

"So you'll –?"

He shook his head. "I don't know. I want to see her before I decide."

"Thanks." I rose and turned for the door. Looking back, I said, "Don't mind what she says. She thinks you're trying to play God."

His expression didn't change. "If I don't, who will?"

"HOW WAS the harvest?" I said.

Abby laughed. "Fine. Apparently, I'm very fruitful."

"Great. Is the mail here yet?"

"It's on your desk."

I pushed through the door to my office and leaned over the walnut partner's desk that had served generations of the men in my family. The oxblood leather top, inlaid with gold, was bare except for two letters and the afternoon paper. My practice grew smaller each year, as did the volume of mail. None of our boys was interested in the law, and I didn't encourage them. The profession had long since been just a business and, beginning a year earlier, I had referred most of my work to the younger lawyers in town.

I picked up the paper and sat down in the chair by the window. The local newspaper had recently been acquired by the largest chain in the state and it, too, was very much a business. The new owner kept the name, and left the editorial page in local hands, but most of the "news" was wire service copy purchased by the chain and "published" in all its papers. Local news was reduced to a four-page insert, much of which was devoted to arrests and convictions and who was suing whom. A small headline caught my eye:

PARENTS, CLINIC FIGHT OVER BODY

The two-paragraph story, undoubtedly truncated by the police blotter and the grocery ads, didn't make much sense. The parents of a recently deceased four-year-old boy, Joe and Nancy Spiller, had sued Steiner to prevent him from taking possession of the body for an autopsy. It didn't say why Steiner might be entitled to it, but the child had been a product of the fertility clinic. Presumably the autopsy was part of the deal, an idea seemingly confirmed by the final sentence, attributed to the clinic's spokesman: "No one's ever objected before."

I dropped the paper on the floor and closed my eyes. The clinic had originally been housed in one of the old buildings, and it had been in the fertility business for more than eight years. How many babies were assembled during that period of time? How many had died? And, finally, what difference did it make to me?

"I'M NOT going, Harry. I can't."

"Why not?"

"Because I'm not a machine to be tinkered with."

"What are you talking about?"

"Fix a cell here, add a gene there, and you have a new model. A new, improved, not quite human being."

"Alex, all we're trying to do is cure an awful disease. And keep you alive."

"In a Petri dish?"

"No, damn it. In this house. Wherever you are. For your friends and your children and me. And you."

"Harry." She paused. "I wouldn't be me anymore. And it wouldn't be my life. It would be Steiner's." She stopped again. "It would be an — existence, not a life. I don't want to do it."

I was beginning to lose control. "What's wrong with you?" I shouted. "Would you rather be dead? You have billions of cells. We're talking about changing a few bad ones. *You* won't be changed at all, except the leukemia will be gone."

"Harry. Please." She crossed to my chair and knelt beside it. "It won't stop with curing diseases. Pretty soon they'll be changing eyes and hair, and then they'll make people taller or thinner. Babies will be designed. It's — evil. I don't want to be part of the process."

I was very tired. My life had been consumed with seeing her well. Each drug, each procedure had created hope, the flimsy desire for something better, and each time hope — Pandora's illusory gift to mankind — had failed. We had one last chance, and Alex was ready to die rather than take it. Helen's face appeared behind my eyes, and my resolve weakened for an instant, but I resisted.

I shook my head. "That's not it, Alex. You just want to give up." I kissed the top of her head. "We're going to do this. You owe me. And the boys. All this — theology is beside the point. If you die, we'll be alone. You don't want that." I paused. "I don't care if Steiner is Satan incarnate. If he can make you well, we're going to do it."

FIVE

THEY WERE an odd couple. She was not much more than five feet tall, and the giant man-child towered over her. Her clothes were from another era. Without exception, the girls they passed wore shorts and tee shirts and flip-flops, their uniform, careless sexuality on display for anyone who cared to look. Cat Edwards was wearing a white sleeveless dress that almost reached her knees, a broad blue belt cinched around her tiny waist, and low-heeled shoes.

Teddy, too, stood out. The other boys dressed like the girls – he wore a golf shirt and khakis. Even their luggage was different. Instead of the backpacks that turned everyone else into bent Quasimodos, she carried a small leather briefcase, and he eschewed it entirely, opting to carry his books on his hip.

They turned west on College Avenue, and I followed at a discreet distance. At Hill Hall, they spoke for a few seconds on the sidewalk before Teddy went inside. She crossed the street. "Miss Edwards?" She stopped and looked back. "Can I speak to you for a minute?"

She watched me approach, the large gray eyes gauging the degree of bother I might represent. My guess was that the first mention of Teddy would send her running. But how did I know who she was? I had considered the various names I could drop – the Chancellor, the Dean – and finally lit upon one she might not ignore. "My name's Harry Monmouth. Jack Peeler suggested I talk with you." Jack was the College's Athletic Director, a friend since high school. The suspicious face didn't change, but she remained where she was. "I'm conducting a review of the tutoring program, and –"

She spun on her heel and walked away. I hurried to catch up. "I have a class now, Mr. Monmouth," she said. "Goodbye." I considered and rejected the idea of following her, and watched as she disappeared into Phillips Hall.

Fifty minutes later, she emerged. I fell in step beside her. "Okay, it wasn't Jack Peeler. It was the Chancellor." She turned her head, a slight smile on her face, but didn't speak.

She was not the usual consort for a campus hero. Her beauty had to be studied to be appreciated. The raven hair fell almost to her shoulders, and the wide crushed mouth, unpainted, would have been fragile but for the attitude. Up close, her face – the wide-set eyes, heavy brows and determined chin – was unyielding. It might have been the Pope who sent me, for all she cared.

I crossed the street with her before realizing Teddy waited on the other side. Pulling up short, my presence in the middle of College Avenue forced a bicycle – its rider in full regalia – to swerve onto the brick path, narrowly missing a coed who, busily tapping on something in her hand, didn't notice. Back in the street, the rider raised his middle finger and yelled something I couldn't hear. By the time I returned my attention to them, Teddy and Cat were gone.

I passed along the western edge of the quad to Porthole Alley, and pushed through the side door of the College Coffee Shop. At one time an intersection of town and gown, it was deserted. I sat down at the front table, ordered coffee, and stared out the window at High Street. I was interested now, and I owed the Chancellor more than the clumsy effort that Cat Edwards had so easily repulsed. Helen had said something that might help – Cat and Teddy Black came from the same hometown.

I removed the manila folder from my briefcase. Cat had been born and raised in Twin Rivers, a town of 30,000 people 100 miles southeast of New Hope. Rather than attend the local schools, she had been educated at a girls' school in Connecticut where she made excellent grades and starred on the field hockey team.

I nodded at a comment from a letter of recommendation: "Catherine refuses to lose. Any defeat is temporary." She had spent her summers at home, working for something called The Reading Hour, which she described as "a supplemental reading program for children." Her father, a doctor, died right after she graduated, and her mother still resided in Twin Rivers. Cat had stayed home for a year before applying to the College.

I asked for another cup of coffee. I had a rough knowledge of Teddy's biography from the newspapers, and it was hard to see a juncture if there was one. An orphan, he had been adopted in 1995 by an older, childless couple, Paul and Sylvia Black. Schooled for 12 years in Twin Rivers, including the last four at the local high school, his summers had been spent at "sports camps," thinly disguised recruiting tools, at colleges all over the country.

His high school grades and test scores were poor, a circumstance attributed by his teachers to a lack of interest rather than a lack of ability. He had been admitted to the College by way of the Academic Challenges Committee, one of only 25 students in the entire freshman class – all of them athletes – whose credentials would otherwise be summarily rejected. In short, Teddy was an intended participant in Helen's tutoring program.

The College had another category of recruits, called "Scholar Candidates," who had no need for tutors. They were marginal athletes but good students, and there were 20 of them in each class. They were given scholarships and allowed to play on various teams in order to raise the "academic profile" of the recruited athletes on campus. Their sole purpose was to increase the test scores and grade point averages of the athletes as a whole. It was good public relations, and it placated the Organization.

I laid some money on the table and rose. Emerging from the coffee shop, I turned for the office. Helen had suggested that, despite seemingly excellent qualifications, much of the student body was unprepared for college. How would it be, then, to be one of the "challenged" students – 100 of them on campus at any given time – completely at sea? The chosen would move on to the pro ranks. What happened to the rest of them?

I stopped to observe the construction. Another man, standing atop the low stone wall separating the building site from the sidewalk, was doing the same. When he noticed me, he leaped from the wall to the brick path and stood beside me. "This is going to be truly awesome," he said.

"It is?"

"Absolutely. It's the School of Human En-richment." He was short and round, and he wore a tuxedo on a routine Wednesday morning in New Hope. At just over six feet, I was a full head taller. His ruddy complexion, sparse hair and bushy white mustache reminded me of the Monopoly tycoon without the top hat.

He thrust out his hand, but instead of the conventional handshake I expected, he first slapped my palm, then bent his arm at the elbow, hand and fingers pointing skyward. Not entirely certain what to do, but not wanting to appear unfriendly, I bent my arm as well and gripped his upturned hand. We faced each other like arm wrestlers without a table. "I'm Cosmo Ender." He squeezed my hand and dropped it. "Director."

"Harry Monmouth."

"We're the future, Harry. Give the public what they want, I say."

"What does the public want, Mr. Ender?"

"Cosmo. Call me Cosmo. What does the public want?" He winked. "Can you keep a secret?"

"Uh, sure. I guess so."

"Illusion. That's what the public wants."

"So – the Human Enrichment program cre-ates illusions?"

"Oh, no, no, no. Our products and services are very real, very real. And they're very expen-sive, too." He laughed. "No, it's the people who create the illusions." He tapped the side of his head. "In here."

"I don't understand."

"There are many people who don't like the world as it is, Harry. They want it to be better or – different. Traditionally, crudely, they took drugs or got drunk. Very messy, and dangerous, too." He paused. "We do it better."

I looked around. The extraordinary encounter with this outlandish little man seemed unreal. I felt like I had stumbled onto a movie set. "How?"

He smiled. "Ah. That's *my* secret, Harry. Let's just say we make a few tweaks and, *voilà*, life is better."

"Tweaks to what?"

He looked at his watch. "I have to run. Wonderful talking to you."

I watched as he climbed the steps beside Castle Hall and strolled south across the quad, swinging a cane I hadn't noticed before. The sense of unreality remained. Who was this guy really? Was the College actually building a school where Cosmo Ender could sell illusions? Could that really be his name?

Back at the office, I said, "Have you ever heard of the School of Human Enrichment?"

"Sure," Abby said. "And that cute little man. He gave a talk at Memorial Hall a few weeks ago."

"Was he wearing a tuxedo?"

She giggled. "Yes. It was so cute."

"Did he say what the program is?"

She thought for a moment. "I don't think so. All I can remember is something about life getting better for everybody." She laughed again. "And something about bottled water."

I entered my office and closed the door. There was a lot going on. I felt like Rip Van Winkle after his nap.

I picked up the telephone.

AS USUAL, my drive dribbled into the wa-
ter. "There's a drop area over there," Jack said. I
ignored him, and hit a second ball into the lake.
"Why don't you drop one on the other side?" he said.
"Save some balls." I teed up another one, a yellow
ball I had found the last time we played. It seemed
destined for the same fate as the first two, but
skipped off the surface of the lake instead and
wound up on dry land. "Great. You lay five on a
par-four hole."

He tossed a ball on the ground and struck it
casually with his three-wood – one of the conditions
of our monthly match was he couldn't use a tee or a
driver – sending it 100 yards past mine. We
climbed into the cart. "There's still hope," he said.
"You have two strokes here."

Golf was the only game Jack Peeler played at
New Hope High School, and he played it so well
that the College gave him a scholarship. While he
was there, the golf team won a couple of conference
championships, and he was named to the All-
America team his senior year.

His game was the product of talent rather
than diligence, and his professional career floun-
dered when he encountered men who were both
talented and industrious. He had turned to the
business of college athletics and, after stints at var-
ious schools around the country, was tapped to run
the Athletic Department at the College after his
predecessor was forced out by the football scandal.

I was 35 when I first picked up a golf club,
and the game had evaded me ever since. After los-
ing serious money for a few months, I had lowered

the stakes to a level where it didn't matter how badly he beat me. "The Chancellor says the football team's going places this year," I said. "Is he right?"

He nodded. "If we stay healthy, we might run the table."

"All because of Teddy Black?"

He watched me slash the yellow ball into a pine forest on the other side of the fairway. "Pretty much."

I resumed my seat in the cart. "So if something happened to him . . ."

"Don't even think about it."

We stopped beside his ball. I took four clubs from my bag. "I'll see you on the green," I said. Trudging toward the woods, I heard the clear, crisp click of a well-struck iron, a sound I had never produced. Three stokes later, I joined him on the green. His ball was two feet from the hole. "Is that for par or birdie?"

He laughed. "Does it matter?"

A few minutes later, we sat over drinks in the clubhouse bar. He laid the scorecard down. "You owe me a buck and a half," he said.

"I'll pay for the drinks."

"Okay."

"Have you got a handle on the Athletic Department yet?"

He sighed and his shoulders slumped. "It's hard to say. I don't have anything to do with the games we play. It's all about managing people. And money." He paused. "It's not much fun."

"How much money?"

"Our budget this year is $75 million."

"Wow. Where does it come from?"

"We have 28 teams, men's and women's. Two of them – football and men's basketball – generate revenue. Forty-seven million dollars last year. The rest comes from fees, donations and the general fund."

"Really? I thought football paid for itself. That it funded the rest of the athletic program, in fact."

"Not by a long shot."

I waved at the bartender. After he delivered more drinks, I said, "The Chancellor told me the Organization's investigation is finished."

"Yes. The kangaroo court will hand down its verdict tomorrow."

I smiled. "You mean we didn't do anything wrong?"

"No. We did plenty wrong. I mean the penalty will be assessed by the same people we compete against every day." I nodded. "And that penalty's only the tip of the iceberg."

"How so?"

"The rules require that our players be students, too. The tutoring program is the single largest expense we have. This year alone, just to make the Organization happy, we've added 20 writing tutors, 10 –" he raised his hands to make quotation marks in the air "– reading, writing and learning specialists, and a full-time tutor coordinator whose job is to recruit, train and supervise tutors. It's insane."

"But necessary?"

"Absolutely. If we're going to be part of the Organization."

"On the subject of tutors, I'm interested in one of them. Cat Edwards. Do you know her?"

"We have more than 100. The name doesn't ring a bell."

"She's Teddy Black's tutor."

He stared at me. "Harry. Please. Don't – don't mess with Teddy Black."

"It's not my idea, Jack. The Chancellor asked me to look into it."

"Why?"

"She seems to be more than a tutor. He's worried about it." We drank in silence. "All I want to do is talk to her, and she's ducking me."

We were quiet again. Finally, he decided. "If something *is* wrong, you come to me first. Before the Chancellor, before anybody. Okay?"

"Well –"

"It'll be my ass, not the Chancellor's."

"Okay."

"She comes to practice every day. I'll leave your name with the people at the gate. That's the best I can do."

"All right. Thanks."

"And keep this in mind: Millions – hell, maybe billions – of dollars depend on Teddy Black, not to mention the lunatics we used to call fans. I wouldn't want to be you if something upsets that apple-cart."

THE SINGLE-STORY brick building on West High Street – headquarters of the *New Hope Chronicle* – was always the new building to me, even though it had stood for nearly three decades. Its predecessor, a much larger structure on Bishop Street, had been partially destroyed by fire in an effort to cover up the crime that tarnished my family. The fire was arson, but the arsonist was never charged because he was dead when the crime was finally revealed.

I stepped into a small office that looked out to the street. A striking blonde woman turned her head from the laptop that was the only thing on her desk, and smiled. "Harry."

"Hi, Samantha."

"How's Alex?"

"Not very well, I'm afraid."

"I'm sorry."

I'd met Samantha Clarke the same day Alex finally agreed to marry me. Samantha proposed that we dally before the nuptials. My ego was pleased but, in love with Alex and the idea of love, I declined. Unfazed, Samantha became my friend, and helped me survive a crisis that threatened my marriage before it started. News anchor for a local television station when I first knew her, she had climbed the ladder to the cable network in Atlanta and, for a few shining moments, to an anchor chair in New York.

She had stepped down recently because of lines in her face and rumors of drug use that were never substantiated, and returned to New Hope where she assumed the editorship of the *Chronicle*. She had free rein to opine on local, state and national affairs, a responsibility she took seriously. In just a few short months, she knew everyone and everything, on campus and in town.

I sat across from her. A few years younger than me, she was still a beautiful woman. The full figure was firm, the hair luxuriant, and the features more than pleasing. She regarded me for a moment, a pensive look on her face, before getting down to business. "Your friend Cosmo Ender interests me greatly."

"Why?"

"Because he's – what's the word – *elusive*. And fascinating."

"Meaning what?"

"After you called, I went through the past issues here. There was nothing. Even the announcement about the new building didn't mention him or the School of Human Enrichment. It was just a 'research and development center associated with the leisure industry.'" She gestured toward the laptop. "He does show up on the Internet sporadically. That's what's so odd." She paused. "I found five isolated stories. I made copies for you." She handed me a slim sheaf of paper. "They aren't about him. He's just mentioned in passing." She paused again. "He seems to be an entrepreneur."

"What does he do?"

"Well, it's hard to say. He promotes ideas."

"Ideas? Is there much money in that?"

"Must be. He's fabulously wealthy. He started in Europe, and came over here in the '80s." She leaned back in her chair. "He made his first big bundle with the bottled-water craze."

"Why is that an idea?"

"The notion is that it's healthier or tastes better than tap water, neither of which is necessarily so. It costs three or four hundred times what tap water costs. Ender got in at the bottom, promoted the idea, and sold out for millions." She pointed to the pages in my hand. "He's behind every fad diet that's come along in the past twenty years. Tattoos were his idea. Organic foods. You name it. He's never the guy in charge – he's an 'investor.'" She paused. "He bankrolled all of those huge Christian churches back in the '90s."

"Why is he here? Why associate with the College?"

"I don't know. Given his history, though, there's money to be made, whatever it is." She smiled. "It's very, very curious. I'd like to know."

I grinned. Cosmo Ender would need all his elusiveness to avoid Samantha Clarke. "Well, keep me posted. I'm curious, too." I rose and turned for the door.

"Harry?"

"Yes."

"Tell Alex I'm thinking about her."

SIX

THE PRACTICE fields – acres of grass marked with grids and goalposts plus a full-sized artificial surface – were located a few hundred yards south of Tower Road, adjacent to the soccer fields and the track and field complex. A chain-link fence, nine feet high with five rows of barbed wire at the top, enclosed them completely. Canvas attached to the fence denied prying eyes. Each of the eight gates was padlocked when the facility was not in use, and guarded by two armed policemen when it was. "I'm Harry Monmouth," I said.

The man minding the gate gazed at me suspiciously – I was not the usual sportswriter or pro scout ordinarily admitted – before consulting his clipboard. "Can I see your ID, please?" I gave him my driver's license. He examined it carefully, shifting his eyes from the license to my face and back several times. Satisfied finally, he pawed through a box and handed me a laminated card with a cord attached to it. I slipped it over my head and passed through the gate.

The offensive team – in shorts, helmets and shoulder pads – was working on pass routes against an array of linebackers and defensive backs who remained stationary while the receivers ran their patterns and caught the balls thrown by Teddy Black. As I watched, he zipped a tight spiral to a receiver streaking down the sideline 50 yards away.

She was sitting on the second row of a short set of bleachers reading a book. I sat down beside her. She turned her head toward me, pushed the large sunglasses to the top of her head, and said, "I guess you do know Jack Peeler." I nodded. "What do you want, Mr. Monmouth?"

"Miss – Ms. Edwards –"

"Miss is fine."

"Miss Edwards, the Chancellor is concerned about your – relationship with Teddy Black, and he asked –"

"What? That I'm sleeping with him?"

"Well, uh –"

"Tell him to go to hell."

"That's – that's not it exactly." I hesitated. "He's worried you're so close you might go too far on the tutoring side of things."

"You mean write his papers? That sort of thing?" I nodded. She smiled. "You can tell the Chancellor Teddy does his own work. He goes to class, and studies, and he takes his own tests." She paused. "He's a real student. Unlike some people."

"Who?"

She shook her head. "Ask Jack Peeler."

"Are you talking about the football team?" She didn't respond. "Miss Edwards, there's –"

"Why don't you call me Cat? And I'll call you Harry."

"Okay. The College has a lot at stake with this team, Cat. If someone's breaking the rules –"

"Don't hand me that bullshit, Harry." She gestured toward the field. "Those guys are playing by the rules. They do what they're told."

"Then what's the problem?"

"The problem is we're talking about two different sets of rules."

"What do you mean?"

She shook her head again. "You should talk to Peeler. Or the people running the tutoring program."

She turned away from me and gazed out at the field. Teddy was running the hurry-up offense now, peppering the defense with bullet passes from one sideline to the other. "He sure can play," I said. She nodded. "You must be a big fan."

She stared at me. "I loathe it."

"Then why do you do this?"

"That's my business."

On the way home, I considered my dilemma. The mission was accomplished. Teddy Black's tutor had assured me he was the student-athlete the College claimed he was, and I believed her. I could spruce it up a bit – maybe talk to a professor or two, or his academic advisor – and put it in a nice neat package the Chancellor could file away, ready to be retrieved if necessary. As was so often the case, though, my "investigation" had revealed another rock that might be turned over, and I was reluctant to know what was beneath it.

THE OVERSIZED hospital gown gave her the appearance of a wizened child. The lines at the mouth and eyes seemed exaggerated, and the wispy brows and lashes added to the illusion. "You can get dressed now, Mrs. Monmouth," said Steiner. "We'll be next door."

I followed him into a small, drab room furnished only with a desk, a few chairs and a black metal filing cabinet. He spoke into the telephone, then sat down behind the desk and began to write. "Can you help her?" I said.

He looked up. "Let's wait for her, Harry. It's her decision, and it's complicated." I nodded and dropped into a chair. I was exhausted. Steiner, on the other hand, was as crisp and vital as a teenager on his first date.

Alex joined us a few minutes later. Steiner rose as she entered the room, and pulled another chair close to the desk. After she was seated, he resumed his place and continued to write. I reached for her hand. It was cold and brittle, and the veins so prominent now throbbed beneath the gossamer skin.

He laid his pen down and looked at her. "Do you want to live, Mrs. Monmouth?" I almost protested the brutality, but held my tongue. Alex was used to my sermons on life and death. Perhaps she needed to hear it from someone else. "The leukemia has overwhelmed your white blood cells. You have a cancerous tumor in your brain, and there's evidence it's spread to your lymph nodes. I'm surprised you're still alive."

That was too much. "Frank, don't –"

"I'm sorry, Harry. Mrs. Monmouth. We have to tell the truth here." He gazed at her. "The fact is this is a research project, and you're an excellent subject. The disease and all its manifestations are as widespread as I've ever seen in a live body. You'll die soon if nothing is done. You may die anyway." He stopped. "Do you want to live?"

"Yes, but . . ."

"But what, Mrs. Monmouth?"

Her voice strengthened. "I don't want to be – something else. I'd rather die."

He stared at her again, eyes blinking like signal lamps. "I'm not talking about turning you into something else. I alter cells to cure disease. If the treatment works, you'll be disease-free. I don't want to make you into something different."

"But you could?"

"Why would I? And what difference does it make? It's just medicine."

We sat without speaking. "What do you do?" I said.

"I'll tell you what I do with mice." He paused. "In patients with leukemia, the bone marrow produces mutant white blood cells. They don't die, and they crowd out the good blood cells. It deprives the body's tissues of oxygen, and generates uncontrolled bleeding. The immune system won't function properly."

Someone knocked on the door. Steiner opened it and, seconds later, set a small cage containing a single white mouse on the desk. He continued: "I take normal immune cells from the patient's blood, infuse them with special molecules, and reintroduce them into the body. The molecules make the immune cells much more potent. They persist and multiply, and each one of them kills thousands of cancer cells." He looked at Alex. "It's very hard on the patient. There's a battle raging inside you, and you feel it. Fevers, pain, what have you. There are analgesics to make it easier, but they diminish the effect of the treatment."

"How long does it take?"

"The treatment?" She nodded. "It takes two minutes to introduce the new immune cells." He pointed at the mouse. "That little fellow was eaten up with cancer. Three weeks after I gave him the new cells, he was cancer-free."

"Three weeks?"

"Yes. It'll take longer for a human being."

Her expression revealed the limits of her skepticism. She had endured over a year of painful, intrusive procedures, and she was sicker now than when she started. Two minutes and three weeks – twice that many if necessary – were nothing. It was a miracle, not medicine, if it worked. "Are there side-effects?" I said.

He nodded. "The new cells kill healthy cells, too. Injections are required to control them. It's part of the treatment."

"So – a shot once a month?"

"Basically, yes."

"How much does it cost?" said Alex.

"Nothing. This is a research project funded by the American Pharmaceutical Association. You're just another mouse." He removed the glasses and rubbed his eyes. "I have every reason to believe the treatment will work, but I can't guarantee it. Side-effects in human beings might be different. But, as I said, without it your prognosis is very poor."

Alex and I looked at each other. She was human, too. She wanted to live, and a relatively pain-free, convenient path to life was within her grasp. It really *was* medicine, just like radiation and chemotherapy and marrow transplants. The vague ideas about the morality of gene manipulation gave way. She turned to him. "All right."

He smiled. "Good. There's one more thing. This is our secret for the time being. There are protocols I'm – overlooking." He rose. "We'll begin immediately." He held out his hand, and she took it. Pausing at the door, he drew a document from his inside coat pocket and gave it to me. "I'll be back in a little while, Harry. Look that over while I'm gone."

ALEX WAS too tired to eat. I helped her undress and, ignoring the terrible purple bruises on her body, slipped the flannel nightgown – worn on even the warmest summer nights – over her head. She put her arms around me and buried her face in my chest. "Are we doing the right thing?"

"Yes. Now lie down. I'll bring you a cup of soup."

She sat on the edge of the bed. "Why is he doing this? Couldn't he get into trouble?"

Those were my questions, too, and I didn't know the answers. I stated the obvious: "He's doing it because he's an egomaniac who thinks he's God. God can't get into trouble." She was sound asleep when I returned with the soup.

I poured a glass of scotch and climbed the stairs to the single large room on the third floor. At one time my grandfather's study, Alex had converted it into a playroom for the boys. When they no longer needed a playroom, I reclaimed it. I sat down behind an old Queen Anne desk and considered the day.

Steiner was no humanitarian, and he barely knew us. Yes, he was undoubtedly pleased to have Alex as a specimen, and the result of her treatment – good or bad – would certainly be of value to the American Pharmaceutical Association, but it was also certain he was skipping a few professional steps between the white mouse and Alex. With respect to Project Sickle Cell, all kinds of papers and meetings and studies were necessary after the animal experiments, and even then he wanted a controlled clinical trial before he began treating patients. He was infusing Alex with his special immune cells on Monday morning.

I picked up the document he'd left with me. It was a Civil Complaint filed a week earlier in the Superior Court of Azure County. The plaintiffs, parents of a dead four-year old boy who had been "conceived" in Steiner's clinic, sought damages for negligence "in excess of $1 million," plus an order denying Steiner the child's body for an autopsy. "I want you to handle this matter for me," Steiner had said. "The hearing on the autopsy is set for tomorrow afternoon. It's cut and dried." He stared at me. "It's in the contract."

It was, of course, impossible for me to refuse. The idea of quarreling over a dead body was repulsive, and neither side – the scientist who had created it and the parents who had purchased it – seemed especially admirable. But Steiner was going to raise my bride from the grave, and it would be ungracious and impolitic to decline his request. "Is there a file or something?" I said.

"Yes." We rode the elevator to his office and sat in silence while his secretary copied the contents of a slim folder. "This will all be confidential, correct?" he said. "You will keep my secrets if you learn them?"

I nodded. "It's part of my job."

"Good." He handed me the file. "This autopsy is important to my work, Harry. Very important. I want that body by Monday morning."

I shuffled through the pages. The "contract" was actually a series of consent forms signed only by the parents. The documents seemed to cover every stage of the process – medications, egg retrieval, embryo transfers and so on. Each one provided a history of the science, a summary of the risks, and an acknowledgement by the parents that they knew all there was to know and wanted to go ahead anyway.

The most troubling one was called "Consent for Adverse Outcomes." It purported to instruct the parents on the likelihood of everything from ectopic pregnancy to chromosomal abnormalities, and required them to agree they understood the complex issues described in the form and were ready to proceed. This one-sided "contract" was valid, and enforceable, too, as long as it didn't go too far. That would certainly be the question at the hearing tomorrow.

An entire paragraph was necessary to ensure no impediments to an autopsy "in the event said child dies before his fifth birthday," and it was the only provision in all the forms that required the parents' initials. Autopsies were usually performed because the law required them, but nothing prevented a parent from seeking one or assigning his right to do so, regardless of how repugnant such an agreement might be. Still, it could shock someone's conscience and, if that someone was our judge tomorrow, Steiner – and, by extension, Alex – might be in trouble.

I pondered the differences. We had no contract, and Alex's treatment was free. Abby's father was paying $25,000 for her babies. Combined with the professional risk, Frank Steiner was doing us a very big favor. Why?

I turned to the other, now almost insignificant, item on my plate – the potential academic problem inside the football program. Cat Edwards had raised the possibility, and suggested that Jack Peeler knew all about it. I was pretty sure Jack wasn't responsible for whatever it was – he'd been at the College for less than six months – but he had insisted that any wrongdoing be brought to him first. I would worry about that when there was something to say. Helen had a mole inside the tutor program.

It was after 10:00 P.M. I hesitated, then found the phone book and dialed her number. A familiar but unexpected female voice answered: "Hello."

"I – I was calling for Helen Tanner. Is she there?" Who was that?

There was some murmuring in the background. Helen came on the line. "Hello."

"Helen, it's Harry."

"Yes?"

"I spoke with Cat Edwards this afternoon. She hinted at a problem with the tutor program." I paused. "Didn't you tell me you had a couple of your people in the program? That one of them raised the issue of Cat and Teddy?"

"Yes."

"I'd like to talk to him. Or her. Can you –?"

"It's a her. Hold on a second." She returned a moment later and gave me a name and phone number. "It's a cell phone," she said.

I smiled. "Who is she?"

"A grad student working on her thesis."

"In what?"

"English Lit." She paused. "Tell her to call me if she wants to."

"All right. Thanks."

I laid the receiver down. I knew that first voice – Samantha Clarke.

SEVEN

THE ORGANIZATION'S report was front-page news. In addition to the expected sanctions, the College was fined $500,000 and forced to fire several employees whose only crime was insufficient knowledge of the Organization's rulebook. A series of petty scarlet letters were also imposed. All College publications – media guides, recruiting brochures, anything related to the athletic program – would henceforth include, in bold letters, an explanation of the 22 victories forfeited, and – like the air-brushing of deposed dictators – all references to the dismissed players and coaches would be expunged from campus.

The head coach, already unemployed, was admonished to likewise erase the forfeited games from his record, and any institution with the temerity to hire him was required to note the forfeits in *its* promotional materials. The sanctimony was obscene. One particularly risible comment referred to an "unscrupulous world populated by those looking to 'cash in' on college athletics," this from a cartel whose members squeezed billions from the athletes in their charge.

"Hot lines" had been established, ostensibly to alert College officials of any future irregularities, actually to make it easier for the Organization to fix blame. The Athletic Director, for example, was required to inform the Chancellor of a potential rule violation "immediately." Failure to do so was a breach of the Organization's rules, and grounds for dismissal.

The College responded by mostly ignoring the findings and talking up the current season, which was unaffected by the sanctions. The Chancellor announced that the College had hired an outside firm to help the players "in the agent selection process," as well as a public relations outfit to "guide us as we navigate the complexities of bigtime athletics." The *mea culpas*, endemic before, were forgotten.

There was the usual moaning from the academics: "These unavoidable consequences of an out-of-control athletic program tarnish the College's reputation. Something must be done." Multiple reports and recommendations prepared by various committees since the investigation began – now gathering dust on the shelf to which they'd been relegated – were cited.

Jack Peeler responded with a suggestion designed to silence the critics: "The diversity of our student population is enhanced by our student-athletes." Confronted with this all-encompassing rationale, one they alluded to every day, the professoriate sputtered.

Near the end, the Chancellor took a gratuitous swipe at the players involved. "The individuals responsible for these sanctions have lost their eligibility and created serious problems for the College. The damage they've done to themselves, their teammates and their school is irreparable."

The players, of course, had engaged in the ordinarily laudable process of selling their services to the highest bidder. Virtually every enterprise in the country – unbound by the edicts of the Organization – did the same. The College itself was a bastion of commerce. The irony would go unnoticed by the College's adherents.

I heard the telephone ring. "Mr. Monmouth's office," Abby said. Then: "Please hold." She leaned in the door. "It's Samantha Clarke."

"Thanks." I lifted the receiver. "Hi, Samantha."

"Harry, I need to talk to you. What are you doing this afternoon?"

"I have to be in court this afternoon."

"Tomorrow, then. At my office. Say, 9:30?"

"All right. What's it about?"

"It's about Cosmo Ender. And friends."

"What friends?"

She laughed. "I'll see you in the morning."

I passed into the outer office. "I'm going to lunch. Then the courthouse. I may not be back today."

Abby nodded. "Remember, I won't be here Monday or Tuesday. I'm getting pregnant."

I paused. "You know, it's not risk-free. There've been some – problems."

"I know."

"Don't you think you could try it the normal way for another year or two?"

She shook her head. "This might be our only chance at the clinic. I can't give that up."

"Well – okay. I'll see you Wednesday."

I turned west on High Street, past the sorority houses and the fraternity houses and the Presbyterian Church. On the other side of Anderson Street, I paused in front of the Post Office. According to the *Chronicle*, the building had been leased to the Sunday Convocation, a church for atheists. Its spokesperson said the "services," borrowed from the Episcopal Church, were for those who were "spiritual" rather than "religious."

God, of course, wasn't mentioned – denial of God was the unifying theme. The notion that Man was their God, and that their disappointment in Man had left a void now filled by rituals they had previously mocked, also went unsaid. I made a mental note to drop in one Sunday.

At the corner of High and Division, I turned into a small, crowded restaurant called Franky's. "My name's Monmouth," I told the boy behind the podium. "I'm meeting a young lady named Vera Carr."

He pointed. "She's at the table in the window."

She turned her head as I weaved my way through the tables and chairs. She wasn't actually a "young" woman. Attractive in a sultry sort of way, she was on the far side of 30, her dark hair cut close to her head, her eyes and lids defined by blue mascara and eyeliner. The sullen mouth was a slash of red. "Ms. Carr?" She nodded. I sat down across from her. "Thanks for coming. I appreciate it."

She looked around the room, a fretful look on her face. "I'm not sure I can help you."

"Well then, we'll have a nice lunch anyway." I picked up the menu and, after a moment's hesitation, she did the same. We were quiet until the waitress came to take our orders. "Dean Tanner tells me you're writing your thesis," I said. "What's it about?"

"It's called 'Social Media and the End of Literature.'"

I smiled. "Would that be from the author's point of view, or the reader's?"

"Both."

The waitress delivered our drinks, white wine for her, sweet ice tea for me. "Have you talked to Dean Tanner about this?" She nodded again. "I understand you're tutoring a couple of the football players."

The uneasy look returned. "Yes."

"Do they take it seriously?"

"I – I guess so. They show up on time. They seem to pay attention." She paused. "They're very polite."

"How does the system work?"

"Each tutor has one or two players. All sessions are held in the Snopes Center. I meet with them for an hour and a half four days a week."

We drank without speaking until the food arrived. "Does it do them any good?" I said. She didn't answer. We ate in silence. I tried again: "Ms. Carr, I don't really care if the program is effective or not. I'm trying to find out if there's anything wrong with it. Anything that might cause more trouble for the football team."

The color rose in her face. "It's people like you," she said in a low, angry voice, "who are the problem. Not the tutor program."

"I'm not –"

"The goddamned football team is all that matters. Those kids –"

"Wait. That's not my attitude. I've been asked to make sure the program is complying with the rules. They're all Rhodes Scholars as far as I'm concerned." She went back to her salad, and I picked at my fish.

The silence dragged on. She looked up. "That's not the case, as I'm sure you know." She paused. "You asked me if the program was doing the students any good. The answer is no."

"Why not?"

"Neither of my guys can read. They can't write, either. It's hard to pick up on the nuances of Virgil or Shakespeare if you can't read or write." She put her fork down and leaned toward me. "I don't believe they're alone. I suspect most of the players on the football team shouldn't be in college at all. It's – distressing."

"But how do they cope? How do they take tests and write papers and – and read the text-books?"

"I don't know. Everything is very carefully compartmentalized. I have nothing to do with their academic performance beyond my time with them." She turned her glass up, then lifted her purse from the floor and rose. "Thanks for lunch."

"Have you told anyone else about this?"

"No, but – somebody needs to do something. Maybe I will."

I watched as she made her way to the door and out to the street. If Vera Carr's suspicions were correct, there *was* a problem with the tutor program. If the players couldn't read or write, extraordinary measures would be necessary to keep them eligible to play football. I approached the bar. "Can I use your phone?"

The bartender was amused. "Sure." I dialed Helen's office. She wasn't there, so I left a message with her secretary. I stepped outside, and turned toward the courthouse.

THE PLAINTIFFS' attorney was already in the courtroom and, just as I had taught her, she'd claimed the table nearest the jury box. There would be no jury today, but it was a worthy habit for all occasions. She turned her head as I crossed the bar through a low swinging gate, a smile becoming a frown and then a smile again. "Harry. What brings you here?"

I wanted to kiss her, but opted for professional decorum instead, so I squeezed the proffered hand and sat down at the other table. "I'm representing the Defendants in your case, Missy."

"I thought you retired."

"Not yet. My bar dues are paid in full." The dead boy's parents sat beside her. I'd seen them recently at the West End Mosque. I knew the Spillers – his father had been a few years ahead of me in school. They were simple people, struggling for a family their neighbors took for granted, and their appearance at the mosque had surprised me. "Hello, Joe. Nancy." They refused to look at me.

The bailiff entered the room and stopped in front of the bench. "All rise." Judge Robert Hood – Bob to his friends, Bobby to his old friends – came through a door, and climbed to his perch overlooking the room. Other than a gathering bulk, he was little changed from the boy I'd known for 50 years. He smiled when he saw me, the bulging eyes wider. "Well, Mr. Monmouth. Welcome."

"Thank you, sir."

"Are you participating in this hearing?"

"Yes, sir. I'd like to enter an appearance for all the Defendants." He nodded. I turned to the court reporter seated directly beneath him. "Harry Monmouth for the Defendants. 401 East High Street. 792-2425. Bar number 7797."

Bobby turned his attention to Plaintiffs' counsel. "All right, Ms. Farrell. It's your motion. Proceed."

Melissa Farrell was the daughter of another old friend who had died – drunk, broke and alone – in Las Vegas 25 years earlier. Her mother had left both of them five years before that, and Missy had grown up with an alcoholic uncle in Milltown.

A few of her father's friends, including Bobby and me, coalesced to ensure she was healthy and educated. She had worked in my office for several years before striking out on her own. Successful and driven, she had a reputation for unbridled tenacity, especially in confrontations with those she regarded as powerful. She relished a fight with the Frank Steiners of the world.

Her arguments were as anticipated. Her clients were desperate for a child, and signed whatever Steiner put in front of them. The idea of allowing him to "experiment" on the boy's body was repellent. The law shouldn't lend itself to enforcing bargains with the devil, though she didn't use those exact words.

As I listened, a possible compromise formed in my head. The purpose of an autopsy was to determine the cause of death. The Spillers' real complaint was that the procedure would be performed by Steiner in the privacy – make that the "secrecy" – of his temple on the hill. If it was done by someone else at another place, I suspected the plaintiffs would withdraw their objections.

Bobby Hood's thoughts had turned in the same direction. After Missy finished speaking, he said, "What if I permitted the autopsy, but only if somebody else performed it? Would that be acceptable to your clients?"

Her quick response told me – and him – that it would, indeed, be acceptable, but she didn't want to say so until the negotiations were complete. "That's certainly something we'd consider, Your Honor."

Bobby turned to me, smiling. "What about you, Mr. Monmouth? Can you persuade your client to accept that?" He glanced at the clock. I had persuaded many clients to compromise, and I'd never refused to try when he suggested it.

"No, Your Honor."

He stopped smiling. "Why not?"

The reason was I knew, without being told, that Steiner would never accept it, and any suggestion that he do so could adversely affect my wife. It seemed irrational, but I was sure I was right. Steiner wanted a secret autopsy performed by him. Anything less would be failure on my part, and the repercussions might be catastrophic.

"The Spillers signed a contract, Judge Hood. They both initialed the paragraph permitting Doctor Steiner to do the autopsy. In exchange, they received a valuable service, one that Doctor Steiner has strived to perfect for many years. The autopsy is a critical element of his work. It might reveal something that would enhance the prospects of other childless parents." I paused. "There's no claim here that the Spillers were defrauded, or that they were unable to understand what they were signing, and that's because neither circumstance exists. They simply ask you now to allow them to change their minds. That's not your job."

He was surprised. We had been friends and colleagues for many years, occupying the same classrooms from kindergarten to law school, and practicing our profession in the same little town. We studied for the bar exam together, took the test in the same room and the oath at the same time. We'd been drunk together countless times, chased the same girls, and celebrated victories and mourned defeats. I had never lectured him about his job, whatever it was at the time, nor had I ever been unwilling to at least consider any proposal he made. "Well, what about maybe having an observer –?"

"Judge Hood." I had to make him understand. "This is an extremely important matter." He stared at me, the perplexed expression becoming thoughtful. I was trading on our friendship, and he knew it. Maybe someday I could explain. "Extremely important."

He nodded. "Very well. Motion denied. Draw up the Order, Mr. Monmouth." He left the room.

Missy was stunned, not by the outcome but by the swiftness of its rendition. She was not permitted the usual rebuttal, and most of the comfortable wheedling between bench and bar had been forsworn. My performance puzzled her, too, and she did not yet understand the basis for Bobby's ruling. After ushering her obviously distraught clients from the room, she returned. "Please get the Order in quickly, Harry. I may take an appeal."

"I wish you wouldn't. You won't win."

She looked at me closely. "Is everything okay? Is – Alex all right?"

I considered a confession, but couldn't bear to be weak in her eyes. "I'm fine, Missy. I'm – Alex is as okay as possible."

She frowned. "I won't appeal if you don't want me to."

I let the relief show in my face. "No, no. Do what you think is right for your clients."

The walk back to the office was longer than usual. I felt the resentment again – two people I loved had compromised themselves because I wanted them to – and pushed back. Alex had always been our strength. She'd been County Attorney for ten years, and sat on Bobby Hood's bench for ten more. She had raised our children, and coaxed some maturity from me, and now the genes she was so proud of had laid her low. Her life was in my hands. I was her champion and, no matter the losses I suffered, I would do whatever was necessary to see that she lived.

Abby was gone. I had two messages, one from Helen, the other from Samantha. Samantha had cancelled our meeting in the morning because of a "field trip" she had to take, Helen wanted me to call. I dialed the number.

"Hello."

"Helen, Harry. I had lunch with Vera Carr today. She says her players can't read."

She laughed. "I'm sure they don't read very well, Harry. That's why they need tutors."

"I don't believe that's what she meant. She said that most of the team shouldn't even be in college."

There was silence at the other end of the line. "They take standardized tests. They have to make a minimum score to get in."

"What about the Challenge Committee kids?"

"Even they have to be able to read, Harry. They'd never get by in class if they couldn't. It's silly."

"Can you get me their class schedules? Just the freshmen?"

"Sure."

"Thanks. I'll pick them up Monday after-noon. Is that enough time?"

"Yes."

"Great. Thanks again."

I leaned back in my chair. Helen was right. If a kid couldn't read, his teachers would know it. It was a simple matter to check with a few of them who would undoubtedly assure me that, of course, their students could read. What did I take them for? Armed with those assurances, I could deliver my report to the Chancellor with a clear conscience.

I heard the outside door open and, seconds later, Wes Vaughn stuck his head in the room. "Hey," I said. "What brings you to the pale side of town?"

He smiled and squeezed into the armchair on the other side of the desk. "Just doing a little evangelism."

"Evangelism? Where?"

"The new church up the street. At the Post Office."

"Any luck?"

He shook his head. "I've found my God. They're still looking for theirs." I nodded. "They're not sure about the sickle cell business, though. I'm speaking there Sunday."

"Preaching?"

He shook his head. "Debating."

"Who?"

"I don't know. Somebody who disagrees with me."

"I may have to come see that."

He leaned forward. "Have you talked to Steiner?"

"Yes."

"And?"

"Let's just say he's going to try to help us."

He nodded. "Are you sure?"

"It's her last chance, Wes. I have no choice."

We contemplated each other in silence. "Is death so bad?" he said.

"I don't know. I do know that whoever is re-sponsible for us made us want to live." I paused. "More than anything."

He nodded again. After a moment, he said, "I'm going to sue the College."

"Why?"

"To make them stop Project Sickle Cell."

"Project Sickle Cell hasn't hurt you. You'll have to find –"

"We've already started contacting people who've been through the treatment."

"But – they've all been *cured*, for God's sake. No one's been harmed."

"You don't know that. That's the trouble. We have no idea what this gene manipulation does to the rest of the body. Or to our children." He paused. "We won't know all the risks until some-thing goes wrong. It might affect generations. We can't leave this stuff to scientists and drug companies."

"The legislature passed a bill explicitly authorizing the program and subsidizing the cost."

"Is that supposed to make me feel better?"

I smiled. "Nobody forced those people into the program. They can do what they want with their own bodies."

He shook his head. "This isn't about one person's rights, Harry. They're meddling with the whole race. The human race." He took a deep breath and let the air out slowly. "Will you take it on?"

"I can't. I have a – a conflict." He frowned. "I already represent Steiner in another matter." I paused. "You know Missy Farrell, don't you?" He nodded. "Call her. It's right up her alley."

EIGHT

I SWITCHED off the radio. The football team, paced by Teddy Black's five touchdown passes, had just annihilated a ranked opponent on the road. When the new polls came out on Monday, the College would be at the very top.

I was restless. After leaving a note for Alex, I walked into town. Work on the School of Human Enrichment was languid. I watched a few men with transits and wooden stakes mill about the site, then dropped onto the bench across the street from the Post Office.

Because the game was played on the opponents' turf, High Street was less crowded than the week before, but the selection of people – seemingly permanent now – was the same. They had been superimposed on the landscape, transforming the street and the buildings and the sidewalks into a Potemkin façade, a two-dimensional canvas of ersatz life painted in various shades of uncertainty.

My friends and I had grown up without irony. We acquired it, of course, but we had known something else. The new denizens of High Street, steeped in the "wisdom" of a common, monochrome culture imposed by those who profited from it, had not. No longer allowed to find meaning for themselves, they were force-fed – like geese about to give up their livers – the prejudices of people with the power to do so. They questioned nothing except the motives of those who resisted.

The unmistakable figure of Cosmo Ender emerged from the Post Office building, and paused on the top step. I knew immediately he would be Wes Vaughn's opponent in the debate tomorrow. Who else could give so rousing a defense of modernity, of which gene manipulation was the current exemplar? DNA was the Midas gold, the genie in the lamp who granted every wish. Give the people what they wanted, never mind the aftermath. Frank Steiner, of course, could provide a more nuanced rationale, but he would never condescend to debate anyone, certainly not Wes Vaughn.

Ender stared straight at me. I raised my hand, but – perhaps contemplating one of his remunerative schemes – he didn't wave back. I thought of Samantha, and looked at my watch. Maybe she was back from her field trip. I rose and turned west.

On the other side of Division Street, I stopped to observe another new building. Years before, New Hope High School had occupied the site. The town had sold the property to the College, which promptly began work on an eyesore atop acres of asphalt called Academy Square. The noise and dirt and general chaos were unremitting, and the graceful old building – surrounded by excavation and fences and construction equipment – was destroyed the day I graduated. It was the first intrusion into New Hope proper.

But not the last. Its citizens were banished to pods – freeways and housing developments and shopping malls – where they turned inward and forgot what New Hope had been. Their children, once educated only a block or two from campus, disappeared from the streets and sidewalks, and knew nothing of the time when they routinely walked the College's paths, and played on its fields and diamonds and courts. New Hope had been hollowed out, its charm dissipated, and the new people and the new money came and went, indifferent to the wreckage left behind.

Academy Square itself was an unrelieved disaster, but it took the College and the town decades to admit it. Now, the rotting piles of brick had been razed and the cracked pavement removed, and a new project, an eight-story condominium called The High, had just recently been completed. The marketing campaign harked back to the time when the village and the people were one, but The High was still about the dollars.

A plot of land in the middle of town that once belonged to everyone, and a school that educated its citizens and bound them to one another, were irretrievably lost, regardless of the nostalgic ad campaign. The implicit acknowledgement that something important had vanished was patent.

Samantha was not in her office. I leaned in another door. "Is Ms. Clarke around?"

The young man turned reluctantly from his computer screen. "No, sir. She's out of town."

"Do you know where she's gone?" He shook his head. "When's she coming back?"

"She said she'd be here Monday."

"Okay. Thanks."

WHEN IT was the Post Office, the big room had an enclosed counter with "windows" along the left wall and banks of metal boxes for mail on the right. The space in between was empty except for a single round table where patrons could write addresses and apply stamps. The counter and table had been removed, but the boxes, fixed in brick and plaster, remained. A mural depicting a bogus version of the founding of the College was still on the wall just inside the doors.

The Sunday Convocation had managed to find two dozen mahogany pews which were arranged on either side of a narrow middle aisle. A curved dais, elevated a foot above the tile floor, had been built at one end, and there was a metal lectern on one side and a wooden podium on the other. Ornate gilded armchairs lined the back of the platform, occupied presumably by the "priests" of the atheist church. Cosmo Ender sat in the chair on the far right. Wes had not yet made an appearance.

His little flock, however, was well-represented. I estimated they were 25 or 30 percent of the packed congregation. The bowdlerized rituals had concluded, and people were looking at their watches.

Wes appeared in the doorway. Dressed in a white robe and sandals and carrying a wooden staff, he looked like Moses in *The Ten Commandments*. The sound of the staff striking the floor as he walked up the aisle reverberated in the stunned silence. If the Sunday Convocation was seeking a faux religious experience, he would recall the real thing.

He stepped onto the dais and waited. After a long moment, a woman rose from her chair and said, "Mr. Mohammad?" He nodded. She crossed the platform and offered her hand. Turning her head, she said, "Doctor Ender, would you join us?" He and Wes shook hands in the usual way.

They turned to face us. She was taller than Ender and, of course, much smaller than Wes. "Ladies and gentlemen, as you may know, there have been great strides in medicine arising out of the mapping of the human genome. Gene therapy is increasingly seen as the future of disease prevention and cure. In our own community, a controversial treatment for sickle cell anemia is ongoing. People differ in their opinions."

She looked at Ender. "Doctor Cosmo Ender is Director of the School of Human Enrichment at the College. He tells me the school will soon offer a variety of programs using a process he calls temporary gene substitution. He has several patents pending in the area of therapeutic gene enhancement."

She turned to Wes. "Mahmoud Mohammad is imam at the West End Mosque. He opposes Project Sickle Cell. I understand he will file suit shortly to try to stop it." She paused. "Each man will have five minutes to outline his position, after which we'll throw the floor open for questions. Doctor Ender?"

Ender filled his five minutes with unobjectionable platitudes that came down to this: Gene therapy was the logical extension of everything man had sought from the beginning. We had eradicated smallpox and polio with vaccines and drugs. Why not destroy other diseases, like sickle cell anemia, with gene therapy? Completely at ease, he wore a red carnation in the lapel of his tuxedo. He looked like a toastmaster.

Wes took less time, limiting himself to a discussion of the uncertainty of the science. He avoided religion until the end. "I believe in Allah. You say you do not, and yet, you come together in this place. Why? Do you seek the salvation you deny? This – science promises a false salvation. It wants to explain who we are, our morality and our fate, and how we can alter those things." He drew himself up. "We do so at our peril. These scientists are manipulating genes, not creating them. Someone else is the creator."

Eager hands were raised. The woman pointed. A young man, probably a student, stood up. "Neither one of you talked about babies. Can't we fix it so that kids aren't born with deformities and stuff? Doctor Ender?"

Ender smiled. "Oh, yes. We can do amazing things to prevent children from falling victim to their genes. It won't be long before all the familiar problems – birth defects, mental retardation, heritable diseases – can be fixed before a baby is even born. Generations of deficiencies will disappear." He smiled again. "Unwanted cells can be pruned from the family tree."

"How long will it be?"

Ender shifted his eyes toward Wes. "That's – unclear. Some think it's a step too far."

"Messing around with reproductive cells or embryos is a bad idea," said Wes. "It's one thing for an adult to agree to gene therapy. Changing another human being's cells before he's born, which will alter everyone who comes after him, is something else."

"No parent should pass on deadly genes if he doesn't have to," said Ender. "What do you say to a child who's dying of an inherited disease that could have been prevented?"

"It's Allah's will."

"It's not about religion. It's about life."

Wes shook his head. "The life you promise is fraudulent. Allah made man in His image. Man will make man in *his* image. They cannot coexist."

"How can you object to curing disease?"

They had forgotten their audience. "We're not just talking about disease," said Wes. "That's only the nose of the camel under the tent. Manipulation of an embryo's cells will lead to all sorts of abuses. It will refine children, not repair them."

"Why is that an abuse?" said Ender. "What's wrong with improving the species?"

"Who said anything about *improving*?" Wes roared.

"Well – you did. We could refine genes to make our kids better."

"According to who?"

"I – I don't understand. I mean taller, stronger, smarter. More beautiful."

"And what happens to the shorter, weaker, dumber kids? The ugly ones? This treatment won't be free. Ninety-nine percent of the children born into the world won't get it. The ruling class will be even smaller than it is now. What then?"

Ender wasn't backing down, but he seemed a bit apprehensive as Wes loomed over him. "I don't think this is a political –"

"Of course it's political. It's about who tells who what to do."

The woman, who had receded into the background, finally intervened. "Gentlemen, I think we have more questions." She pointed again. "Yes?"

A black woman rose from the first row. "Doctor Ender, we already have two kids. If we had another one, could he be – improved?"

"Certainly. Each newborn is a different –"

"Martha," Wes said. "Why would you do that to your family? You'd have two normal kids, two normal parents and one supposed superman. How would that work out?"

"Well," she said, "I guess –"

"And what if you wanted another child, and there were new bells and whistles? How would your first superman feel? Add to that the fact that these engineered children will live decades longer than their siblings, and –"

"Is that true, Doctor Ender?" she said.

He nodded. "We'll be doubling life spans very soon."

"How will we sustain that?" said Wes. "Our water, our air, the food supply – how will we live?"

"Technology in other areas will adapt. It always has, and . . ."

They were off again. I stopped listening as the questions and debate raged around me. I was pulling for Wes, but his side of the argument wasn't very compelling. Even his own people couldn't resist the allure, and who could blame them? Ender and Steiner were offering life, more and better, and perhaps even a kind of immortality. All Wes had was the status quo, which didn't look so great now that more and more people – even those in other pews – had lost their belief. The now was much more enticing than the hereafter.

Some people embraced change, others resisted it. I was among the latter. The past, frozen in time, could be examined, its less attractive bits ignored – change was chaos beyond my control. Change over the years, of course, became part of the past I accepted, a circumstance I usually ignored when something new turned up.

Gene therapy was more change than I ever imagined, and Alex's illness had forced me to reconsider. How could other people, who wanted change or didn't care, be expected to reject – for themselves or their children – beauty, intellect and long life? It was all the old religions wrapped into one, and a tiny voice inside was wondering what it could do for me.

The debate was winding down. Wes and Ender were shaking hands again, and people began gathering their things. It seemed that Ender's new venture involved "temporary gene substitution." Would he tell me more?

I rose. "Doctor Ender?"

He turned. Everyone in the room paused. "Yes, Harry?" he said, as if we'd known each other all our lives.

"What does your gene substitution program do?"

He faced the crowd again. "The Chancellor and I are holding a press conference next Wednesday. But I'll give you a hint. With our therapy, people will no longer have to be who they are. Or, they can be themselves at some other time. The human experience will be enhanced immeasurably. Temporary gene substitution will liberate mankind."

I waited for Wes at the door. "Nice outfit," I said.

He didn't smile. "We're going too far too fast, Harry. No one remembers yesterday, let alone the last two millenniums. I'm here to remind them."

I turned for home. The past year had been consumed by Alex's illness. Tomorrow would mark the end of that one way or the other, and life would change. Already, I was being forced out of the self-imposed solitude – Teddy Black, Steiner's lawsuit – and, if Alex survived, our lives might again achieve something approaching normalcy, though "normal" would certainly be new. Cosmo Ender was a curiosity Samantha would probably explain.

As I crossed Capital Street, a police car raced past me. Its whining siren and flashing lights proclaimed the urgency of its errand. Seconds later, an ambulance and another cruiser roared past. Terrified they might be going to my house, I began to run but, when all three turned right on Castle Lane and continued down the hill, I relaxed and settled into a fast walk.

At the corner, I debated whether or not to follow them, and opted to check on Alex first. The house was dark and cold on a bright sunny afternoon, and she slept like the dead. She stirred when I smoothed her hair, but didn't wake up. I left by the kitchen door and walked down Castle Lane.

The blue lights were still turning and, as I approached, a State Police car joined the others. There was an old stone amphitheater at the bottom of the hill where Boundary Street, Club Drive and Castle Lane intersected. Once the summer home for a student theatrical group, it was now reduced to hosting weddings and birthday parties, and the students had been replaced by a professional repertory company more to the taste of the corporate lions who came and went. Their glittering new playhouse was only steps away on Club Drive.

The outdoor theater was just west of, and contiguous to, a forest of almost 100 acres called Castle Park. My first real job, the summer after my freshman year in high school, was clearing branches and undergrowth from its trails, picnic areas and floor. Some of the trees were more than 200 years old, but it was neglected now, and the College was looking for a buyer.

The police had congregated in front of the stage. I decided against joining them, and sat down on the top step – soil and grass held in place by gray stone – instead. As I watched, two officers bearing a canvas litter emerged from the woods. They laid it on the elevated stage, and drew a white sheet from the top half of what looked like a woman's body. A man I recognized as the Azure County Coroner bent over it.

Another man I knew, Sheriff Jeff Farnham, looked up and saw me. He hesitated, then motioned for me to join them. Curious but oddly reluctant, I paused, too, before climbing to my feet and walking down the steps.

Jeff met me at the bottom. He was a big man, bigger than me, and he took care of himself. His black hair was cut close to his head, and the tone of the soft drawl was official. "A woman's dead, Harry. Probably within the last 12 hours. Did you notice anything unusual down here? Cars? People?"

I shook my head. "Who is it?"

"We don't know yet. There's no identification." He looked over his shoulder.

"How'd she die?"

"Struck in the back of the head."

I approached the little knot of men surrounding the body. The sheet had been replaced, but the coroner nodded to me and pulled it down to her neck. The red and blue makeup was still in place, but the pouting mouth was slack and the eyes closed. I felt Jeff beside me. "Her name's Vera Carr," I said. "She's a graduate student at the College."

"A friend?" said Jeff.

"No. I met her day before yesterday."

He touched my arm. "Let's take a walk." We climbed the steps and started up the hill. "Why did you meet her day before yesterday?" he said.

"We had lunch at Franky's. I wanted to ask her some questions."

"About what?"

"Teddy Black."

His thick brows shot up. "Teddy Black?"

I nodded. "She's a tutor for the football team. The Chancellor asked me to check out – something."

"What?"

We'd reached the corner. The Chancellor's House was a block away. "I'd be glad to tell you, but I think it would be wise to bring him into the conversation." The Sheriff had every right to demand an answer now, but the Chancellor was a very important person, and Teddy Black was – well, Teddy Black. Vera Carr's murder couldn't be allowed to interfere with the football team.

NINE

I PULLED the car to the curb and pointed. "Look. Abby and David." We watched as they dis-appeared inside the temple. "Both of the women in my life left to the tender mercies of Frank Steiner."

Alex smiled. "Second thoughts?"

"No. You'll only be here a few days." I reached for the sleek leather bag purchased ex-pressly for the occasion. It was a product of fine materials and craftsmanship, and it would grow more handsome as it aged, a message not lost on Alex when I gave it to her.

We stopped at the reception desk. She took the bag from me. "I'll take it from here, Harry."

"Don't you want me to go with you?"

She shook her head. "You've brought me this far. I need to take some responsibility for myself."

I nodded. "I'll see you tonight."

"No. I think it might be a little – hard. There's no reason for you to suffer through it." She paused. "I'll be home soon."

"Yes. Yes, you will." My eyes welled up again, and one or two drops slipped free. She wiped them away with a finger. "No more tears. Everything's going to be fine."

I watched as she stepped into the elevator and the doors closed behind her. She had pushed her doubts aside and, whatever pain was coming, she'd never give in to it. If Steiner failed, it wouldn't be because of her. I made my way slowly back to the car.

A few minutes later I parked in front of the courthouse and climbed to the second floor. Bobby's secretary looked up as I entered. "I need a favor," I said. She smiled. "Abby's – out today and I need the order from Friday's hearing." I dropped my hand-written version on her desk. "Do you mind?"

"Of course not." She glanced at it. "I'll have it for you in a minute."

"Thanks. Just give it to Judge Hood. I'll –"

Bobby leaned into the room from his office. "Harry. Can I see you for a second?"

"Sure." I braced myself and stepped over the threshold.

He didn't say a word about the hearing. Instead, he probed in his friendly, familiar way, trying to discover what was wrong. I resisted. When he understood that I wouldn't tell him, the conversation turned first to Alex and then the football team. As I rose to leave, he said, "Jeff says you were at the crime scene yesterday." I nodded. "And you had a meeting with the Chancellor?"

"Yes." The Chancellor had been irritated that Jeff Farnham was in on the Teddy Black inquiry, but I didn't care. Vera Carr had been very uncomfortable at Franky's. After a vague explanation from me, the Sheriff had tactfully avoided more than the most cursory questions, and it was left that I would do my thing and he would do his. Should our paths cross, we would deal with it then.

Bobby was curious, but again didn't push. "If there's anything I can do, let me know."

I took the stairs to the third floor and entered the coroner's office. "This is the order for the Spiller boy's body," I said, handing him a copy.

"Thank God," he said. "Would you like to take him with you?"

I ignored the gallows humor. "I'll have somebody from the clinic call you." I paused. "What's the story on the Carr woman?"

"It's not complete yet. She died from a blow to the back of the head sometime between midnight and eight o'clock Sunday morning."

"Murder weapon?"

"We haven't found it. She was struck twice. One was blunt – the scalp was barely broken. The other one had an edge to it."

"Like an axe?"

"Not that sharp." He paused. "Not that serious, either, but it broke the skin. She lost some blood."

"Are you saying there were two weapons?"

"No. I'm just answering your questions."

"Which one killed her?"

"We're waiting for the autopsy, but I'm 99 percent sure the blunt instrument did the job."

"Left-handed or right?"

"Right."

"Was she robbed?"

"Maybe. There was no purse."

"Anything – exotic so far?"

He nodded. "There was evidence of ejaculate in the vagina. Hers."

"Semen?"

"No."

"Rape?"

"No signs of it."

I considered that. Vera had had sex before she was killed, but her partner left nothing behind. That could mean any number of things. I ran through them in my head.

"She wasn't killed in the park," the coroner said. "Her body was dumped there."

"How do you know?"

"Like I said, she bled from the wound to her head. There was no blood where her body was found. Not a drop."

"Anything else unusual?"

"Well – I don't know about unusual. She wasn't wearing any underwear."

I hesitated. "About the Spiller boy – how many other dead kids have you delivered to the clinic?"

"Nine. Five girls and four boys."

"How old were they?"

"I don't remember exactly. Most of them were infants. There was a little girl who was about two."

"How'd they die?"

He smiled. "I asked Steiner to send me his reports. He doesn't have to, but he does it anyway." He paused. "They're not autopsy reports exactly – they don't say why those kids died. Not in plain language anyway." He stopped again. "He's a smartass. He knows I can't understand that crap. I don't even try to read them anymore."

Back at the office, I called Steiner. "I have the order for the boy's body," I said. "I'll send you a copy."

"Good. What happens next?"

"I talked to the coroner a few minutes ago. He's waiting for instructions from you."

"All right. Thanks."

"Have you injected the cells?"

"Yes."

"Is she okay?"

"So far. I'll call you when I have more information."

"Thanks."

I held the button down for a second and dialed another number. "Samantha Clarke, please."

"I'm sorry. She's not in yet."

"Would you ask her to call Harry Monmouth?"

HELEN WAS out sick. "I'm supposed to pick up some paperwork from her," I said.

The woman behind the desk nodded and extended another manila folder. "These are the class schedules you asked for." She handed me an envelope. "And that's a note from the Dean saying you're authorized to observe in the classroom. Just show it to the instructor."

"What – what will they think I'm doing there?"

"They probably won't give it a second thought. We have accreditation people and recruiters in the classrooms all the time."

The Chancellor was waiting at the bottom of the staircase. I followed him into his office. "I spoke with the Chairman of the Board of Trustees a few minutes ago," he said. "He's worried the press will tie this woman's death to the football team."

"Doesn't he have better things to worry about?"

He ignored me. "The Organization's investigation is behind us now. We don't need something else."

"What are you saying?"

"I'm saying the less we hear about Vera Carr, the better. And the tutoring program." He paused. "I appreciate whatever you've done, Harry, but circumstances compel me to call a halt."

"I'm nearly finished. All that's left is to visit some of the faculty."

"No. Just drop it."

My walk home took me by the outdoor theater. I resumed my seat on the top step and considered the Chancellor's change of heart. In a sane world the Chancellor of the College would want to know if a woman was killed because of corruption in his domain but, since it might affect the football program, he'd chosen ignorance instead.

It was all of a piece. When the story about the Organization's investigation first broke, the College's initial response was: "Who can we sue and for how much?" followed by: "This is hurting recruiting and fund-raising." The last refuge before bowing to reality was: "Everybody does it." Behavior that would never be tolerated on the academic side of things was wished away so as not to offend the vast, influential constituency of the football team. The tail wagged the dog.

Inside the house, I tried Samantha's office again, but she still wasn't there, nor had she been in touch. Slightly alarmed, I looked up her home number and dialed it, to no avail. As the receiver settled back into its cradle, the telephone rang. "Hello?"

"Harry, it's Frank Steiner."

"Is everything okay?"

"Well – yes and no."

"Meaning what?"

"Our readouts say the new cells are working. The cancer is being destroyed. She's on track to be cancer-free in five or six weeks."

"But?"

"But she's in terrible pain. Her temperature never goes below 103 degrees and spikes higher. The nerve endings all over her body are hypersensitive. She can't even wear a hospital gown." He paused. "The temperature, especially, is life-threatening. We have to do something. I'm trying to cure her, not kill her."

"But – wouldn't that affect the treatment?"

"I'm going to induce a coma. I believe it will reduce the fever. The pain will still be there, but she won't feel it. I don't think it'll interfere with the treatment."

"What does she say?"

"I haven't talked to her. I'm telling you."

I had no options and he knew it. We lived at his sufferance. "All right. I want to see her before you do it."

"Fine. Be here in an hour."

I OPENED my umbrella. Thunder rolled in the distance, and a jagged bolt of lightning – miles away in reality – appeared to strike Steiner's temple as it came into view. The ancients had used their temples to make sacrifices to the gods. How far had we come in 25 centuries?

I took the elevator to the third floor and pushed through the door to his office. He wasn't there. I crossed the room and looked in the open door to the laboratory. He was standing at the far end of a metal counter peering into an elaborate microscope. "Frank?"

He turned his head. He looked different, and I realized he wasn't wearing his glasses. "The cancer count keeps going down," he said. "She's winning that battle." He stood aside. "Look." I leaned over the microscope. Globular forms swarmed in fluid to no purpose I could see until, looking closer, I noticed that many of them – after contact with others – simply disappeared. "This is a big day for medicine," Steiner said. "The same procedure can be used to fight dozens, hundreds, of debilitating diseases. All that remains is to learn how to control it."

"Fever and pain?"

"Yes. And maybe other things we don't know about yet. Your wife's a brave woman. I admire her very much."

The price for his admiration was pretty high, but it was we who had come to him. "What are you going to do?"

"Body temperature is controlled by the brain. I'm going to use an anesthetic to induce an unconscious state. I hope that will cause the brain to stop reacting to the chemicals that cause the fever." He paused. "It worked on the mouse."

"What – impact will that have on the rest of her?"

"We'll treat her as if it were a real coma. Her vital functions will be monitored, she'll be fed through tubes."

"How long?"

"I'm not sure. The destruction of the last cancer cell should be the outside."

"Where is she?"

He pointed to a closed door a few feet away. "Please don't discuss this with her. I think she's willing to suffer the pain. I'm not."

Her eyes were shut tight, the lips pressed together so hard they almost disappeared but, somehow, she looked more vital than she had in months. Bathed in sweat, she was naked except for a pair of cotton panties. The disease had taken its toll on her body but already, only a few hours after the new genes were introduced, the desiccated flesh was alive. I wanted to touch her, but didn't.

"Alex?" The eyes opened. "Don't talk." She blinked. "The cancer cells are dying. I saw it myself." She reached for my hand. Maybe I imagined it, but the grip seemed stronger, or perhaps she was just trying harder. I stood there for a few seconds. "I'll be back tomorrow." I turned away.

"Harry?"

"Yes?"

"Kiss me."

Steiner was standing by the door when I left. I wanted to thank him, truly thank him, but the words wouldn't come. "I'll be back tomorrow," I said again. He nodded and entered her room, closing the door behind him.

The rain had stopped. Still stunned, I walked down the hill, contemplating the magic I had seen. Despite all the talk and reports from the sickle cell project, I was really a skeptic. It was just science fiction, or a new religion. Now I was a believer.

At the bottom of the hill, I continued north on Division Street rather than turn toward home. I cast the perils of our brave new world aside for the moment. I had good news, and I wanted to share it.

I turned left at High Street. Samantha lived in one of the penthouses at The High. As I approached I saw a familiar face – Jack Peeler's – exit the front door and hurry across the street. He turned west, away from me.

I ignored the crowded plaza with its banal artwork and trendy coffee bars, and entered the lobby. The security guard, perched on a stool behind an imposing marble desk, was a former Azure County Deputy Sheriff. "Hey, Mike."

"Mr. Monmouth. How you doing?"

"Fine. I just saw Jack Peeler. Does he live here?"

"Yeah. He moved in last week. Fourth floor."

I nodded. "I'm going up to see Ms. Clarke."

He indicated the guest book in front of him. I signed my name and noted the time. When the elevator doors opened, I entered and pushed the button marked "PH." There were only two units on the top floor, one of which was still unsold. I rang the bell and, after a moment or two, touched it again. I knocked and tried to speak through the door. "Samantha? It's Harry." And then, inanely, "Are you okay?"

Descending to the lobby, I considered recent events. We'd met at her office the previous Wednesday, five days earlier. The last time we spoke was Friday morning when she scheduled a meeting to discuss "Cosmo Ender and friends," and she'd called later that day to cancel it because of a "field trip." On Saturday, the boy at the *Chronicle* said she planned to be in the office Monday, today, but calls to home and office went unanswered.

She was only a few hours beyond her estimated return, but something was wrong. She'd been bursting to tell me about Ender, and she had a paper to get out. Mike turned away from his small television set as I stepped from the elevator. "Not home?" he said.

"Apparently. When was the last time you saw her?"

"Last night. About eight o'clock."

"Was she alone?"

"No. She had another woman with her."

"Who?"

He shook his head. "I don't know." I reached for the guest book. "It won't be there. We don't make guests who come in with a resident sign in."

"Have you ever seen her before?"

"No."

"What did she look like?"

He smiled. "Good looking for her age. Tall, fair. Red hair."

I nodded. "When did she leave?"

He thought for a second. "Maybe an hour or two later."

"I think something's wrong. Do you have a key?"

"Well –"

"I'll be responsible."

He opened a drawer and withdrew a key. We were quiet as the elevator ascended again. He rang the bell and knocked on the door. "Ms. Clarke?" Inserting the key, he turned the lock and pushed the brass lever down. The door swung open.

The kitchen was immediately to the left, and there was a powder room on the right. A short hallway opened into a large room with high ceilings and hardwood floors. A cluster of blonde furniture was grouped around a square coffee table, and chairs and ottomans – ebony covered with white leather cushions – framed the fireplace. A baby grand piano stood beneath a winding staircase against the far wall.

I'd seen some of it before, though I'd never been there. The local media, agog at the presence of a former anchorman in their midst, had greeted her arrival with huzzahs all around, and the *Chronicle* had published a two-page spread dedicated to her and her new home. There were pictures of Samantha at the fireplace, Samantha at the piano, Samantha on the staircase – the new doyen in her salon. The prose gushed.

"Samantha?" I called. I looked at Mike. "I'll check upstairs." I took the steps two at a time. There were two doors off the open landing, both leading to bedrooms and connecting baths. The double doors at the end of the hall were closed. I pushed one open.

The drapes were drawn and there was no light, except for a few embers in the fireplace. I could barely make out a figure outlined on the bed. I flipped the switch next to the door. Samantha lay outstretched, her head thrown back on a pile of pillows. Her robe was open, revealing the naked body beneath it. A syringe and needle dangled from her arm like a dart thrown poorly at a dartboard, and a large bent spoon, darkened by flame, lay on the bedside table. A tiny amount of liquid remained.

An elaborate Swiss clock on the mantel chimed the hour.

I lifted her wrist. Her hand was cold, the arm stiff but not rigid. After pulling the robe closed, I walked out to the landing and leaned over the iron rail. "She's dead. Call the Sheriff." Mike reached for a phone next to the stairs. "Don't touch anything. Go downstairs. I'll wait up here."

Back on the first floor, I sat on the edge of the sofa. Samantha's companion yesterday sounded like Helen Tanner. Samantha had answered the phone when I called Helen a few days earlier. The needle seemed to confirm the rumors from New York. What did Helen know about that?

There was a shabby book on the coffee table. I lifted it carefully. The raised white letters on the maroon cover read: *RiverLife – 1961*. I flipped the front cover over. It was a library book, checked out from the Twin Rivers Town Library two days before. The title page proclaimed that it was the 1961 edition of the yearbook for Twin Rivers High School. It was odd. Twin Rivers had been on my mind, but Teddy Black was just a glimmer in the cosmos in 1961.

I heard the unneeded sirens undoubtedly headed this way. Samantha's field trip was Twin Rivers. Why? And why had she come away with this book? I opened it. The first section contained the retouched photographs and achievements of the members of the senior class and, appended to each one, a literary phrase intended by the editors to characterize each particular life. It was one of the cruelties of an earlier time no longer tolerated.

There was a post-it affixed to a page beginning with "Alma Jane Doakes" and ending with

"Alexander George Farris." I examined all eight pictures closely – one of the faces gave me pause, and I recognized one of the names. "James Francis Edwards" had become a doctor, and his daughter's name was Catherine. What was Samantha's interest in James Edwards?

I checked the index. The only other reference to Edwards led me to a photograph of the Chess Club, two beaming young men holding a tall loving cup. Edwards was wearing his glasses this time, and he stood a head taller than his teammate, a boy named Gerry Ender. I studied the images for a few seconds, then turned back to take a closer look at "Gerald Wilhelm Ender." The quotation beneath the picture read, "Rebellion lay in his way, and he found it." I imagined less hair and a ruddy complexion, and a bushy white mustache. I wasn't certain, but there was a good chance Cosmo Ender had once been a chess champion at Twin Rivers High School.

BOOK TWO

Till swollen with cunning, of a self-conceit,
His waxen wings did mount above his reach,
And, melting, Heavens conspir'd his over-
throw – Christopher Marlowe

ONE

AS A rule, I avoided hospital rooms, but the chamber in which Alex had lain for weeks wasn't in a hospital. It had all the paraphernalia – tubes, rails on the bed, even a slight medicinal odor – but, tucked away in Frank Steiner's private laboratory, the bustle and the noise and the germs were missing. I came to see her each evening, though she never knew I was there.

Steiner, too, was a frequent visitor. He was the scientist and she the specimen, but I sensed that his attentions exceeded the requisites of the doctor-patient relationship. I had surprised him several times at her bedside, and fresh flowers appeared daily. He made no excuses, and I asked no questions.

Alex lay comatose, perfectly still, like a queen atop her funeral bier, but her body was more alive each day. The statistics of the disease Steiner issued were unnecessary. Her skin was firmer, the complexion fresher, and the portents of death were gone. The cancer had made her old – its cure would restore her vigor. It was now only a matter of killing the last few cancer cells and awakening her from the coma, and the marvel would be complete. Already my mind was turning to the rest of our life.

I had lots of time to think. Despite the pub-
lic lamentations on her behalf – a public that in-
cluded Alex – I had consigned her to death, and
been unfaithful in my mind, a secret kept even
from me. I had contemplated with little conscience
a life with someone else. Why? Did I really want
Alex to die so I could indulge some imagined virility
that likewise lived only in my head? And, if that
were so, was it evil – a terrible flaw in me – or only
innate? Which was worse?

Whatever the truth, my latent plans had
been set aside. Only the guilt remained. Alex
would live, and our most pressing problem was an
explanation for her recovery. I held her hand for a
moment before leaving the room.

Steiner was at his desk. He was quiet until I
reached the door. "Harry?" I looked back. "Where
are we in our legal proceedings?"

I'd been "retained" to represent him in Wes
Vaughn's suit against the College. Steiner wasn't
named in the litigation, but he was certainly an in-
terested party. The Chancellor had wanted to hire
me as well, but Steiner – to my great relief – had
vetoed the idea. "The plaintiffs want Project Sickle
Cell to stop until the case is decided. There's a
hearing in the morning. I plan to attend." I
paused. "Where do we stand, in case somebody
asks?"

"It's immaterial to me. If something's wrong,
the damage is already done."

"You mean, it doesn't matter if it's 400 peo-
ple who might be screwed up, or 4,000?"

"That's correct. What about the other thing?
The Spiller child? I assume that's still going on."

"Yes, they still want money. I received some discovery requests this morning. I sent you copies."

"What does that mean?"

"They want to see every document you've created since the beginning of time, and they want you to answer some written questions. It's standard procedure these days, unfortunately."

He stared at me. "I won't do it. Make it go away."

I shook my head. "You'll be forced to produce them one day. And answer the questions. If you want to maintain any credibility with the Court, you'll cooperate now."

His eyes blinked in code again, and then he smiled. "You mean provide them with *something.*"

"No. I mean do what the rules say."

He nodded, the smile still on his face. "Of course," he said without a hint of conviction, leaving the clear impression that it would be a cold day in hell before Missy Farrell saw anything meaningful from the files of Frank Steiner.

I ran into Abby in the lobby. "How'd it go?" I said.

"Everything's fine. There are two babies in here —" she pointed to her midriff "— a boy and a girl. My due date's in June."

"So I don't have to start looking for a new secretary yet?"

She laughed. "Not yet. You have a few months."

We parted on the plaza, she for the parking garage, me for the walk through campus to the house on High Street. It was only Thursday, but the parties had already begun. The football team, number one in the nation for the sixth consecutive week, was undefeated. The frenzy in the media — radio, television, the Internet — was unprecedented.

Teddy Black was without peer. He led the country in all the numbers kept for quarterbacks, and was on track to break every mark in the Organization's record book. He and Cat had so far maintained his privacy, but the pressure was mounting nationwide for a closer look at the young phenom. In an effort to discourage would-be "journalists," the College had assigned a squad of campus policemen to escort them in public.

Vera Carr's murder was still unexplained. Samantha Clarke's, though, had been resolved — death from a massive overdose of heroin administered by her own hand. Whether intended to kill or not no one could really say, but there was evidence that the troubles in New York weighed more heavily than she let on.

The Sheriff's office and the coroner inclined toward suicide — I did not. Samantha was chasing a story and nothing, certainly not the contemplation of her own death, would be permitted to interfere. Helen Tanner was questioned — Samantha had been fine when she left her — and nothing was made of the high school annual borrowed from the Twin Rivers Library.

Samantha had made two phone calls the day before she died. The first was to Helen, the second to Jack Peeler. When asked about it, Jack said that, like everyone else in the news business, she was looking for an interview with Teddy Black. He refused her as gently as he could, and she suggested he think again "for his own good." It was a threat he'd heard many times, so he hung up.

The idea that Cosmo Ender played chess at Twin Rivers High School went unexplored because Teddy Black had played games there, too, and I was unprepared to look under that particular rock without thinking about it some more. Samantha had no people and no plans for dying, so she was buried in a plot crowded with my forbears. There was room because – owing to the undisclosed details of a scandal 30 years earlier – neither Alex nor I, nor our children, would finally rest there.

I paused to gauge the progress of the School of Human Enrichment. The excavation was finished and the piles driven, and the foundation formed and poured. Steel columns, beams and rebar lay on truck beds. Men in different-colored hardhats swarmed the site, and yellow cranes pointed to the sky. The construction was ahead of schedule, but the College and Cosmo Ender couldn't wait – the School would set up shop shortly in borrowed space at Steiner's clinic.

Ender's press conference had been held on a temporary platform erected adjacent to the construction site. Steiner was on the stage but didn't speak. The Chancellor opened the proceedings. "Ladies and gentlemen, this is a red letter day for the College. The School of Human Enrichment promises a truly unique experience for consumers, as well as a research facility where scientists and scholars can explore the human mind. It will be affiliated with our Applied Genetics department led by Doctor Frank Steiner. Faculty and staff will move freely between the two."

He went on to describe the economic benefits for the College and the state, and to extol the generosity of government and private investors. As I listened, I realized how much Winfred Honeyman had changed. Rather than preside over petty squabbles usually the lot of schoolmasters, he hobnobbed with corporate titans and powerful politicians. Unlike his students and colleagues at the College, important people actually listened to him, or so it seemed. He was playing a role, an actor on an unfamiliar stage, and he liked it. "I'll take a few questions before turning it over to Doctor Ender," he said.

He answered queries about potential profits, the number of jobs that might be created, and the likely increase in tax revenues. About to bring Ender on, he noticed a young woman on the edge of the crowd with her hand raised. The Chancellor pointed. After identifying herself as a reporter for the school newspaper, she said, "Doctor Honeyman, can you explain how this new facility adds to the education we get here?"

It was the first time the word "education" had been uttered. He answered it the way all such questions were answered. "The School of Human Enrichment will bring prestige and influence to the College. Our diplomas will be that much more valuable in the marketplace. And we owe a duty to the taxpayers of this state to create economic opportunity."

Ender, perhaps trying to deflect attention from himself, was dressed in an ordinary business suit. "Experts in the field of genetics," he said, "have understandably concentrated on the prevention of gene-related disease. As the research has progressed, however, science has begun to consider other applications. The vast array of human knowledge outside the medical field – the arts, for example, or the social sciences, even what we call 'amusement' – can benefit from our understanding of the genome." He paused. "The key is the brain. Knowing how the genes in the brain work unlocks our past and enhances our future."

He spent the next few minutes talking about "memory genes" and "emotion genes" and "creative genes" that could stimulate – he used the word "express" – proteins that control how people feel, think and behave. "Of the thousands and thousands of different genes in the human body, about a third are active, and most of those are in the brain. The science is in its infancy, but we've had some success with memory and emotions." He finished with timetables, staffing and the obligatory nod to government and industry, and then called for questions.

A man seated in the first row of folding chairs rose and said, "Doctor Ender, what's the practical value of this research?"

"Well – take memory, for instance. Alzheimer's begins as a disease of the memory. Many psychiatric problems are caused by bad memories, or no memories at all. Our therapy can revive or suppress those thoughts, make them more acceptable to the patient. We can also augment memory for those who want to recall precisely something that happened to them in the past." He smiled. "It's like a movie of your life and you're the star."

"How does it work?"

"Memory is the collection, storage and recall of our past experiences. It can be short- or long-term, reflexive or episodic. When you remember something, the neurons – nerve cells – involved in the original experience, which are located in differ-

ent parts of your brain, fire simultaneously to re-
construct the event. Our therapy is directed at
those neurons."

"How do you pinpoint a specific memory?"
said another reporter.

"Each memory has a unique sequence among
the millions of neurons in your brain. Some of the
cells are devoted to time, others to space. We tar-
get the intersection of time and space. Recent
memories are easy – older ones depend on the pa-
tient's effort to retain them in the first place.
Memories that are personally meaningful are easi-
er to recall."

"What's it like?"

"I'm told it's like being there again. Most
memories are visual, but the treatment enables re-
trieval from the other senses – smell, sound, taste,
texture – as well."

"How long does the effect last?"

"It depends on the duration of what's being
remembered, but the experience we induce will
probably last no more than an hour. The memories
are compressed. An event that lasted an hour will
be recalled in less than a minute. Like a movie
that covers a period of years in 90 minutes." He
paused. "There are two perspectives – you can
watch it, like you're sitting in the audience, or you
can actually be in the movie, playing the leading
role. Or both." He stopped again. "There's another
thing. We believe one person can re-live the memo-
ries of another person. It's what I call temporary
gene substitution." He fell into huckster mode.
"Think of that. You could experience the Battle of
Hastings in the mind of William the Conqueror. I

could walk on the moon. All we need is the right DNA."

A woman in the back stood up. "Aren't someone's memories personal? Even if they're dead?"

Ender recalled himself. "It's still a bit theoretical. And there are some legal problems to work out."

Another man rose. "Do you participate in these treatments?"

Ender laughed. "I'm just a financial advisor."

I waited for a follow-up question, but there was none. His usual part was "investor," but he was the "Director" of the School of Human Enrichment, and he was conducting a press conference on its behalf. The limited role assumed in past ventures had been abandoned. Why?

The rest of the questions addressed the possibilities of temporary gene substitution and how the treatment was performed. As a mere advisor, Ender was suitably vague about the details, and he downplayed the idea that it would be available anytime soon. "It's just one of the areas the scientists at the School will be exploring," he said.

The idea, of course, was monstrous. Whatever prophylactic use it might have, gene substitution was just another term for mind reading. It would allow anyone to snoop into another person's life, the ultimate surveillance tool. All that was required, as Ender said, was the right DNA.

Another exchange near the end caught my attention. In response to a question about himself, Ender began with "I'm a New Yorker born and bred . . ." I'd heard, or seen, those exact words – attributed to the same source – before, in the information Samantha had given me when we first began to wonder about Cosmo Ender. It was true he could have been "born and bred" in New York and still graduate from Twin Rivers High School, but why not mention it, give his identity a local flavor?

Gerry Ender had become Cosmo Ender, and he and James Edwards were friends. Edwards' daughter Catherine was the friend and protector of Teddy Black. All four of them had lived in Twin Rivers. Samantha Clarke made a field trip to Twin Rivers, and sought an interview with Teddy immediately upon her return. She died shortly thereafter. That was too much serendipity to ignore.

HELEN LIVED in a small, secluded cottage on Park Place, only four or five blocks from our house on High Street. Surrounded by a low brick wall covered in ivy, it was situated well off the street, completely hidden by magnolias and dense evergreen shrubbery. The dark gray paint was peeling, and moss grew in the seams of the roof. Windows in three unlighted dormers reflected the moonlight. Stone chimneys rose on either side of the house.

She opened the door before I could ring the bell. "Harry. What are you doing here?"

"I was in the neighborhood. I'd like to ask you a couple of questions." I crossed the threshold into a cramped foyer. She led me to a room on the right, once probably a parlor, now obviously Helen's study. Light from a single lamp revealed shelves full of books, painted wainscoting and a hardwood floor covered by a blue woven rug.

Helen sat behind a kidney-shaped desk, and motioned me to one of the chairs flanking the raised brick hearth. The portrait of her in the white confirmation dress hung over the fireplace. The only sound was the pendulum inside the grandfather clock in the corner.

She was wearing a long black robe and slippers. Her hair was pulled away from the freshly-made face, and gardenia – the scent she'd worn for as long as I had known her – reached my nose. She looked at her watch. "I don't have a lot of time," she said. "What questions?"

Her abruptness startled me, but I plunged ahead anyway. "How did you know Samantha Clarke?"

She blinked. "I barely knew her at all. Why?"

"I'm not sure. I guess I think there's more to her death than we know." I paused. "When did you meet her?"

"She interviewed me for the paper. We go – went to the same church."

I smiled. "Church?"

Her face remained blank. "Yes."

"Which one?"

"Saint Thomas More."

"I didn't know Samantha was a Catholic."

"She wasn't. She told me she liked the rituals."

I nodded. Rituals were soothing in their repetition and familiarity, a common bond among the participants. The notions behind them required belief and commitment. I'd let them go gradually, but Helen's effort to banish them altogether had failed. "Do you mind telling me why she called you?"

She checked her watch again. "She asked me to meet her. I'm on the Admissions Committee. She wanted to talk about the process."

"Anything in particular?"

"Yes. She was interested in the way recruited athletes are treated as opposed to ordinary students." She rose. "Harry, I really –"

"One more thing. Did you mention the Teddy Black business to anyone else?"

"Everyone in the tutoring program knows about Teddy and Cat. Probably the whole College by now."

"No. I mean about my looking into it."

"No."

"What about the idea that the players can't read?" She shook her head. "Okay, thanks." I stood up. "I'll get out of your hair."

Seconds later, I passed through the rusty wrought-iron gate and turned for home. Samantha's visit to Twin Rivers had sparked an interest in the College's admission of recruited athletes, the most famous of whom was the town's own Teddy Black, but I was convinced that Cosmo Ender was her real target. Was there a connection? More to the point, was it any of my business?

Helen had been less than candid. She tried to give the impression that she and Samantha were only casual acquaintances, but Samantha had answered Helen's telephone late one evening a few days before she died, a fact that implied something more. Helen had failed to mention it, to me or the police. Why?

And, bathed and perfumed, she was obvious-
ly expecting a visitor. I crossed the street and
waited in the shadows. Seconds later, a woman
passed me on the opposite side. I couldn't see her
face, but her shape and carriage were unmistakable
– Cat Edwards. I watched as she disappeared in-
side the house. My visit to Twin Rivers, contem-
plated since Samantha's death, could be postponed
no longer.

TWO

THE BATTERED sign read, "Nazareth" and, in smaller letters underneath, "Unincorporated." It was one of several tiny communities, all poor and mostly black, that I encountered on Highway 70 between New Hope and Twin Rivers. Rendered irrelevant by the interstate highway a few miles to the north, they were indistinguishable.

Nazareth began with a liquor store shaped like a cube. The façade was brick, and the windows were barred. It was followed by dilapidated trailers set on blocks and surrounded by rusty automobiles growing from the weeds. Yellow laundry hung from lines stretched between trees or utility poles.

Next was a block of vacant storefronts, and a gas station with an "Esso" sign where the only business now was beer and lottery tickets. Tired men in worn-out overalls, waiting for death to deliver them from the flies and the hot, dusty monotony, sat on benches outside. Sprinkled amongst the desolation were more recent signs of hope, beauty parlors and diners and "antiques" stores, all with "Open" signs on the door and empty parking places out front. Officialdom – signified by an old police cruiser with a single red gumball in the parking lot – was a concrete bunker in the middle of town in need of a new coat of whitewash.

Faith was still alive in Nazareth and the other little towns, but its reach was limited. The old people took the long view and, consequently, the machinations of men were mostly ignored, and the churches – I passed dozens of them – reflected their belief. A better time was coming, and science had nothing to do with it.

The young had been claimed by a "culture" that had no place for them. They knew how to manipulate magic machines that revealed a vicarious world otherwise unknown to them, and they talked only to each other on their cell phones. Like the students at the College, they were customers for those who had something to sell, and the likelihood of becoming something more was slim.

On the far side of Nazareth, I stopped at a place that still had gas pumps. There was a red brick church across the street and, as I filled the tank, a wedding party spilled out of the double doors. The young woman in the long white dress was beautiful on her wedding day, and the groom resembled a toy soldier in his blue service uniform. He had chosen a way out, one of the few available to him, and all he risked was his life.

I walked inside, nodded to the black man behind the cash register and found the facilities. A minute later, I drew a soft drink from one of the coolers and went to the counter to pay him. While he was making change, I noticed three framed photographs hanging on the wall behind him. The one in the middle, seemingly out of place, was Teddy Black in a maroon Twin Rivers football uniform. He was kneeling, his helmet on the ground beside him. The blond hair was close-cropped and the blue eyes hooded, and the expression on his handsome face – like all the others I'd ever seen – was stoic.

The images on either side of Teddy were black-and-white, one a picture of a young black boy, the other a family portrait depicting the same child with his parents, one of whom handed me my change. The woman's features were distinctive, different from the other two.

"You a Teddy Black fan?" I said. He stared at me, but didn't respond. I tried something else. "How far is it to Twin Rivers?"

"Four miles."

"Thanks."

TWIN RIVERS, a once-historic village located at the confluence of the Neuse and Trent Rivers, had thrown in the towel. Like New Hope, it had succumbed to the dictates of commerce, though it followed a different path to achieve that condition. New Hope had been appropriated by its major tenant, but it retained the trappings of what it had been – a small college town in the South – without the overlay of a contrived "identity" designed to make it more appealing to others. There were no festivals or ad campaigns, nothing to disguise what it really was.

Twin Rivers, on the other hand, had undergone decades of "community branding." It had deteriorated in the years after World War II, like Nazareth writ large. Significant structures from its past were torn down to make way for parking lots and gas stations. Streets in the commercial district were widened, separating it from neighborhoods and making pedestrian traffic impossible. Empty storefronts and vacant lots, like those in Nazareth, were the norm.

Rather than give in to despair or abandon Twin Rivers altogether, the town fathers "sold" it to consultants and developers. There was still a Mayor and a Board of Aldermen and a City Manager, but the new owners – armed with corporate capital and government grants – called the shots. The state's seat of government in colonial times, Twin Rivers now billed itself as a "product" or "brand," complete with slogans, logos and "events" for tourists. It was a commodity, and self-marketing was its principal industry.

I stopped first at City Hall, a three-story brick building with arched windows and an outsized clock tower. The Office of Public Records was on the second floor. I found a birth certificate for Gerald Wilhelm Ender, but none for Teddy Black. When I inquired, the blue-haired lady behind the counter was happy to talk about Teddy. She explained that it was a big county – lots of kids back then were delivered by midwives or even fathers who didn't bother to record the occasion. It was almost rote – she had told it all many times before.

I pressed harder. "That was only 20 years ago," I said. "He wasn't born in a hospital?"

She hesitated. We were beyond the glib now. "I don't know." She paused again. "Not here anyway."

"He was adopted by a local family?"

"Yes."

"Can you tell me where his parents live?"

She shook her head. "They're dead. Killed in a car wreck a year ago."

I pointed to Ender's birth certificate. "Would you make me a copy of that, please?"

The offices of the *Sun Journal* were only a few blocks away. Back issues of the paper were preserved on microfilm. I took a pad and pen from my briefcase, and sat down behind the film reader.

I was looking for something in particular, something that wouldn't be included in the index. Armed only with the year – 1995 – I found January 1 and turned to the "Legal Announcements." The type was so small as to be almost illegible. I fiddled with a knob on the side of the reader to magnify the print.

Three hours later, eyes smarting and about to knock off for lunch, I found it on August 5:

A Petition has been filed by Paul and Sylvia Black, 411 Front Street, Twin Rivers, for the Adoption of a male child, a foundling approximately four years old, who was found asleep in Cedar Grove Cemetery on May 14, 1995. Legal notice has been filed and published in accordance with all applicable ordinances and laws, and no parent, relative or guardian has come forward to claim him. All persons having an interest in said child, or in his adoption by Paul and Sylvia Black, are advised to contact the office of the Guardian Ad Litem at the Raven County Courthouse.

So Teddy wasn't just an orphan, he was a "foundling." I'd never heard that part of the story before. The notice was published once a week for the following two months. The address stirred a recollection. I found Cat's file and confirmed it.

Her family lived at 501 Front Street. They were neighbors of Paul and Sylvia – and Teddy – Black.

I considered that while shifting the reader to May 15, 1995. There was nothing, so I moved to May 16. It was on the third page near the bottom:

CHILD FOUND AT CEDAR GROVE

A small boy was found asleep in Cedar Grove Cemetery this past Sunday afternoon. According to Doctor James Edwards, who discovered the child lying just inside the Weeping Arch on one of the tabletop gravestones of the Taylor family, the boy appeared healthy but disoriented. He was unable to recall his name or who his family was, and had no idea how he came to be at the cemetery.

Authorities have requested that anyone having information about the child to please contact the Sheriff's Department as soon as possible.

There were initials at the end of the report: "DR." I checked the newspaper's roster, but found no name that matched. Flipping through a few more stories in 1995, I saw it: Deborah Raines. There was no further news about Teddy's mysterious appearance – the adoption petition was the next item on the microfilm.

The next mention of the Blacks was under a photograph where they were identified as the parents of the local Little League MVP. He was already taller than his father.

Teddy Black took up more than nine pages of the index, so I looked for other people first. As expected, there was nothing about Frank Steiner and only a single entry for Gerald Ender, a photograph taken at a high school reunion in 1995. The hair was thicker and still had some color in it, but the man smiling into the camera was undoubtedly Cosmo Ender. His old friend, Doctor James Edwards, stood beside him.

Newspaper accounts of Edwards reflected the usual activities of a family doctor in a small town – births, deaths, service on local boards and work for civic associations – but his personal life went mostly unexplored. Cat was mentioned a few times, and the sole references to her mother were as the wife or widow of James Edwards.

Paul and Sylvia Black likewise went mostly unnoticed until Teddy started doing big things on the football field for Twin Rivers Junior High School. They were mentioned more and more frequently as the years passed: Pictured with Teddy after a big American Legion game, quoted extensively after Twin Rivers won the state basketball championship and, of course, part of the mass speculation about where Teddy would play college football. Mrs. Black was the booster – her husband, while always "proud as punch" over Teddy's achievements, remained in the background.

I found a few items about Paul Black that were unrelated to his son's athletic exploits, all in connection with his position as Comptroller of the Bank of Twin Rivers. The last one, dated almost 16 years earlier, involved the near-failure of the bank. The reason for the trouble – unpaid loans whose collateral had been severely overvalued – required a highly-publicized audit and intervention by the state. The bank managed to right itself, but later stories about the recovery didn't mention Black. Sylvia had been a successful real estate broker.

The report of their deaths was on page B-6, just before the classified ads. It was perfunctory – Paul Black had lost control of his car on a rain-slicked highway, and they perished when the automobile crashed into a live oak at 70 miles per hour. Their joint obituary was also cursory – it felt like something had been left out. He'd once held a responsible position in town, and she'd been a more than dutiful spouse. Nothing had happened in either life after they adopted Teddy and, other than listing him as their only survivor, there was nothing in the story about him either.

Already familiar with Teddy's athletic prowess, I searched the stories about him for something different, and came across one, written when he was a freshman in high school, about his musical talent. A pianist, he had turned in a bravura performance at a local recital. The author of the piece, a music professor at the College invited to observe, gave him a rave review: "His technical proficiency was flawless, but it was the seamless transitions and flow, particularly in difficult selections like the Rachmaninoff and Straus concertos, that marked young Mr. Black as a talent to be reckoned with. We'll be hearing more from him." I looked through the index again, but saw nothing else about music.

I took Ender's birth certificate from my briefcase. He was born at Twin Rivers Memorial Hospital in 1943. His mother was Ilse Ender, and the space for the father's name was blank. The attending physician was Doctor Beauregard Lee. According to the index, the hospital was still in operation though it had moved into a new building nine years earlier. Beauregard Lee had died in 1975.

On my way out I stopped at the reception desk to inquire about Deborah Raines. The young woman had never heard of her. "Has anyone been here for 15 or 20 years?" I said. She smiled and allowed as how they had several "older" people on staff. "Who?"

She rummaged in a drawer, and withdrew a one-page in-house telephone directory. Using a pen with red ink, she checked off several names and handed the sheet of paper to me. "Thanks," I said. "Can you tell me how to get to Front Street?"

Outside on the sidewalk, I turned north on Raven Street. I was disappointed at the lack of information about Cosmo Ender, and the few bits of news about Teddy Black and the Edwards family seemed unimportant. Teddy's discovery at Cedar Grove Cemetery was intriguing, but what possible connection could there be between an abandoned four-year-old and Ender?

Paul and Sylvia Black were more interesting, if only because of the melancholy that appeared to hang over them, especially after they adopted Teddy. I'd seen at least a dozen photos – the eyes were dull, the smiles unconvincing – that belied the joy they claimed to feel in their son's achievements.

Front Street was part of the town's historic district. The lots and houses were large, and they looked across the Neuse River half a block away. Many of them had black and white markers, touting antiquity and former owners and presidential visits, planted near the curb. One of those was Number 411.

I climbed the steps to the porch and knocked on the door. No one answered. Shielding my eyes against the glare, I peered through a window into an empty room. If the house belonged to Teddy now, he had apparently decided not to live in it.

Further on, the house next door – Number 501 – had a marker, too, and grounds four times that of its neighbor. There were hints that it began as a classic Georgian Revival mansion, but some-where along the way had become a Southern Colo-nial. Its façade was white wooden siding, and it had a profusion of columns, gables and porches, all the trappings of upper-class affectation in a small Southern town. Another building appeared through the trees, several yards to the left and be-hind the main house. I could just make out a "For Rent" sign next to the steps.

I turned up the walk to the main house. The steps led to a faux round portico, supported by four sets of double columns, which formed part of the porch roof. The bell in the center of the massive door required that it be pulled rather than pushed. A woman, whose face startled me for an instant, opened the door. "Yes?"

The coffee-colored skin and full white apron suggested she was not the mistress of the house. "I'd like to see the place you have for rent," I said. "Is there someone –?"

A woman's voice came from another room. "Anita, who is it? Another reporter?"

"No ma'am," Anita called. "Someone askin' about The Dependency." There was no response.

"The Dependency?" I said.

"That's what it's called." She untied the apron and draped it over the banister behind her. Plucking a key from the table next to the door, she said, "Come on."

I followed her around the front of the house. Partially enclosed by latticed brick walls, The Dependency was a small two-story frame structure set atop a high brick foundation. There were five windows in the front – three up and two down – and a screened-in porch. We passed through a gate and climbed the steep steps. "They's two bedrooms and a full bath upstairs," Anita said as she inserted the key into the lock, "and two parlors and a kitchen downstairs. They's all furnished."

"Why is it called The Dependency?"

"Because it was built for slaves." She pushed the door open. We stepped into a narrow hallway that contained a staircase and little else. She remained by the door as I pretended to inspect the parlors. Each one had dark pine flooring and fireplaces surrounded by painted mantels. The overstuffed furniture – leather in one room, floral print in the other – was worn, and the walls were bare. "Both fireplaces work," she said.

We passed the staircase and entered the kitchen. The purple linoleum was shiny, and the appliances, cabinets and fixtures looked like they'd been there from the beginning. Only the refrigerator had been purchased within the last two decades. I looked at Anita inquiringly. "Everythin' works here, too," she said. "The stove's gas."

We took the stairs. There was a closed door directly across the hall. It didn't open when I turned the knob. "They's some family stuff in there. Miz Edwards ain't got round to movin' it yet." The bedrooms were spare, and the bathroom between them was the most modern room in the house.

"What's the rent?" I said.

"You'll have to ask Miz Edwards about that."

We returned to the main house, this time through a side porch that opened into a large kitchen. A glass-topped table with four chairs included a view of the river through a bay window and avenue of oaks. Anita pulled one of the chairs out and said, "Wait here, please." She left the room.

I'd had no intention of renting the cottage when I rang the doorbell, but now I was considering it. There were things I still wanted to do here: Try to find Deborah Raines, look further into Paul and Sylvia Black and, most especially, continue the search for the connection between Cosmo Ender and Teddy Black that I was sure Samantha had found. And there was now another puzzle awaiting explanation. I looked at my watch – I needed to get back to Alex.

"Mister?" Anita gestured. I rose and followed her down the hall.

We passed through a doorway on the left. The large room was a combination library and sun porch. Two walls were filled with books from floor to ceiling. A black Steinway, its lid propped open, stood in a corner, and the portrait of a stern man with white hair that reached his collar – not James Edwards – looked down at us from his place over the mantel.

The back wall was all windows. The view, elevated a few feet, was a garden with boxwoods and brick walks and fountains and pools. Sun poured through the glass and a round skylight in the middle of the ceiling.

The room was marred by a low bed pushed against one of the bookcases, a small television beside it, and a noisy icemaker next to the door. The scent of cut flowers, hundreds of them gathered in huge vases placed on the floor and other horizontal surfaces, was overwhelming. A woman in a wheelchair, glass in hand, watched as I entered the room.

I approached her. She shifted the glass to her left hand and extended her right. "I'm Virginia Edwards," she said.

"Harry Monmouth."

"Can I offer you a drink?"

"Uh – sure."

She glanced at Anita, who was still standing by the door. "Would you fix Mr. Monmouth a drink, please? And freshen mine." She looked back at me, brows lifted.

"Scotch on the rocks," I said.

"Sit down, Mr. Monmouth," Virginia Edwards said. We were quiet while Anita took ice from a crystal bowl, opened a cabinet and poured scotch for me and vodka for her. "Thank you, Anita." The lady of the house took a long pull on her drink. "You're interested in The Dependency?"

"Yes, ma'am." The "ma'am" was merely habit. She was no more than 40 years old and, despite the disability that kept her in a wheelchair, a stunning woman. The daughter's understated beauty was conspicuous in the mother. The black hair that fell over her shoulders was lustrous, and the dark gray eyes were bright and clear. Her delicate nose turned up slightly. The mouth, crushed like Cat's, was painted a pale pink that highlighted the glowing complexion. Her voice was soft, and she spoke in a cultured Southern accent that refused to conform to the homogenized sounds the rest of us made.

"Do you live around here, Mr. Monmouth?" she said.

"No. I – we live in New Hope."

"Making a move?"

I shook my head. "My wife's been ill. I'm looking for a place where we can rest and relax until she's ready to pick up her routine again."

She nodded. "It's quiet here. There are several good restaurants within walking distance." She seemed to wince at the word "walking."

"What's the rent?"

She hesitated. "Five hundred dollars a month."

"That's certainly reasonable."

"When would you like to move in?"

I calculated. "In a week, I think."

She nodded again. "Anita will have it ready for you."

Despite my need to return to New Hope, I was in no hurry to leave. "You have a beautiful home."

"Thank you. It's been in my family for more than 100 years. I've lived here all my life." She paused. "My husband died a year ago, and my daughter's at the College, so it's just me and Anita most of the time."

"She lives here?"

"Yes. I – I need a lot of attention now."

"I see your neighbors have moved." She frowned. "I made a mistake and went there first."

She closed her eyes. "Yes. The Blacks are gone, too."

I could barely hear her. "The Blacks?"

The eyes opened. "Yes."

"Any kin to Teddy Black?"

"They were his parents. His adoptive parents." She stopped. "They're dead now."

"Is Teddy the reason you have reporters down here?" She nodded. "Have you met my friend Samantha Clarke? She's a reporter. From New Hope."

She turned her head. "Was that her name, Anita?"

"Yes, ma'am. I think so."

Virginia turned back to me. "She was here a few weeks ago."

"She's dead." There was no reaction from Virginia beyond a slight widening of the eyes, but Anita – who had remained to rearrange bottles and glasses and maybe listen to our conversation – made a noise she tried to conceal. After a second, she hurried from the room.

I looked at Virginia. "It must have been pretty exciting to live next door to –"

She turned the chair abruptly toward the bed and pushed a button at the end of a white cord. I heard the sound in the hallway. She looked over her shoulder. "I'm sorry. My energy's not what it should be." Anita reappeared in the doorway, her features distressed. Virginia didn't notice. "Mr. Monmouth is leaving," she said. "We'll see him again next week."

I stood up. "Thanks for the drink." There was no response.

THREE

I SLIPPED the empty flask into my coat pocket and joined the crowd in the aisles. The juggernaut that was the College football team rolled on, having just beaten one of its chief rivals by 42 points despite using the second team for all of the last quarter. Teddy Black had performed as usual.

The reaction in the stands had surprised me. It was mostly as expected – unbridled cheers and chest-thumping, as if the fans themselves were performing on the field – but there were also whispers about "fairness" and the superfluity of Teddy's teammates. A man sitting behind me summed it up: "It's like he's playing the game by himself."

The national media had spent the weekend in New Hope. Puzzled and unhappy over Teddy's solitude, there were dark musings about the reason for it. One broadcaster, speaking from an empty, fully-lighted stadium on Friday night, alluded to rumors of steroids and other chemicals. The College countered immediately with the news that Teddy was tested before and after every game by a representative from the Organization. A writer for one of the country's few remaining major newspapers speculated, jokingly, that he came from another planet. The College let that one pass. It was only a matter of time until some enterprising reporter, following the path I'd taken, discovered the circumstances of Teddy's adoption, and then the questions would really begin.

Outside the stadium, I turned west toward The High. The law required that Samantha's possessions be accounted for and distributed to those entitled to receive them. I had persuaded Bobby Hood to give me charge of the reckoning. Samantha had left much behind except, apparently, someone to inherit it.

She had a single checking account at the Bank of New Hope, but her principal asset managers – brokers, lawyers, accountants – were still in New York. I'd provided Abby with the list, and now possessed copies of the various statements reflecting Samantha's considerable wealth. Not only had she died without a will, all of the beneficiary designations were the same – "Estate." No potential heirs had come forward, and the requisite notices in the newspaper were ongoing. The open maw of the state, ever ready to gorge on the leavings of its subjects, would probably swallow it all.

I waved to Mike and crossed the lobby to the elevator. Samantha had done me a great service many years before, and I wanted to return the favor. Her death was too easy to explain. That she died of a heroin overdose was beyond question, but I was convinced she had not intended to kill herself, that her trip to Twin Rivers – and whatever she discovered while she was there – was somehow responsible for her death.

I wandered through the rooms. In an effort to confirm Samantha's habitual drug use, and perhaps determine who supplied the heroin, the Sheriff's people and the State Bureau of Investigation had made a thorough search. They found no samples of the drug itself beyond what was left in the spoon, and removed a single set of utensils – the spoon, the syringe, a length of rubber tubing – from her room. Otherwise, the condo was undisturbed. The Twin Rivers yearbook remained on the coffee table in the living room.

I opened every cabinet and drawer in the place, shuffled through her closets and examined each book and piece of bric-a-brac, and came up empty. Not only was there nothing to shed light on her death, there was almost nothing to illumine her life. The cherished detritus that most people acquire and preserve was missing.

There were a few tokens of her rise and fall in the news business. A golden statuette of a winged woman holding a giant, stylized atom over her head rested on the nightstand next to her bed. It represented great achievement in her profession, and the idea it would be sold to some stranger at auction was depressing.

I walked down the stairs. My search for nothing in particular had turned up nothing, and the specific item I hoped to find had eluded me as well. Samantha's red Porsche was parked in the garage, but the keys were gone. The experts couldn't find them, and neither could I. Car keys, and the others often collected on the same ring, were seldom far from their owner. Her wallet had not been recovered either, and there was speculation it might be in the locked car.

Another unusual circumstance in our age of unceasing communication was the dearth of electronic gadgets. There were no computers, laptops or tablets, and the only portable telephone was an ancient cell that did nothing but send and receive phone calls. The police, accustomed to the trove of personal information cached in such devices, were disappointed.

I took a small key from the kitchen counter, stepped outside and walked to the end of the hall. The garage elevator carried me to a mailroom adjacent to the parking garage. The penthouse mailboxes, larger than the others, were at the end of the row. There was no name on the box next to hers – the other penthouse apartment remained unsold. After withdrawing her mail, accumulated since the Sheriff's final visit, I returned to her living room.

Perched on the edge of the sofa, I spread the mail on the coffee table. There wasn't much – the last few bills, a couple of magazines and a large envelope from something called Uniworld. Uniworld was a cruise line that carried passengers on the great rivers of Europe. A few days before she died, Samantha had reserved a suite for two on the River Baroness. She and her companion would travel up the Seine, from Avignon to Paris, over the Christmas holidays. Part of my brain registered the need to retrieve the substantial deposit, while another wondered who the other person was – recent events provided a clue, but I was not yet ready to confront it. It seemed unusual that someone about to commit suicide would plan a $20,000 cruise.

One of the bills made me smile. It was from the local music store, New Hope Sounds. Alex and I had rented trumpets, clarinets and violins with which we hoped to civilize our children from New Hope Sounds and, when our efforts failed, the people at the music store always overlooked the scratches and broken agreements and took the instruments back.

Inside the envelope was a statement for $150 for "cleaning and tuning 1 1921 Starr baby grand piano." There was a handwritten note at the bottom: "This is a wonderful instrument and a beautiful antique. It was a privilege to work on it."

I approached the piano and sat down on the bench. The sheet music on the rack was a gospel arrangement of *Amazing Grace*. I played a few notes – the piano was in perfect tune. It was another thing that argued against her suicide. Tuning a piano was the last thing a person in that frame of mind would do.

Absently, I pushed the bench back and caught the legs on a rug beneath it. It tumbled backward, and so did I. The top fell open, scattering sheet music everywhere. Stunned, I lay there for a minute, then untangled myself from the bench, set it upright and began gathering the sheets of paper.

A framed portrait, evidently kept in the bench, was lying face down amongst the music. I picked it up and turned it over. The smiling face of a beautiful young girl looked at me from behind the cracked glass. The heavy, elaborate frame was made of Sterling silver polished recently enough that I could see my reflection in it.

For an instant, I entertained the notion that she was someone important to Samantha, someone who might be entitled to her things. Then, almost as quickly, I dismissed the idea. After disassembling the parts that held the picture in place, I saw it was not a photograph, but a thin cardboard rendering of a model intended to sell expensive picture frames. If Samantha had bought it to enshrine anyone in particular, she failed to get around to it.

My next stop was the *New Hope Chronicle*, three blocks further up West High Street. There was no one now behind her desk, and something else was missing – the laptop. I searched the desk and didn't find it. The police had been there, too.

The young man I'd spoken to before was down the hall, still glued to his computer screen. "My name's Harry Monmouth. I'm looking after Ms. Clarke's estate." He nodded, his attention divided between me and the monitor. "Has anything been taken from her office?"

"I don't think so."

"What about her laptop?"

"No."

"It's not on her desk." I paused. "When was the last time you saw her?"

He sighed and turned toward me. "The day she died. It was a Sunday. Around noon."

"Did she have the laptop with her?"

"I don't – No, wait. She gave me a project, and said I could take her computer home if I wanted to. So I guess she left it." He smiled. "I didn't need it."

"What was the project?"

He frowned. "I don't see why you –"

"I'm Samantha's representative, duly appointed by Judge Robert Hood. I'd hate to tell him you were uncooperative."

"Well – she wanted some research on one of the bigwigs at the College."

"Who?"

"A guy named Steiner."

Were the lines beginning to merge? "Did you do it?" He nodded again. "Where is it?"

"In her mailbox." He pointed. "At the end of the hall."

"Did she say anything else? Why she needed the Steiner info?"

"No. She made a phone call and left." He paused. "I think she had to leave a message."

"Who'd she call?"

"I don't know. A woman called back about an hour later."

"Who was it?"

"She wouldn't say. But she gave me her number. It's in the mailbox, too."

"Could you hear what Samantha said?"

"No."

I paused in the doorway. "What do you do around here about locking up?"

"There are eight – seven – of us. The last one out locks the doors."

"Was anybody else here that day?"

"Nobody's ever here on Sunday except me and Ms. Clarke."

"Did you lock the doors when you left?"

"Yes."

I walked down the hall, took a fat folder and a message slip from Samantha's mail slot and returned to her desk. After a moment, I picked up the phone. "Sheriff Farnham, please. It's Harry Monmouth."

He came on the line. "Hi, Harry. What's up?"

"I'm trying to gather Samantha Clarke's things. You guys went through her stuff at the office, didn't you?"

"Yes."

"Did you take anything?"

"No."

"Was there a laptop on the desk?"

"No."

"Do you know any more about the wallet and keys?"

"Nope."

"Okay. I'll contact the dealer about a key to the Porsche. Probably on Monday. I'll let you know."

"Thanks. I'll want somebody there."

My suspicions were becoming certainties. If Samantha's death was accidental, or even intentional, there was still no reason why her computer should be missing. A thin plastic case that weighed only a few pounds, it served as typewriter, postman, filing cabinet and diary. It was a repository for all she chose to keep, a detailed record of whatever life she wished to preserve, and it had been taken by someone who wanted to keep all that – or maybe just part of it – hidden.

I looked at the message slip again. There was a number and an extension, and the "returned call" box was checked. I was pretty sure I knew the caller's identity, but I lifted the receiver and dialed the number anyway. A voice answered: "Spencer Hall." That was enough. Cat Edwards had returned Samantha's call a few hours before she died.

I LEANED back in my chair and opened the folder. The boy at the *Chronicle* had summarized its contents. Frank Steiner was born in Geneva, Switzerland in 1943. He'd moved to New York with his parents as an infant at the height of World War II. It seemed that both parents were well-educated, but there were no details.

After the war, father and son returned to Switzerland, the mother having died of some undis-closed illness. Steiner went to school in Switzer-land, Germany and England, and began his career in genetics. At the age of 49, he came back to the United States, joined the Harvard faculty and con-tinued to develop the various aspects of his work. Ten years later, he moved it all to the College.

The rest of the summary described the suc-cess he had achieved. There were setbacks – a small percentage of children born in his fertility clinics had died – but he was unquestionably one of the foremost genetic therapists in the world.

I flipped through the computer print-outs, searching for more personal information. There was nothing about his wife beyond the fact that he had one, and there were no children. His years in Europe were little more than a line or two in his biography. He'd received the equivalent of a bache-lor's degree at the University of Ingolstadt, and studied medicine and genetics at King's College, Cambridge, and later at the University of Jena. I smiled – all three had been around far longer than Harvard.

Something in the description of the school at Jena, located in the German state of Thuringia, caught my eye. One of its most famous, or infa-mous, alumni, was Fritz Astel, author of a book called *Heredity and Racial Hygiene*. A primitive geneticist, Astel had been a leader in Germany's eugenics movement in the 1930s, and participated in the Nazi experiments intended to exterminate the Jews. He'd committed suicide in 1943. Steiner, an infant at the time, kept a copy of Astel's book in his office.

THE WHITE marble gleamed in the moon-light, the columns a phalanx shielding the priests from skeptic and believer alike. Once firmly among the former, I was a full-blown convert. I still wondered about the magician, but not the magic.

I met Steiner at the elevator. Wordless as we climbed, he stepped into the corridor and turned toward his office. I followed. He paused at the door to the laboratory. "We're almost done," he said. "I think you'll be pleased." He opened the door to her room, and stood aside to let me pass.

Over the past weeks, I'd seen Alex in several prone positions, but tonight she was regal once more, flat on her back, arms forming a cross over her chest. She wore a white silken gown, nothing like the hospital attire in which she had spent so much time in recent days. The wires and tubes were gone, and the transformation I had observed day-by-day remained, enhanced if anything. The disease that had ravished her was beaten.

I stood in the silence, gazing at my wife. "The cancer's gone," Steiner said. "The collateral damage – skin, hair, that sort of thing – has been cleaned up, too."

"When – when can she –?"

"I stopped the anesthesia a couple of hours ago. She'll come out of the coma gradually. It'll probably take a few hours."

"I'll stay."

He nodded. "She'll have to be here for another week. The immune cells need to be managed. I'll monitor her for any signs of relapse."

"Then what?"

"After that, I want her to come in once a month until further notice." He paused. "Have you thought about what you're going to say?"

I nodded. "It's a miracle." He smiled. "Nobody knows she's here. Everyone in town is used to not seeing her, so the past few weeks haven't raised any questions. I told the kids we were leaving it in God's hands, which – which I guess we did." He laughed out loud. "What about you?"

He shook his head. "It would be unwise to publicize this now." He stared at me. "Things may still go wrong." He glanced at Alex. "As soon as Mrs. Monmouth is completely out of the woods, I'll commence the protocols designed to hamper the real scientists and protect the fools."

I smiled. During Alex's treatment, Steiner had become almost human. Now, with her recovery an astonishing feather in his cap, he was reverting to type, but it no longer mattered to me. Pride was the deadliest of the seven sins but, as far as I was concerned, he had every reason to be proud.

"I have something for you," he said. "You can look it over while you wait." We returned to his office. He pointed to a large cardboard box on the floor. "The documents the Spillers demanded." He laughed again, and reached inside his coat. "And the answers to their questions," he said, handing me a sheaf of paper. "I'm sure it will all be very helpful."

THE VIGIL at her bedside was surreal. All the old tales of defeating death – dispensations from the gods, miracles at the hands of saints, the kiss of a handsome prince – were parables in which superhuman beings intervened to alter the implacable mortality of nature. Whatever else he was, Steiner was one of us, and Alex's resurrection was not a myth. The world was altered irrevocably. The search for cures was over, and the life and death we had known since we knew anything were different. What would we do?

And who would Alex be? Her body, ravaged by a terrible disease, had been restored but, when she went to sleep, she belonged to the old world where disease was problematic and death often the result. She would awaken as the first lady of a new place where disease was vanquished and death deferred. How would she cope? And what would she think of me? I was of the old order, untouched by genetic absolution. Who would we be?

I turned my attention to Steiner's box. As expected, its contents would be no help to Missy and her clients. Ninety percent of it was medical jargon, formulae and endless calculations, all written in a shorthand that only a scientist, maybe only Steiner, could decipher. The rest was mostly correspondence, papers and formal presentations only slightly less impenetrable. The idea that any of it might demonstrate wrong-doing on Steiner's part was ludicrous.

The last few pages were a series of brochures describing panel discussions and speeches he'd given after he joined the Harvard faculty in 1992, all designed to promote the fertility clinic he wanted to establish and the gene therapy he was perfecting. As I browsed the pamphlets, I noticed something they all had in common: Each presentation was "sponsored" by Ender Enterprises, the umbrella organization used by Cosmo Ender to consolidate his immense wealth. The School of Human Enrichment wasn't Frank Steiner's first collaboration with Ender.

Musing on the confluence of science and money, I saw Alex's right arm slide from her chest. Seconds later, the left arm did the same. I rose and approached the bed. When her lids began to flutter, I bent and kissed her lips. I wasn't the handsome prince, but I could claim to be the go-between.

Her arms went around my neck in a fierce embrace she didn't want to end. I slipped my head loose, and took her hand. "Take it easy," I said. "Steiner hasn't cleared you for sex yet." Surprised at the thought – sex had been sporadic for years – I understood its genesis. She wasn't just cancer-free. She was firm and luminous, the blue eyes were clear, and the gray in her hair was now silver. The lines in her face were softer, the brows and lashes more prominent. My response to her touch – a growing thickness between my legs – was almost embarrassing. It was the last thing I expected.

She smiled. "I'll apply for conjugal visits."

She looked around, a question on her face. I recounted the deep sleep. "The cancer's gone. You have to stay another week. Then you can go home. Or – we may take a little vacation."

"To where?"

"We'll talk about it later." I moved toward the door. "Steiner's in his office. I know he wants to see you."

FOUR

THE RED Porsche yielded nothing. Samantha's most personal things – her wallet and her computer – were still missing, along with her keys. The Sheriff's inquiry was at a dead end. He decided to go along with the coroner's verdict, perhaps because his investigation into Vera Carr's murder had come up empty. The prospect of two unresolved deaths on the books was unappealing.

Bobby Hood had called a halt to Project Sickle Cell, and the dudgeon was high. What did he know about sickle cell? How could he stop a process that was finally liberating the black community from the pain and death of a disease ignored for so long? Children remained untreated. Only the cruelest bigot would issue such an order. That it might be only temporary provided no consolation, and Bobby's chances in the next election were bandied about.

Side effects in those who'd been treated were ignored by the critics. Newspaper photographs depicted a pale rash, or stain, on the skin of some of the earliest patients, and bits of hair were falling out. There were also complaints about sensitivity to the sun – several were wearing sunglasses for the first time. Steiner had dismissed the problems as inconsequential, "probably caused by an allergic reaction to the drugs used in the post-treatment procedures." Nevertheless, Bobby cited the effects as one of the reasons for his order.

Missy Farrell came in for her share of criticism as well. Heretofore a tilter against sanctioned windmills, and lauded as such, she had somehow lost her way. Suing the College was bad enough, but challenging its most enlightened undertaking was too much to bear. Speeches and rallies resumed.

Missy was undeterred. She packed the preliminary win away, and plotted a course to make it permanent. She found time for the Spiller litigation, too. Phone under my chin, I sat back to listen. "Harry," she said, "who's running this case? You or Steiner?" Steiner was, but I denied it. "This stuff you sent over here is completely unresponsive. Did you even look at it?"

"Yes."

"I want you to try again. I don't want to have to get an order from Judge Hood."

"Missy – Frank Steiner's a difficult client. Bobby's the only leverage I have. Go ahead and get your order. I won't oppose it."

There was silence on the end of the line. "I don't understand this," she said at last. "I've seen you fire clients for less. What's going on?"

I owed – really owed – Steiner the best defense I could provide. His obduracy would make it harder, but it was a small price to pay. And I was convinced that Missy would never prove negligence on his part. "Have you really analyzed your case?" I said. "You'll need expert testimony, good expert testimony, to win. Who's going to testify about artificial insemination against Frank Steiner? In front of an Azure County jury, half of whom probably work at the College?" She was quiet again. "The autopsy was the real reason you filed suit. The autopsy's over. Why don't you just drop it?"

"There's something *wrong* about your client, Harry," she said softly, "and I'm going to find out what it is." She hesitated. "I'll tell you something – you'll hear about it soon enough anyway. Steiner swears in these interrogatories he was born in Geneva in 1943. I've checked. No one named Frank Steiner was born in Geneva in 1943."

I considered that. "There was a war going on in 1943. The Swiss were bombed by both sides. Records, assuming they were kept at all, get lost."

"The immigration people *here*, where no bombs fell, have no record of Steiner and his parents ever coming to New York." She paused. "That's two lies. How many more are there?" She hung up.

I leaned into the outer office. Abby looked up from her book. "Call Immigration and Naturalization in Washington. It's called something else now, I think. I want to talk to somebody about their immigration records during World War II."

A few minutes later, I lifted the receiver. After an exchange of salutations, I said, "Do you have access to the names of people who came over here in 1943?"

"At the click of a mouse."

"Great. How many Steiners do you have? S-T-E-I-N-E-R."

"Hold on." She was back in a few seconds. "Ten individuals. Four families."

"What sort of information do you have on them?"

"Age, sex, race. Where they came from. Where they entered the country. Where they went. Names of relatives or friends already here."

"How many pages is it?"

"For all of them?"

"Yes."

"Um – 22."

"Are they on paper somewhere?"

"Yes."

"Can you fax them to me?"

"Sure." I gave her the number. Thirty minutes later, I stood beside the fax machine and plucked the pages as they emerged. Back in my office, I lowered myself to the leather chair and lifted my feet to the ottoman. Missy was right – there was no Steiner family arriving from Switzerland in 1943. But Ilse Steiner embarked at Bremen and landed in New York, and quickly moved a few hundred miles south, to a quiet little town where her cousins, the Enders, lived. It was called Twin Rivers.

I WAITED on the steps outside Phillips Hall. She appeared in the middle doorway, and I raised my hand. "Cat." She turned her head. "Can I talk to you for a second?"

Surprised, her eyes shifted to the other side of the street where Teddy, flanked by two campus policemen, was emerging from Hill Hall. She hesitated, then shook her head. "I can't, Harry. I have another class."

"In an hour then? At the College Coffee Shop?" She began to walk away. I called after her: "I spoke with your mother a few days ago."

She stopped. I caught up with her. "All right," she said without looking at me. "In an hour."

She was a few minutes late. I ordered another cup of coffee, and she asked for a glass of iced tea. "Why are you harassing my mother?" she said.

"I wasn't harassing her. We were talking business."

"What business?"

"I'm going to rent The Dependency."

Her eyes grew larger. "Why?"

"Rest and relaxation. My wife and I need to get away."

She stared at me, lips pursed. After the waiter delivered the ice tea and coffee, she said, "What did you want to talk about?"

"Do you know Helen Tanner?"

Her gaze remained steady. "She's one of the deans at the College, isn't she?"

"Yes."

We sat for a moment in silence. "Well?" she said.

"Is that all you know about her?"

She nodded. "Why would I –?"

"I saw you go into her house last Thursday night."

Even in the dim light, I could see the furious blush, but she maintained a precarious control. "That's – that's not true. It wasn't me."

I had imagined, because Helen knew Samantha better than she would admit, and because Cat – a lifelong citizen of Twin Rivers whose father was Gerry Ender's chess partner – seemed to know Helen, that between them they might shed some light on Cosmo Ender and why Samantha was dead.

Helen had denied knowing Samantha, and now Cat claimed not to know Helen, both of which were demonstrably false, but further inquiry along those lines seemed pointless. "What can you can tell me about Gerry Ender?"

She was surprised again, and cautious. After a few beats, she said, "Why on earth do you want to know about Gerry Ender?"

"Humor me. Please."

"Gerry Ender was a friend of my father's. He moved away before I was born."

"Did he ever come back?"

"Yes. He used to visit every few months. He always stayed with us." She paused. "In The Dependency, as a matter of fact."

"When did those visits start?"

"I can't say for sure. I was a little girl, maybe five or six."

"Was there a reason he came to Twin Rivers?"

"I was at school most of the time. All I know is, he came to see my father."

"When was the last time you saw him?"

"A year ago. At Dad's funeral. But . . ."

"But what?"

"Anita – that's the woman who stays with Mother – says he's been back several times since."

"Why?"

"To see her. My mother."

I nodded. "Why can't she walk?"

"She has multiple sclerosis."

"When did it start?"

"When I was six. 1995."

"How did your father die?"

"He had an aneurysm."

She was relaxed now, soothed by the familiar, happy to answer questions unrelated to Helen Tanner. "Your mother told me that Teddy lived next door. Were you friends?"

The wariness returned. "I hardly knew him when we were kids."

"Did you know about his adoption?"

"What about it?"

"Well, the cemetery and your father and –"

"I don't know what you're talking about."

I nodded again, and rejected the urge to ask more about Teddy. "What about his folks?"

She shook her head. "They were just strange."

"What do you mean?"

"They didn't seem to do anything except go to Teddy's games."

"What do you know about Ender's people?"

"Just that they've been in Twin Rivers a long time."

"Do you know Cosmo Ender?"

"No. Who's he?"

"What about Frank Steiner?"

"He's the genetics guy, isn't he?"

I nodded. "Have you met him?"

"No."

"Did you ever see him in Twin Rivers?"

"Not that I know of. I don't know what he looks like."

Except for questions about her and Teddy, which would probably go unanswered, I was nearly done. "Did you know Samantha Clarke?"

"I know who she is. Or was."

"Have you ever spoken to her?"

"No. She called me once. About Teddy."

I nodded again. "How long has Anita worked for your mother?"

"All my life. Longer."

"Does she have a son?"

"I don't think so. Why?"

THE RIDE to the state capital, on the old road, took an hour, and the search for a parking place for Samantha's Porsche another 15 minutes. The Department of Banking and Commerce was located in the old Capitol building, a Greek Revival structure with a dome and Doric columns. I passed through the bronze doors, entered the rotunda and consulted the directory. Climbing to the second floor, I walked halfway round the gallery and turned down a hall.

I expected microfilm at best, but the young woman who greeted me led the way to a nest of aging computers, none of which was occupied. The room was dry and dusty, like the Deed Room at the courthouse. She apologized several times for the outdated equipment. I assured her that if it were any newer, I wouldn't be able to operate it. After a brief tutorial involving indexes and key words, she left me alone.

I clicked the cursor and typed "Audit of Bank of Twin Rivers – 1995." After some whirring and sputtering, the file appeared on the monitor. It was more than 600 pages with the appendices and attachments, so I placed the cursor in a new box and typed "Paul Black." There were 102 references to Black, most of them in a 40-page section entitled "Results of Investigation." I found the first page and began to read.

An hour later, I knew what the Twin Rivers *Sun Journal* had refused to print or, more likely, never knew. Black and his wife Sylvia had defrauded the bank to the tune of some $720,000. The scheme utilized inflated assessments of real estate on the edge of the historic district – owned by straw men for Sylvia Black – to borrow large sums from the bank where her husband ensured there would be no scrutiny. They used the proceeds to buy still more land.

The bet was that the property would increase in value by several orders of magnitude, thereby allowing the Blacks to sell it, repay the bank and turn a tidy profit. When that scenario failed to materialize, the bank was left with loans in default backed by nearly worthless collateral. After the land was sold, and the Blacks' bank accounts wiped out, a deficit of almost $500,000 remained.

I scrolled to the next page, and the one after that, but there was nothing more about Paul and Sylvia Black. I tried different key words and turned up nothing. Finally, I clicked on the section called "Audit Closed – December 31, 1995." It was only a couple of paragraphs to the effect that the bank's books were "now balanced," and no further action was necessary. The $500,000 had been found.

I returned to the box and typed "Gerald Ender" and "Cosmo Ender" and "Frank Steiner." Nothing. I tried "James Edwards." Still nothing. About to surrender and depart, I remembered another name – "Virginia Edwards." She was mentioned three times, first as a member of the bank's board of directors and then as its majority shareholder.

The last reference was to a sale of Bank of Twin Rivers stock transacted on September 30, 1995. Virginia Lee Edwards had sold some of her stock – enough to cede control of the bank – for $500,000, a premium price for an enterprise in financial trouble. The buyer was Ender Enterprises. There was no mention of a "gift" or "donation" from Mrs. Edwards, but there was little doubt that the money from Ender had saved Paul and Sylvia Black from prison.

It also seemed likely that the Blacks' adoption of the foundling from the cemetery was a consequence of Virginia's "gift." There were too many events in close proximity – the audit, Teddy's discovery, the adoption and the $500,000 – for any of it to be coincidental. And Cosmo Ender, Chairman of Ender Enterprises, had attended his high school reunion about the same time. Samantha could have easily drawn the same conclusions.

If my surmise was correct, what was it about an abandoned little boy that drew such interest from the Edwards family and perhaps Ender as well? And why involve the Blacks? It would have been easy for James and Virginia Edwards to take the child in.

I found another file. The Bank of Twin Rivers had been chartered in 1933. Its founder and sole shareholder at the time was Beauregard Benjamin Lee. Curious, I looked up the Twin Rivers Memorial Hospital. It, too, had been founded by Beauregard Lee, and his daughter Virginia still owned it lock, stock and barrel.

I looked at my watch. Alex and I were having supper in her room at the clinic, and I was going to be late. I hurried from the building and, in an effort to make up the lost time, opted for the interstate highway between the capital and New Hope, a choice I instantly regretted.

In a traffic jam halfway down the entrance ramp, there was nothing for it but to grit my teeth and think of excuses. Alex always took the interstate – maybe I could blame her. As I crested a hill, I saw the police cars and emergency vehicles in the distance. It was going to be a long wait. I pulled into a rest area and switched off the engine.

With time on my hands, I decided to do my own search of Samantha's car. The dashboard looked like a cockpit. Knobs and dials and buttons, all with mysterious German appellations, begged to be turned and pushed and twisted. Mindful that one of them might operate the ejector seat, or at least some kind of warning klaxon, I located each one in the owner's manual before touching it.

There was a black button on the driver's armrest that wasn't mentioned in the book at all. The urge to push it was overwhelming – maybe a clown's head would spring from the middle of the steering wheel, or a propeller might rise from the roof and carry me over the mass of metal that blocked my way.

I pushed it. Nothing happened. I pushed it again, and this time the leather top on the armrest between the seats slid smoothly back, revealing a metal box secured by a combination lock. On the assumption that Samantha probably never changed the tumblers, I squeezed the catch and lifted the lid.

At first I thought the cavity, undetected during the earlier search, was empty. Closer inspection, however, revealed a small white envelope pushed upright against the side of the box. "Sa-mantha," in a tight classic cursive, was written on the sealed envelope, and it was apparent there was an object inside. When I opened the envelope and turned it up, a wide golden wedding band fell into my hand. There was no inscription and, when I tried it on my pinky finger, it wouldn't slide past the first knuckle.

FIVE

I WAS near the end of my story. "Steiner and Ender have been doing business together for years. Samantha had a file on Steiner, but I didn't think he had anything to do with her or Twin Rivers. Now I'm not so sure."

"I don't suppose there's any question that Ilse Steiner became Ilse Ender?" Alex said.

"I'm going to check when we get there, but I doubt it. I think she left New York as Ilse Steiner and arrived in Twin Rivers as Ilse Ender." I paused. "Six months later, Gerry Ender was born."

"Could they be brothers?"

"Steiner and Ender?"

"Yes."

"Well, they're about the same age. And I guess there's a slight resemblance. But why would one be Ender and the other Steiner?" She shook her head. "I'll check on that, too."

We rode in silence. "The real question is," she said, "why all the rigmarole? Why would Steiner, or whatever his name is, lie about his parents and where he came from?"

I had no answer to that, but there was a chance that, sooner or later, Missy Farrell would. Citing the discrepancies in Steiner's biography, she had obtained an order from Bobby Hood requiring that Steiner be fingerprinted. Outraged as always at Missy's "prying," Steiner had insisted that I appeal the order. After I advised that an appeal was almost certainly fruitless, he said, "How long will it take?"

"The Supreme Court won't even allow the appeal. It'll take them at least 60 days to say so."

He nodded. "Go ahead then. Do it."

The papers were duly filed, much to Missy's aggravation. Actually acquiring his prints, of course, would be easy, though they might not be allowed in evidence without the order. Steiner's fingerprints were on the documents he'd submitted, for example, and the draft answers to Missy's questions. Making them appear, and lifting or photographing them, was five minutes work for an expert.

I pulled into a service station across the road from a red brick church. "Why are we stopping?" said Alex. "You just got gas."

"I want something to drink. Can I get you anything?"

"No, thanks."

Someone else was working the cash register. "Who are they?" I said, gesturing toward the pictures.

She turned her head. "The one in the middle is Teddy Black. He's a big star on the football team at the College. He went to high school in Twin Rivers."

"What about the other two?"

She looked back again. "One's the owner and his family. The other's just the kid."

"When were they taken?"

"I don't know." She paused. "The little boy died."

"When?"

She shook her head. "A long time ago."
"They look familiar. What's the name?"
"Moore."
I nodded. "Thanks." I turned away.
"Don't forget your Coke," she said.

It was like a jigsaw puzzle with pieces from another mixed in. Before attempting to fit them together, you had to decide which ones belonged to your puzzle. The woman in the photograph, Anita Moore, was Virginia Edwards' maid. I had no idea if she was part of the puzzle or not.

"MIZ EDWARDS," Anita said, "wants you and Miz Monmouth to join her for cocktails this evenin'. Six o'clock."

"We'll be there, Anita. Thanks." She closed the door behind her. There were signs of recent activity at The Dependency. The windows had been washed, and the sitting rooms smelled like furniture polish. A bottle of a good red wine rested on the kitchen counter, along with an unsigned note in blue calligraphy: "Welcome. I hope you enjoy your stay."

The room at the top of the stairs was still locked. When I mentioned it, Anita said, "Miz Edwards says she's sorry. She just don't have the energy to clean it up. She says she'll reduce the rent."

Alex was pleased with the gardens and the view, but dubious about our quarters. "It's just a place to sleep," I said. "Your rehab will be fresh air and long walks and no worries."

It was doubtful she required any rehabilitation at all. Her last week at the clinic had been uneventful, and the healthy glow remained. Her hair had almost regained its former thickness and luster. The plan was to commute to New Hope as needed. Her first injection was Saturday, five days away. "I'm going to help you with your adventure," she said. "I've been so worthless for so long . . ." She picked up my briefcase. "Let's make a list."

I smiled. "There's a game table on the porch. We can sit out there."

The screened-in porch overlooked Virginia Edwards' formal garden. The perfume of giant tea olives, posted like sentinels at each intersection of the walkways, suffused the air, and the splash of fountains combined to mask the noise beyond the gates. A few yards away, Virginia's glass wall reflected the late afternoon sun. A shallow ramp beside the steps reminded of her affliction.

I poured two glasses of wine while Alex arranged the contents of my briefcase on the table. "What's this?" she said, holding up the envelope with Samantha's name on it.

"Take a look. I found it in her car."

She slipped the ring onto the finger where she wore her own wedding band and held up her hand. It fit perfectly. "I didn't know Samantha was ever married," she said.

"Neither did I."

We spent the next hour making a list of the things we might do in Twin Rivers. I considered our "adventure." What were we doing, exactly? Samantha had died of a drug overdose. She injected the poison herself. Yes, she had Cosmo Ender in her sights at the time, but so what? It was a story, but I was no journalist. I was a part-time lawyer with a refurbished wife who needed my attention.

All the things I'd learned, the history and the lies and the inconsistencies, were interesting but,

to what end? None of them changed the circum-
stances of Samantha's death. Completely absorbed
by Alex's struggle to survive, I was left without
purpose when Steiner induced her coma, so I creat-
ed one to occupy myself. I was a dilettante, a Peter
Wimsey without monocle or title.

I watched Alex happily dividing up our
tasks. Tomorrow I would return to the archives I
had examined before, and she would track down
Deborah Raines. We had conducted many joint ex-
ercises over the years – our children, our careers,
our lives – comparing notes and examining each
overturned stone. With every success our marriage
was better, and when we failed, we failed together.
This was the first effort in our new life, and we
would see it through, however quixotic the adven-
ture might be.

Anita called to us from the kitchen porch.
"Mr. Monmouth. Y'all come through the garden.
Miz Edwards is waitin'." We wound our way
through the parterres and pools and statues. As I
raised my hand to rap on the glass, Anita opened
the door and ushered us inside.

I made the introductions. Alex sat down
next to Virginia while I helped Anita with the
drinks. The portrait of Beauregard Lee looked
down at us. I delivered the drinks and, already
deep in conversation, they ignored me. I examined
the bookcases.

They were very different people. Alex was a
Yankee who had insisted on a career despite the
four children we began our marriage with, Virginia
was a belle who had presided over a wealthy
Southern family, but they had one thing in com-
mon. Their blood was blue. Each woman was ac-

customed to the deference accorded her, and each one – in her own way – accepted it as her due. They recognized each other, and the reticence that might have otherwise come between them was missing. I fixed another drink and sat down on the piano bench.

Virginia turned her attention to me. "Cathe‑rine called last night," she said, an edge in her voice. "She said you seem very interested in our family."

I had prepared for this. "A friend of mine, a journalist, died a few weeks ago after a visit to Twin Rivers. I mentioned her before – Samantha Clarke. She was doing a story on a man named Cosmo Ender. You know him as Gerry." I paused. "I think Samantha's death and Cosmo Ender may be related." She gazed at me, unblinking. "He's visited your home. What can you tell me about him?"

She shook her head. "Nothing. He was James's friend."

"He's your friend, too, isn't he? Now?" A faint blush appeared on her cheeks, but she made no response. I tried something else. "What's he have to do with Teddy Black?"

She smiled. "I don't know what you mean."

"What about Teddy and Cat? What's their deal?"

"Catherine doesn't confide in me, Harry. She's decided to watch over him for reasons of her own. He has accepted it. That's all I know."

Whatever she really knew, she was unwilling to share it. Gesturing toward the Steinway, I said, "This is a beautiful piano. Do you play?"

She nodded. "My father bought it for me when I was a girl."

"I understand that Teddy's great on the piano. Have you ever heard him play?"

There was a subtle change in her expression. The faux frankness gave way to uneasiness, lips tighter, eyes narrowed. "No."

THE NEXT day, Alex and I went about our appointed tasks, and met for lunch at a restaurant called Baxter's. Virginia had recommended it. "It's on Pollock Street. There's a big cast-iron clock with four faces right outside. You can't miss it." The clock was indeed a notable landmark – I could see it from a block away.

"Her name's Deborah Allen now," said Alex. "She's not working anymore. I'm going by to see her after lunch."

"Good."

"Did you find anything?"

"Well – there were no brothers, Steiner or Ender. No Frank Steiner, no Ilse Steiner, no Steiners at all, in fact. One interesting thing – according to her obituary, Ilse Ender was Beauregard Lee's nurse for 30 years. Virginia's father."

"When did she die?"

"Nineteen ninety. I'll bet Virginia knows something about her background. Why don't you ask her in a roundabout sort of way? She might talk to you."

She hesitated. "Okay. But I – like her."

"It's not about her, Alex. I don't know why she won't help us, but I can't imagine she had anything to do with Samantha's death."

"All right."

We studied our menus. "Where are your glasses?" I said.

She touched her face, brow creased. "I don't know." She searched her purse. "I must've left them at home."

My morning had turned up two more items, neither of which was yet part of the puzzle. After striking out on the Ender and Steiner queries, I checked the back issues of the *Sun Journal* for Samantha Clarke. There was only one item, just a few months old. The *Journal* had reprinted the Sunday spread on Samantha that appeared in the *New Hope Chronicle* right after she became its editor.

I'd let my eyes drift over the photos and text, my mind on other things, when the picture of Samantha at her baby grand piano roused a recollection. Just above the keys, propped up next to the music rack, was a framed photograph. I recognized the silver frame, but the image inside was too small to make out.

The other item was even less consequential. Almost as an afterthought, I went to "Obituaries" and typed in "Moore." I expected nothing – the death of a young Nazareth resident was unlikely to make the *Sun Journal* – but there it was, in the edition for October 31, 1994. Jamal Moore had died of an infection acquired at Twin Rivers Memorial Hospital while having his tonsils removed. His physician was James Edwards. The picture was the same as the one behind the cash register at the service station in Nazareth.

THE WEEPING Arch was really three arches, the tallest one in the middle, each with wrought-iron gates open to the public. Like the paneled wall that enclosed the cemetery, the entryway was made of coquina, cement with shells quarried from the nearby rivers. A drop of water fell on my head as I passed beneath the middle arch – the porous material absorbed rainwater and released it a "tear" at a time.

More than two centuries old, Cedar Grove Cemetery lay only a few blocks west of Front Street. Its oyster-shell paths wound around burial plots enclosed by brick, marl and concrete block, and massive red cedars – their moss dragging the ground – provided intermittent shade. The scent was damp earth.

The Taylor family lay inside a low wall of marl topped by a metal rail. I imagined a little boy curled, asleep, atop one of the tabular tombs. It seemed an unlikely place to nap.

The Confederate memorial rose in the distance. I wandered amongst the stones, searching for one I didn't expect to find. A familiar figure came toward me, attired in ordinary clothing suitable for a brisk fall day. He wore a Twin Rivers High School cap. "Harry," said Cosmo Ender, "what brings you here?"

Had he been summoned by Virginia Edwards, or was this one of his periodic trips to see her? Or was he just visiting his mother's grave? "My wife and I are taking a little vacation. What about you?"

"This is my hometown."

His demeanor was different. Whereas before he was bluff and hearty, a salesman luring his customer in, now he was wary, almost suspicious, and surprised to see me. "I thought you were born and raised in New York?"

He forced a smile. "I've found that people take New York more seriously than Twin Rivers."

"And the Cosmo?"

"A little comedy's always useful. Where are you staying?"

"We're in a cottage over on Front Street. The Dependency. Do you know it?"

His face tightened. There was antagonism, barely disguised, now. "Yes."

I pushed harder. "I'm conducting an investigation into the legend of Teddy Black. Have you ever heard it?" He shook his head. "He was abandoned in this cemetery 15 years ago. Your friend James Edwards found him. Did you know that?"

"No."

"He never mentioned it?"

"No."

"I've come across several Enders. Ilse. And Gerry." He made no response. "Frank Steiner tells me you've been in business together a long time."

He smiled again. "That's very unlikely." The clumsy lie about Steiner seemed to relieve the tension, and he was Cosmo Ender again. "This is the most historic cemetery in the state," he said, his gesture taking it all in. "Many notables are buried here. Can I give you a tour?"

"No, thanks. I'm looking for one occupant in particular. A little boy."

"I'm very familiar with this place. What's his name?"

"Moore. Jamal Moore."

He stared. "You won't find him here. There are no blacks buried in this cemetery."

"How'd you know he was black?"

The features stiffened again, but only for an instant. "Greenwood Cemetery's just up the street." He paused. "It was nice to see you, Harry. Have a good vacation."

I watched as he disappeared behind the trees, considering the wisdom of what I had done. The premise of my quest was that Samantha's death was related to her investigation of Cosmo Ender. Now the object of that inquiry knew some-one else was curious. Ender was not the bizarre little promoter I'd first met at the building site for the School of Human Enrichment, but who he really was remained to be determined, and now he knew I'd taken Samantha's place.

I walked to the northernmost boundary of the old burial ground and exited onto Cypress Street. The single gate to Greenwood Cemetery was a block away. Not nearly as well preserved as the white cemetery – tombstones placed haphaz-ardly, leaning or fallen, and weeds and trash and even graffiti – Greenwood was built specifically to accept blacks from Cedar Grove. In a particularly virulent outburst of Jim Crow, the town fathers of Twin Rivers had segregated the graveyards by moving black bones, most interred before the Civil War, from one cemetery to the other. The separa-tion remained, despite decades of decrees. Life was fleeting, death eternal.

A pink granite stone, clean and polished as if it were new, rose up in front of me:

JAMAL MOORE
1990 – 1994

It stood alone, surrounded by low-lying shrubbery and newly-trimmed grass. The contrast with the rest of the place was stark. A young black boy from Nazareth lay beneath the finest marker in the cemetery, and his plot of land was well tended. Was that a sign of the regard of family and friends, or something else?

I SIPPED my drink, watching Alex wend her way toward me. A full moon cast the garden in shades of gray, a maze between Virginia Edwards and our sanctuary on the porch. Alex climbed the steps and pushed through the screen door. "Why are you sitting here in the dark?" she said.

I switched on a lamp. "No reason. It sneaked up on me." I paused. "How was happy hour?"

"Delightful, actually. When she forgets about the wheelchair, she's – delightful."

I nodded. "Anything interesting?"

"Well – I don't know. Let me tell you about Deborah Raines – Allen – first."

"Okay."

"She wasn't really a reporter for the paper back then. She wrote an occasional feature story – historical pieces, old homes, that sort of thing."

"Why'd she get the Teddy Black story?"

"Her family and Virginia Edwards were old friends. Doctor Edwards called her himself."

"Did she go to the cemetery?"

"No. She came here."

"Here?"

"The Dependency. Teddy stayed here until he was adopted."

"Really? Isn't that a little out of the ordinary?"

"I got the impression that suggestions from James or Virginia Edwards were pretty much accepted around here. They – she – has her finger in a lot of pies."

"Did Deborah talk to Teddy?"

"She says she tried, but he couldn't, or wouldn't, speak."

"Why not?"

"He was only four years old, I guess. Everyone was a stranger."

"But he talked to Edwards?"

"Apparently."

"And told him he didn't know who he was or who his parents were, and so forth?" She nodded. "And Edwards passed it along?"

"That's what she said."

"Was anybody else there?" Alex shook her head. "Did she ask Edwards any questions? Like why he was at the cemetery, for instance? Or why he decided this little boy needed his attention?"

"She didn't mention it."

"Did she tell you anything else?"

"No. Wait – she had a camera, but Edwards wouldn't let her take a picture."

I stood up. "I need another drink. What about you?"

"A glass of wine would be great."

Back on the porch, I said, "So, basically this woman just wrote what Edwards told her?"

"Yes. I think so."

"And whoever's in charge of – of orphans around here just accepted it?"

"I guess."

"It's hard to believe the social services bureaucracy, even here, didn't intervene somehow." I smiled. "Would you care to look into that?"

She smiled back. "I'd be happy to."

"Good. I think the Guardian Ad Litem's office would be the place to start." I paused. "There's another thing." I told her about Jamal Moore's gravesite. "The town keeps track of the owners of the burial plots. Would you mind checking on that, too?"

"Not at all."

"Thanks."

"What are you doing tomorrow?"

"There's been a lot of dying around here recently. I'm going to see the Sheriff, and maybe the coroner, about Paul and Sylvia Black. And James Edwards." I took a sip of my drink. "Now tell me what you and Virginia talked about."

The telephone rang. When Alex saw I was going to ignore it, she hurried into the house and picked up the receiver. "Hello." A pause. "Yes, Bobby. Hold on." She leaned out the door. "It's for you. Bobby Hood."

I sighed and walked inside. "Hey, Bobby. What's up?"

"Harry, I'm sorry to disturb your vacation, but – Helen Tanner's been arrested. She's asked for you."

"What's the charge?"

"Murder. The murder of Vera Carr."

SIX

I TOOK the interstate to save time, and this time it worked. Traffic was light, and 80 miles per hour seemed slow. Bobby knew nothing about the details of Helen's arrest – Jeff Farnham had called him, and he called me. Helen was spending the night in the Sheriff's holding tank. The bail hearing was scheduled for the next day.

Alex had elected to stay behind. While I prepared to return to New Hope, she recounted her conversation with Virginia about Ilse Ender. After giving birth to her son, Ilse worked as a nurse at the new Twin Rivers hospital. Impressed by her skills, Virginia's father had hired her for his private practice. Her husband, Gerry's father, was killed in the war.

I added another job to Alex's list. "You don't just walk into a hospital and say 'I want to be a nurse.' She must have had something to prove she was qualified. Maybe the hospital still has it." Alex would keep working on the puzzle while I tried to help Helen. If necessary, she would rent a car and drive herself to her appointment with Steiner.

I smiled at the thought of her. We had abandoned the non-essentials of our love-making – the anticipation, the caress, the kiss – years ago, and invested the energy in other aspects of our life we deemed more important. Sex had become routine, then dull and, finally, tedious. Realizing that something important was missing, we'd planned "special" occasions to revive the ardor and then, unfulfilled, returned to the status quo. When Alex fell ill, even that was too much.

Things had changed since her awakening. It wasn't like when we were kids – it was better. We had lain entwined, naked, on her bed at the clinic, heedless of the possibility that Steiner might open the unlocked door. Last night we had celebrated her renewed life with what could only be called a splendid, leisurely debauchery. Her vigor was remarkable – invariably, I was the one who cried hold. It was actually beyond remarkable, but I kept the disquiet at arm's length.

The carillon was chiming 11:00 P.M. as I turned north on Division Street. The Sheriff was waiting just inside the door. "Up a little late, aren't you?" I said.

"Bobby told me you were coming. I wanted to make sure you got in to see her."

"Thanks. What can you tell me?"

He smiled. "Not much. The County Attorney told me not to talk to you."

I shook my head. In most cases, the question at a bail hearing was whether or not the defendant was likely to flee the jurisdiction, and it was rare for bail to be denied. The state always opposed bail in capital cases, but its burden then was more serious. In order to keep Helen incarcerated, the County Attorney was obliged to show Bobby Hood why a conviction was likely, and he wasn't taking any chances. "Has she said anything?" I said.

"She says she didn't do it." We passed through a door and approached the old-fashioned cage where Helen was kept. She sat upright on the cot, eyes straight ahead, not a red hair out of place. Jeff unlocked the door. "You can use my office," he said. Still silent, she rose and followed us.

After he left, I said, "Why did they arrest you?"

"I didn't kill Vera Carr."

"I believe you, but I need to know why the Sheriff thinks you did." She didn't respond. "Where were you?"

"At home."

"Tell me everything that happened."

"It was a little after five. The Sheriff and two of his men came to the door. He said he wanted to talk to me about Vera's death. And he wanted to search the house."

"Did he have a warrant?"

"Not that I know of."

"But you let them in anyway?"

"Yes."

"Okay. Then what?"

"They weren't there five minutes when one of the deputies called from my study. He was lifting a blue rug I keep in front of the fireplace. There were stains on it. The Sheriff wanted to know what they were."

"What were they?"

"Blood."

"Whose blood?"

"Vera Carr's."

I blinked. "Did you tell them that?"

"Yes."

"Why did Vera bleed on your rug?"

"She came by to talk about her lunch with you." She smiled. "She didn't think you had the right attitude. She tripped on the rug and fell against the hearth. It didn't seem very serious – she wasn't unconscious – but there was a lot of blood. I cleaned the wound, and when the bleeding stopped I tried to bandage it. Unsuccessfully."

"How come?"

"To get a bandage to stick I had to cut her hair. She said no."

I considered. "Was there another injury to her head? A big bump, or maybe a bruise?"

"No."

"Did you tell Farnham all this?"

She shook her head. "After I told him it was Vera's blood, things became a little more – confron- tational. He told me about remaining silent, and getting a lawyer and all that. When I refused to answer any more questions, he arrested me."

I nodded. "Do you know why they came to see you in the first place?"

"No."

"Was there any reason why you *might* want to kill Vera?"

The caramel eyes narrowed. "Of course not. Why would you ask me that?"

"Motive. It's important to the cops."

"Well, it's silly. Vera was one of our tutors. That's all."

I asked a few more questions pertinent to tomorrow's hearing. About to return her to the Sheriff's custody, I said, "By the way, when did Vera's visit happen?"

She stumbled a little this time. "It was a Saturday evening. Just – just before she was killed."

"Really? What time did she leave?"

She hesitated again. "I don't remember ex‑actly. Eight o'clock?"

"Where was she going?"

"Home, she said."

"Which is where?"

"One of the graduate dorms. Cobb, I think."

I nodded. "Okay. I'll see you tomorrow." I gave her a quick hug. "Don't worry."

I stopped at the office, reluctant to go home without Alex. After pouring a drink, I sat down by the window to consider the case against Helen Tanner. Her story was plausible up to a point. A fall against the hearth would account for the shal‑low cut the coroner had described, and the blood would have fallen on Helen's rug instead of the leaves in Castle Park. The bricks might reveal evi‑dence of the accident. Helen lived on the northern border of the park, and Vera's dorm was just south of it. The shortest way home was along one of its paths where someone killed her with the blunt in‑strument that struck the fatal blow.

But the timing was wrong. A walk through Castle Park would take 15 minutes at most, mean‑ing that Vera would emerge onto Club Road around 8:15 P.M. The coroner had pegged the time of death at midnight at the earliest.

And there was no accounting for the ejacu‑late the coroner had mentioned. Female ejacula‑tion was controversial, not least in legal circles. Some claimed there was no such thing, but the lo‑cal medical examiner disagreed. Chemical markers had been discovered that distinguished it from the male version, and from other fluids generated by a woman's body during sex. The science had been used sparingly, most often in defense of a man ac- cused of rape. What was its significance here?

The easy answer was that Vera didn't go home at all, that she had achieved a serious orgasm sometime before midnight, and that someone had killed her with a club between midnight and 8:00 A.M. She must have had a partner for the sex – the alternative seemed ridiculous. Was he – or she – the killer, too? And how did Vera wind up in Cas- tle Park?

The bail hearing tomorrow would be an up- hill fight. Helen had admitted that the stains on her rug were Vera's blood. The body was found a few hundred yards from her house. That might be more than enough to keep her in jail.

THE COUNTY Attorney was a young man, and *State v. Tanner* was his first murder. He chose to make the case for keeping Helen behind bars with sworn testimony rather than rely on his own eloquence and powers of persuasion, which might allow me to explore issues of interest to the de- fense. Judge Robert Hood would hear the evidence and decide.

Although Helen had been in custody for less than 24 hours, word of her arrest had spread. Rep- resentatives of the press and other media were in the courtroom, as were members of the local bar with time on their hands. Missy Farrell was in the gallery, and so was Winfred Honeyman. They were not sitting together. While we waited for the bailiff to deliver Helen, the Chancellor leaned across the bar and said, "Harry, this is absurd. Helen didn't kill that woman."

"I agree."

"The publicity will be terrible. Can't you do something?"

"Win, right now I'm just trying to get her out of jail pending the trial of this case. Unless they drop the charges, which isn't very likely, we have a long way to go." I could tell the idea disturbed him. Not only would the bad press linger, it was possible that Helen, a potential murderess, would be back at her desk in South Building tomorrow.

He rallied. "Can she afford to pay you?"

I shook my head. "We haven't gotten that far yet."

"Well – the College will guarantee your fees and expenses."

"Great. What about her bail?"

"We'll pay that, too."

"Thanks. I'll tell her."

Helen, in the same blue dress she'd worn the night before, came through a door on the left and sat down beside me. The Chancellor patted her arm, and returned to his seat.

"All rise," cried the bailiff with more self-importance than usual. Bobby entered the room and took his place behind the bench. The bailiff announced the business of the day, asked God to look after us, and then said: "Please be seated."

The coroner was the first witness. He was led through everything in his report except the sex, and I thought I knew why – it didn't fit the state's case any better than it did mine. When it was my turn, I said, "You examined the victim's body, didn't you? Including the vaginal cavity?"

The County Attorney was on his feet. "Objection, Your Honor. That's beyond the scope of the direct examination. And it's irrelevant to the issue of bail."

Bobby looked at me. I began, "Well –"

"Harry." Startled, I looked around. It was Helen, her face so twisted as to be almost unrecognizable. I leaned toward her. "Drop it," she whispered. "Please."

Nonplussed, I turned back to the judge. "I, uh, withdraw the question."

Bobby smiled. "Good. I was going to sustain the objection anyway." Everyone laughed.

I looked back at Helen. Her head was bowed. I returned to my seat as Jeff Farnham took the stand. Suppressing the turmoil in my head, I tried to listen.

"Sheriff Farnham," said the County Attorney, "tell the Court about your visit to the Defendant's home yesterday afternoon." Jeff responded with the blue rug, Helen's admission that the blood was Vera Carr's, and her refusal to cooperate after the rug was found. "Where is Dean Tanner's house located?"

"It's on Park Place," the Sherriff said. "On the edge of Castle Park."

"The victim's body was found in the park?"

"Yes."

"How far from Dean Tanner's home?"

"No more than a quarter mile."

"Thank you. No further questions."

I stood up. Jeff Farnham had been a year ahead of me at New Hope High School. A product of Milltown, he had refused to accede to the class arrangements in place at the time, and carried off a daughter of one of New Hope's finest families. Law enforcement was the family business – his father had reined me in on several occasions when we were kids. "Sheriff, why did you visit Helen Tanner yesterday?"

He looked at the County Attorney, then back at me. "When we first spoke to Dean Tanner, she indicated that she and the victim were only acquaintances. Our investigation turned up evidence that she and the dead woman were – more than that, and there might have been a quarrel."

I nodded. "What evidence?"

The County Attorney rose once more. "Objection. Irrelevant. Defense counsel is trying to prepare his case now. This is a bail hearing."

"Mr. Monmouth?" said Bobby.

"The state has a serious burden at a capital bail hearing, Your Honor. It shouldn't be permitted to hide behind vague allegations about 'evidence.'"

Bobby nodded. "Overruled."

"What was your evidence, Sheriff?"

"Well – we received a note."

"From who?"

"I don't know."

"An anonymous note?" He nodded. "May I see it?"

Jeff turned toward the County Attorney again. After a moment's hesitation, the young man rose and said, "Judge Hood, defense counsel wanted to know why the Sheriff went to Dean Tanner's home. Now he knows – the Sheriff received an anonymous note. The contents of the note are irrelevant to this proceeding."

"Your Honor," I said, "the state wants to keep this woman in prison indefinitely, but doesn't

want to tell us why. This note's going to be pro-
duced eventually. Why not now?"

Bobby considered. "Overruled."

The County Attorney crossed the room and
handed me an envelope addressed, in block letters,
to the Sheriff. I withdrew the folded sheet of paper:

SHERRIF – HELEN TANNER AND VERA
CARR WERE <u>VERY</u> GOOD FREINDS – THEY
HAD A FIGHT – YOU SHOULD LOOK INTO IT.

I held the note up. "This came in the mail?"

"Yes."

"When?"

"The morning before Dean Tanner was ar-
rested."

Something about it didn't ring true. I
dropped the note on the table, and turned back to
the witness. "Did Dean Tanner object to allowing
you and your men into her home?" I said.

"No."

"Did she impede your search in any way?"

"No."

"Was the rug hidden?"

"No."

"It was right there in front of the fireplace,
wasn't it? In plain view?"

"Yes."

"Does that sound like a woman with a guilty
conscience, Sheriff?"

"Objection! Now he's arguing his –"

"Withdrawn," I said. "Was there any evi-
dence of a body being dragged through the park?"

"No."

"Ms. Carr weighed about 130 pounds, didn't she?"

"Yes."

"Do you suppose the defendant just threw a 130-pound corpse over her shoulder and carried it a quarter of a mile?"

"I don't know."

"Pardon me, Your Honor." I returned to the table, and flipped through a yellow legal pad without seeing the pages, deciding. "You mentioned a quarrel, Sheriff. What was it about?"

The County Attorney stood up again. "It's not relevant, Your Honor. I object."

"The Sheriff specifically —"

"Overruled," said Bobby. "The witness said there might have been a quarrel between Ms. Carr and the accused. So does the note. I'll allow the question."

"Well, Sheriff," I said, "what was the quarrel about?" He hesitated. "Well?"

"It was about — love, I guess. A lover's quarrel."

There it was. I should have left it at that, but I wanted to punish her. "What are you talking about?"

"I spoke to some of the victim's friends. She and Dean Tanner were — lovers, but — there were problems."

I knew about Helen and Cat, and now Helen and Vera. I had resisted it because Helen and I had been lovers, too, and how could she "love" a woman after once loving me? The same ego, the same self-absorption, that laid claim to her virginity so many years before had blinded me. I'd even had a new affair with her in my head, confident it would be a reality if I so chose.

An hour later, I sat in the courtroom alone. Bobby had denied Helen bail, and she was already on her way to the women's prison in Orangeburg. I had questions, lots of questions, but decided to defer them, which was just as well because she had nothing to say. Vera Carr was more than just a tutor.

For much of my life, sexual bent was a given. Religion had redefined human nature, and behavior going back to the beginning of humanity was proscribed. The law, and the opprobrium of neighbors, kept people in their closets. When I was a boy – and Helen was a girl – homosexuality was never mentioned except in the most hyperbolic, pejorative way. In an age and place riddled with bogies, "queers" were the ultimate other. The oppression was widespread but, because it was deemed so beyond the pale, mostly unspoken.

And then God lost His clout, and sex took His place. At one time, not so long ago, sex was personal. But sex sells, in every way imaginable, and – as enforced modesty was abandoned – the salesmen grew ever bolder, until nothing was truly prohibited. Sexuality, once more private than sex, was displayed – defiantly at first, increasingly with brio – amongst angels on pins arguing about "rights" and "wrongs." The closets were emptied, and then some.

Helen Tanner, though, had never overcome the circumstances of her birth. Her religion, her parents' religion, was more powerful than the others despite its shortcomings, and the trappings – emptied of conviction – lingered. All the mysteries had been explained, but she still went to church and her portrait, in a white confirmation dress, hung over the mantel. She had risked time behind bars because her parents, and her parents' friends, still lived. The worst torture imaginable was to be revealed for who she was.

But it was more than that. The pain in her face had convinced me it was more than rules and the opinions of others. I had to find out what it was.

SEVEN

I LEANED in the Sheriff's doorway. "Jeff?"

He raised his head. "Come in, Harry. Sit down."

"Have the forensics people been to Helen's house yet?"

"They're going this afternoon. Guys from the State Police lab."

"Ask them to pay special attention to the edge of the hearth. That's what caused the cut on the back of Vera's head."

He stared. "All right. Anything else?"

"You have access to the FBI's fingerprint repository, don't you?" He nodded. "Does it include non-criminals? Job applicants, security checks, that sort of thing?"

"Yes."

"Foreigners?"

"Not necessarily. You need to check with Interpol to be sure."

"How long does it take?"

"Do you have the actual prints, or do we have to find them?"

I held up a sheet of paper. "You'll have to find them."

"Is it about the Tanner case?"

"No. Completely unrelated."

"Then it'll be sometime next week at the soonest."

"That's okay. A week's fine."

"Is there a time period? It might speed things up."

"Yes. Nineteen forty-three to the present." Infants didn't really have fingerprints, but why take the chance? Steiner had become more mysterious than Ender, and I wanted to know why. The information collected in the fingerprint archives might provide a clue.

I pointed the car toward Orangeburg, 13 miles north of New Hope. I had viewed Helen through a flawed prism for more than 30 years, an accumulated memory that had to be revised. The first order of business was to start again with the death of Vera Carr. When that was over, I would be guided by what Helen wanted to do.

I had puzzled over the state's reluctance to "out" her, and decided that the County Attorney was just a good lawyer trying to do his job, not always a given. Strictly speaking, the sexual preferences of victim and accused were irrelevant but, as soon as Helen was charged with Vera's murder, the countdown to notoriety began. The public's obsession with sex, and its sense of entitlement regarding those in the news, guaranteed that Helen's most intimate secrets would soon be splashed across newspapers and computer screens. My spiteful queries at the hearing had just moved the revelations forward a couple of days. The orgy had already begun.

The discrepancies in Helen's story could now be explained. She and Vera had sex that Saturday evening, and Vera probably didn't leave until midnight. Helen wasn't stupid – the blue rug would've been destroyed long ago if she'd killed Vera. I was sure that traces of hair and blood on the edge of the hearth would corroborate Vera's fall, a much more credible scenario than the state's story. The only thing missing was the killer. Who was awaiting Vera in Castle Park? How did he know she would be there?

Helen was calm, almost catatonic, and her answers to my questions were terse. "When you said Vera left you at eight o'clock, that wasn't right, was it?" I said.

"No."

"It was closer to midnight?"

"Yes."

"Did you hear or see anybody outside the house?" She shook her head. "Did anyone else know she was there?" Hesitation, then another shake. "Helen, you have to tell me the truth. Did anyone else know?"

"No." She paused. "Vera thought she saw someone at the window. I didn't."

"She carried a purse, didn't she?" She nodded. "Did she have it with her that night?"

"I think so."

"Did she have any enemies?"

Another pause. "No."

"Do you?"

"No."

"Was there a quarrel?" She shook her head again. "Do you have any idea who killed her?"

She closed her eyes. "No."

I had one more question, but decided not to ask it. It wasn't relevant to Vera's death, and it would upset her more than she already was.

Ordinarily, a client charged with murder is eager to help her lawyer prove the state wrong. Helen was the exception. She sat across the table, clad in the standard-issue pink smock and slippers, waiting for me to leave. She reminded me of Alex before her rebirth, resigned to death or some sentient version of it. And she still wasn't telling me the truth. "Helen, please. All I need is a little cooperation. I don't think their case is very good."

"It's good enough for me, Harry." She paused. "I'm sorry."

THE STACK of mail on my desk was higher than usual. Most of it was the coroner's report on Samantha's death and the few pages that described the Sheriff's investigation. The minutiae of the coroner's findings – the scars on her arm, the fresh needle marks, the bruise at the crook of her elbow – meant little to me, and the official cause of death – the failure of heart and lungs – reflected the medical profession's insistence on the pedantic. Samantha had been killed by a massive dose of heroin. The breakdown of her organs was just a deadly byproduct.

I picked up the phone. When the coroner came on the line, I said, "Can you walk me through the process that killed Samantha Clarke? I've read your report, and it doesn't help."

"Hang on," he said. "Let me get a copy." He was back a minute later. "Okay, the first part, the scars and so forth, indicate she was an experienced drug user who'd stopped using for a while. There were only two fresh tracks."

"Tracks?"

"Needle marks."

"She injected herself twice?"

"Yes."

"Is that unusual?"

"Ordinarily, I'd say yes. Heroin takes effect within seconds. If the injection's done right it would be almost impossible to do it again." He paused. "I think she missed the first time."

"Missed?"

"The vein. Experienced addicts shoot the drug directly into a vein. It works quicker and better that way. One of the tracks in Ms. Clarke's arm missed. It just went under the skin. That's why there was a bruise."

"Was Samantha an addict?"

He hesitated. "She was a recovering addict. The scars show she was once a heavy user, and the lack of recent marks means she'd stopped for a period of time."

"How long?"

"It's hard to say, Harry. At least six months."

"Do you know how much she actually used?"

"No, but it was easily the largest overdose I've ever seen. Death was almost instantaneous."

"Isn't that hard to do? I mean, doesn't the drug get in the way of the needle?"

"It could. It may have required extraordinary concentration. That's why I think it was suicide." He paused. "Some of the dope was left in the spoon. She didn't measure it. She just used as much as she could."

"Was the needle still in her arm when you examined the body?"

"No. They moved her before I got there."

"So you don't know which injection missed the vein? The first or second?"

"No, but it was almost certainly the first. There would've been no need for the second one, otherwise."

The Sheriff's file held more than expected. Samantha's call to Helen the day before she died – placed at 10:15 A.M. – lasted less than a minute, the one to Jack Peeler – made only seconds later – more than 20. That seemed like a long time to deny an interview request. And there was another call, one that wasn't mentioned in earlier reports. The number was familiar – Frank Steiner's office at the temple on the hill.

I searched the report for follow-up and found none. Samantha had killed herself with heroin, and anything but the most superficial investigation was apparently a waste of time. I was the only one with questions.

The item at the bottom of the pile was a letter from a firm in New York City marked "Personal and Confidential," odd because I knew no lawyers in New York who would have something "personal and confidential" to tell me. Abby had not broken the seal. I opened it.

Minutes later, I emerged from the stucco bungalow and turned west on High Street. Passing through the doors of the *New Hope Chronicle* once more, I found my new friend sitting behind Samantha's desk. "It's only temporary," he said. "Until they find somebody to take her place."

"Do you recall the big spread you did on Samantha when she first came here? In the penthouse and all that?" He nodded. "Who took the pictures?"

"I did."

"Do you still have them?"

"Sure."

"Can I see them?"

I followed him through the warren of offices to a room full of file cabinets. He opened and closed two drawers and found what he was looking for in the third. The picture was larger than the one in the Twin Rivers *Sun Journal*, but I still couldn't identify the people in the photograph. He slipped it into a machine and magnified the image.

The note from New York had confirmed it, but the photo really brought it home. Helen and Samantha, in long white dresses and stylish hats, were seated in a gondola next to the boathouse in Central Park. Their bodies were close, leaning against a red satin pillow. Each woman wore a wide golden band on her left hand and held a champagne flute in her right. The water and the sky were dark, and the brightly lighted boathouse gleamed. The tableau was unmistakable, and the possession on Samantha's face obvious.

The question I didn't ask was answered. Another girl I thought was mine, for a few minutes anyway, had needs of her own. I unfolded the letter and read again the middle of its three paragraphs:

I've been out of the country for several weeks, and was not in the office when your letter arrived. The information my associate provided was correct – Ms. Clarke did, indeed, die without a will. However, she had given me instructions to draft one, leaving her entire estate to Ms. Helen Tanner of New Hope. I understand that Ms.

Clarke died under difficult circumstances, so I thought it proper to bring this to your attention.

It was a classic motive for murder, but Helen was charged with Vera's death, not Samantha's. The case for Samantha's murder was more compelling. Opportunity, means and – depending on Helen's knowledge of Samantha's financial affairs – motive were all there. Was Helen in jail for the wrong crime?

JACK PEELER'S office was larger than the Chancellor's, and much better appointed. I ran the gauntlet of security check-points and gatekeepers, and walked past the trophies and artwork commemorating great moments in the College's athletic past. I looked for Jack's golf trophies, but didn't find them. "How's Alex doing?" he said.

We'd been friends for a long time, but at that moment I was recalling his character flaws, several of which I shared. He favored shortcuts and drank too much, and wasn't above trying to rig life's rules in his favor. Comfort, gained with as little effort as possible, was his watchword.

In short, he was like millions of other people, none of whom could be suspected of killing Samantha Clarke. But he was also in charge of a football team on the brink of winning it all. Any "news" about Teddy Black would be unwelcome. "She's much better," I said. "I think the worst is over."

"Great." He waited.

"Why did Samantha call you?" I said. He gazed at me without responding. "What did she say?"

"She said she wanted to interview Teddy. I said I couldn't help her."

"What else?"

"She didn't believe me. She said if she didn't talk to him, she'd blow the football team sky-high."

"How?"

He cocked his head. "What's it to you? I've already been through this with Farnham."

"I don't believe Samantha killed herself. I'm not even sure it was accidental."

"But –"

"I know what killed her. I just don't know who."

He frowned. "So you've come to me?" I nodded. "She was almost – babbling. She just said if she couldn't talk to Teddy, we could kiss the national championship goodbye."

"Did you mention this to anyone else?"

"No."

Emerging from Jack's palace, I looked at my watch. I would be just in time for the hearing at the courthouse. Missy Farrell had grown tired of our tactics, and asked Bobby Hood for relief.

There were no greetings when I entered the courtroom. Missy was formal, and the hatred on Joe Spiller's face undisguised. Nancy wasn't there. Bobby took his place on the bench, and skipped the usual preliminaries. "All right, Miss Farrell. I've read your motion. What is it you want the Court to do?"

"I want you to do something to get the Defendant's attention, Your Honor. He doesn't take this lawsuit seriously." She gestured toward Spiller. "Mr. Spiller and his wife have lost their only child, and Doctor Steiner couldn't care less. He's contemptuous of them and this Court. The Spillers don't understand it, and neither do I." Spiller began to weep. I pushed a handkerchief at him, but he ignored it.

"What do you suggest?" Bobby said.

"Enter judgment on behalf of the Spillers."

"That's a little – extreme at this juncture. Anything less drastic?"

She nodded. "Order him to come to this courtroom and apologize to Joe and Nancy Spiller. Not for the death of their little boy – they don't expect that – but for his refusal to tell them why. Or to help them find out why."

Bobby turned to me. "Mr. Monmouth?"

Missy was right, of course, but she'd left someone out. Steiner's lawyer had refused to help, too. "I haven't exercised adequate control over my client, Your Honor. I apologize." I tried to get Spiller's attention. "I'm sorry, Joe." I looked back at Bobby. "I'll do better. As for sanctions, we don't do public shaming anymore. Maybe we should. I believe a fine, levied on the Defendant and his attorney, is a better idea."

Bobby leaned forward. "I'll take it under advisement." He turned his head. "Mr. Spiller," he said, "I, too, am sorry for your loss and for the way this case has been handled. Is there anything you wish to say?"

Spiller rose, wiping his eyes with his sleeve. "I don't understand this stuff," he said. "All I know is my wife cries herself to sleep every night and – and I do, too, sometimes, and that – man has never said he's sorry. He's never talked to us at all. That's not right. It's not – human." He paused.

"Why is a man like that alive and our little boy dead?"

A few minutes later, I was on the road to Twin Rivers. Spiller was closer to the truth than he knew. Steiner wasn't human, not in the ordinary sense. The child's death was just something to overcome, and he had no time for emotion. I wasn't much better. I had approached Alex's illness the same way, and failed to recognize the Spillers' pain.

With an effort, I tore my mind from Joe and Nancy Spiller, and considered my conversation with Jack Peeler. I'd begun the adventure with the idea that Samantha's investigation of Cosmo Ender was the reason she died. Now I had a more compelling motive – the football team's quest for the Holy Grail. Anything that threatened Teddy Black would be anathema to any number of people.

That didn't let Ender out of it. I was convinced that he and Teddy shared a past, that the events of 1995 were not a coincidence. Steiner, too, was now part of the puzzle. What did he and Samantha talk about for 15 minutes the day before she died?

Finally, what about Helen? So far, she was the last person to see Samantha alive, and she was undoubtedly aware of her drug habit. If she also believed she was heir to millions of dollars, removing Samantha may have been too tempting to resist.

Leaving Highway 70, I turned north on US 17 and crossed the Trent River. The Twin Rivers waterfront park was just on the other side, and I saw several red and white vehicles, rooftop lights flashing, clustered around one of the boat ramps. A small crowd had gathered, and I joined them.

A woman's body, barefoot and clad in a black dress, lay washed up on the jetty. Two men bearing a stretcher picked their way gingerly over the jagged rocks. After a moment, they motioned toward the shore, and another man joined them. He lifted the body and placed it on the litter and, after some shifting of the burden so that everyone faced forward, they stepped carefully across the rocks and up the concrete ramp. As they came nearer, I stationed myself at the doors of the ambulance to be absolutely sure. It was Anita Moore.

EIGHT

THERE WAS a note on the door:

Harry,
I'm with Virginia. Please come.
          A

I crossed the garden and looked in the door. Despite the hour, they were both asleep – Virginia on her bed beneath a lavender sheet, Alex sitting upright in the wingback chair next to the fireplace. Her features were relaxed, the skin almost unlined. The unease returned – she was beginning to look like the girl I'd married 30 years before. I touched my wife's shoulder. "Alex?"

She opened her eyes and smiled, then shifted her gaze to Virginia. Glancing at the clock, she said, "We've been up all night, Harry. She's only been asleep a few hours." She paused. "Anita's disappeared. Virginia's extremely distraught. I finally had to give her something to make her sleep."

"I'm afraid it's going to get worse."

"Why?"

"Anita's dead. Drowned, I think." I described the scene at the park. "When did you miss her?"

"Around ten o'clock. Virginia was ready for bed, and Anita was nowhere to be found. Virginia called, and I came over to sit with her. She was almost hysterical."

"Did you call the cops?"

She shook her head. "She'd only been gone an hour or so."

"They'll be here pretty soon. Where's Anita's room?"

"Off the kitchen. Through the door on the far side."

I walked down the hall to the kitchen. Despite the bright sunshine outside, her room was dark, the shades drawn. The furniture was spare — a single bed covered in blue chenille, an upright chair, a dresser of cherry veneer. There was an unsealed envelope on the bedside table with a name in block letters: "ANITA." Handling it carefully, I used the tips of my fingers to withdraw the single sheet of paper:

ANITA – SAMANTHA CLARKE TOLD ME ABOUT YOU BEFORE SHE DIED – I WILL RITE THE STORY NOW – MEET ME TONITE AT THE FOOT OF QUEEN ST. – 9 PM – A FREIND

The printing and the misspelled words were familiar. I'd seen them in the courtroom a couple of days earlier. There was something fraudulent about both notes. Someone who couldn't spell wouldn't include an "i" in "friend" at all, and they certainly wouldn't get "Clarke" right. In any event, the two notes added Vera's death to the puzzle.

The doorbell rang. I pushed the note back into the envelope, left it on the table and turned to leave. There was a ring of keys hanging beside the door. I dropped it into my coat pocket, and passed out of the kitchen just as Alex reached the front door. She and the two men murmured in the hall-way for a few seconds, then Alex ushered them into the front parlor. She returned to the sun room and I followed. "The police," she said.

Virginia was stirring. When she was fully awake, Alex said, "There are some men to see you. Policemen."

Alarm showed on her face. "Is it about Anita?"

"I think so."

Alex looked at me. Virginia Edwards had a secret, and I wanted to know what it was. "Anita's dead," I said. "They pulled her out of the river an hour ago." Her beautiful face became a fearful skull – eyes wide, she clapped her hands to her head and opened her mouth like the scream in a Munch painting, but nothing came out. She'd lost her companion, the woman who cared for her for years, but the terror on her face wasn't for Anita. It was more personal. "What are you afraid of, Vir-ginia?" She shook her head. "Tell us. Maybe we can help."

She closed her eyes and sat mute. I looked at Alex. "There's something I want to check on. I'll be back in a little while." I left the house by way of the kitchen porch, skirted the grounds to avoid any official gaze, and walked south. After a few paces, I turned east on Queen Street to the river.

The town's riverwalk did not quite extend to Queen, thus preserving the view from the big house on Front Street. The 25 yards from the bottom of the street to the Neuse River were overgrown with low shrubs and dwarf trees, and a single winding path led the way through it. There was no shore – it was a ten-foot drop from the end of the path to the water.

I tried to avoid disturbing the crime scene, but there was nothing there as far as I could tell. The body had washed ashore a mile downriver. It would have been a simple matter to knock her on the head and drop her into the river, or maybe she was just pushed. However it happened, it appeared that Anita's "freind" didn't want to "rite" the story after all.

ALEX JOINED me on the screened-in porch. "The doctor's there now," she said. "I'll check on her in a little while." She fell into a chair. "I could use a drink."

A minute later, I handed her a glass. "Did she say anything?" I said.

"No. But she's terrified."

"Any idea why?"

She shook her head. "She mentioned Ender several times last night. Not that he's a killer or anything, just – just that they were friends and she didn't want to disappoint him."

"How could she do that?"

"She didn't say. There was also a lot of talk about her husband and the Blacks. About how they died."

"Like what? Foul play?"

"Nothing direct. Just gloomy ideas." She paused. "By the way, I talked to the Sheriff about all the death."

"What did he say?"

"He couldn't tell me anything about James Edwards. Paul Black was drunk when he and Sylvia were killed." She sipped her drink. "There was some question about the brakes."

"What about the brakes?"

"There was water in the fluid. He might not have been able to stop."

"And?"

"Water builds up in brake fluid as a matter of course. It's a question of maintenance."

"Did he check with –?"

"No, but I did." I smiled. "The car was nine years old. The fluid had never been changed."

"Could the water have been added?"

"Yes."

I returned to the kitchen and poured more scotch. When I rejoined her, she said, "What's happened with Helen?"

"Helen is currently at the Women's Institute in Orangeburg." She grimaced. "But she didn't kill Vera Carr. I'm convinced of that." I recounted the hearing and the aftermath without mentioning the sex. I'd come to grips with Helen's sexuality intellectually, but in my gut it was still a slander. A lifetime of sanctioned prejudice couldn't be overcome in a couple of days. Alex would hear about it soon enough. "Did you check on the gravesite at Greenwood?"

She nodded. "It's owned and maintained by Ender Enterprises."

"Well." I considered. "What about Ilse? Was there anything at the hospital?"

"Yes." She left the porch. When she returned, she laid a few pages in front of me. "Her nursing credentials. And a copy of her passport."

I flipped through the pages. Ilse had graduated from a nursing school in Frankfurt, and worked at a hospital in Berlin. A Swiss national, her passport had been issued in 1940 to Ilse Egger. Just before leaving Germany for the United States, the passport had been amended to add her married name, Ilse Steiner. Her emergency contact in Germany was Fritz Astel.

It was the third time I'd seen Astel's name. The first was on the title page and flyleaf of a book in Frank Steiner's office, and the second was included in the information about Steiner that Samantha had requested. Egger, too, was familiar, but Astel's inscription on the flyleaf was addressed to Wilhelm, not Ilse. Her connections were intriguing – Astel would've been tried as a war criminal had he not killed himself first – but none of it seemed to belong to the puzzle.

Jamal Moore, on the other hand, had to fit in somewhere. It was true the boy had died seven months before Teddy was found, but he'd been buried by Cosmo Ender. And now his mother was dead, almost certainly murdered, after telling a "story" to Samantha Clarke.

"I talked to the Guardian Ad Litem, too," Alex said.

"What did he say?"

"No one there was around in 1995. They looked for a file, and couldn't find one."

"Nothing?"

"Nothing."

Of all the remarkable things about Teddy Black's emergence in Twin Rivers, that was the most astonishing – no red tape. It ranked just behind death and taxes, and its absence was a tribute to the influence wielded by the Edwards family. To what end? What was it about Teddy at the age of four that inspired such effort?

"What time are you due at Steiner's tomorrow?" I said.

"One o'clock. Will you keep an eye on Virginia?"

I'd planned to go with her, to ask about his conversation with Samantha, but it could wait. "Sure."

I TURNED the television off. Only the conference championship remained. After that, it was on to New Orleans for the national title, already conceded by the news media and fellow competitors. The gloom was thick over the Meccas of college football, but there was joy in New Hope.

In an attempt to shut down Teddy's passing game, averaging nearly 600 yards per contest, the opposition's defense had played six defensive backs, leaving only two linebackers and three linemen to defend the run. In response, he'd rushed for 350 yards, demonstrating the blinding speed and power only glimpsed before. Combined with the 20 passes he was still able to complete, he accounted for 760 total yards, a conference record by a wide margin.

One play near the end of the first half was emblematic. A defender had managed to deflect one of Teddy's passes at midfield, and Teddy had plucked it from the air himself – bowling over opponents and teammates alike – and sprinted, untouched, into the end zone. One of the boys he knocked down, his own center, had to be carried off the field.

I heard her step outside and walked to the door. "How'd it go?" I called.

Alex looked up. "Okay."

There was an odd expression on her face. "What's the matter?"

Her features grew more composed. "Nothing. Nothing's the matter."

I held up the ring of keys. "I waited for you to get back. I'm hoping one of these will open the room upstairs."

"Where'd you get them?"

"Anita's room."

She followed me up the steps. The door required two keys to unlock it, but it took only a few seconds to find them. I pushed the door open, and stepped inside. The afternoon sun was nearly gone, so I reached for a switch that caused a lamp – located on a metal desk beneath the window on the far side of the room – to light. The only other furniture was a leather chair at the desk whose casters had scarred the pine floor, a refrigerator, and a narrow, unmade bed. A thick book, bound in red leather, rested on top of the desk.

Alex sat in the chair and picked up the book while I checked the closet and refrigerator – both were empty – and then turned my attention to the bed. It was high and short, like a child's, with metal rails. There were steel cuffs on either side, and a device that resembled stocks stretched across the bottom. A similar apparatus was located at the head of the bed. Three heavy leather straps hung from the frame on both sides.

Sleep was not the object. It was designed to confine – to immobilize – its occupant, like the one that restrained the monster in the old horror movies. "Harry?" I turned toward her. "This book is – I don't know what to call it. A diary? Lab notes?" She handed it to me.

It was a binder with loose-leaf pages separated by red and blue tabs. The first tab was labeled "Blood," and the first entry – in a hand I recognized immediately – began "Cambridge, November 3, 1994." Words and formulae and measurements I didn't understand followed.

I turned the pages slowly. The notations continued daily for three months, then appeared every other day, then weekly. On May 13, 1995, the handwriting changed, but the text looked much the same. Still another person wrote the next entry on May 20, and the content was different. Instead of lines of scientific mumbo-jumbo, there were only two words: "First syringe." Page after page, year after year, similar notations – "Second syringe," "Third syringe," and so on – appeared, interspersed with technical words and numbers written by the second person. After each such entry, the syringe count started over.

As the years passed, the time between entries increased until, beginning in 2001, the gap reached six months where it remained. The words changed, too. Syringes were no longer mentioned, just "injections" of differing amounts of "product." The notations in "Blood" stopped altogether in 2006.

The other tabs were labeled "Bones," "Brain," "Eyes," "Fat," "Muscles," "Organs," "Skin," and "All." The notes were the same as those in "Blood," and covered the same time period, except for "All." The pages behind that tab began in 2006, and appeared at 6-month intervals. The last one, in writing different from all the others, was dated June 20, 2010.

"What is it?" Alex said.

The words themselves conveyed nothing, but the binder's import was clear. Teddy Black had been "created" by Frank Steiner, the prototype of the "superman" Wes Vaughn had predicted. The first words in the book were Steiner's. He'd begun the experiment in Cambridge, then moved the child to a small, Southern backwater far from prying eyes. Somehow he'd prevailed on James Edwards to watch the boy and maintain the genetic regime. Cosmo Ender was the middleman.

Questions remained. What role had Paul and Sylvia Black really played? Were their deaths accidental or not? What made Edwards participate? And Jamal Moore was still unaccounted for. His mother had been killed because she knew the story, and it seemed likely that Samantha was dead for the same reason.

Had Steiner learned that his secret was about to be exposed? Had Jack Peeler acted to prevent the damage such a disclosure would cause? What about Teddy? He, too, had a lot to lose. "It's – the future," I said. I muttered a quick explanation, then looked at my watch. "We're expected next door for cocktails."

VIRGINIA WAS fragile but determined to carry on her rituals. "I'd like a vodka tonic, Harry. Alex?"

"I'll have one, too."

I made the drinks while Alex began small talk about Virginia's past 24 hours, plans for Anita's funeral – she would lie next to her son at

Greenwood Cemetery – and the possibility of Cat coming home for a few days. "Will she come for the funeral?" Alex said.

"I don't know. She has exams and – and there's Teddy." Virginia brightened. "Christmas vacation starts next week. I'm sure they'll come home then."

I wasn't so sure, but didn't say so. It was still football season, after all. Taking a deep breath, I said, "When was the last time you were inside The Dependency?"

Her face assumed the flat expression I'd seen before. "Not for a long, long time." Gesturing at her body, she said, "Not since this happened." She looked away. "James used it when he was alive. Anita looked after it."

"Have you ever been in the upstairs front room?"

Her features set even harder. "Not – not since I was a girl."

I held up the binder. "Do you know what this is?" She shook her head, and I waited a few beats. "Did you teach him to play the piano?"

She slumped in the chair, head bowed. When she looked up, tears were rolling down her face. "No," she said in a whisper.

Alex broke in. "Virginia." She turned her head. "We've been in that room." Virginia looked back at me. "We know what happened there. Why were you and – and your family involved?"

She raised herself up and struck the arms of the wheelchair with both fists. "Because of this," she said. "Because of this goddamned chair and these –" she slapped her thighs "– goddamned useless legs. He said he could fix it, that Teddy would lead to a cure, but it had to be a secret."

"Who?"

"Gerry Ender. He told us it would only be a few years, that the scientists were nearly there. I've been in this chair almost half my life." She looked at the piano. "And yes, I taught Teddy to play. He played like an angel. Much better than I ever did."

"So," I said, "Teddy was an experiment to – to cure disease?"

"Yes."

I hesitated. "Didn't you ever wonder about his – skills?"

She dropped her eyes. "No."

"Why were the Blacks involved?" I said.

"Because of Catherine. It would be hard for a child to keep it secret. The Blacks lived right next door, and they owed me a favor."

"Do you know Frank Steiner?" Alex said.

"No."

"Have you ever heard of him?" Virginia shook her head. "Where did Teddy come from?"

"I don't know. He just showed up one day with Gerry."

"Did you know Anita had a little boy?" I said. She nodded. "Did his death have anything to do with this?"

She frowned. "I don't see how. He died before I ever heard of Teddy Black. I went to his funeral."

I nodded and handed her the book. "Can you identify the handwriting?"

She turned the pages. "I don't know who wrote this," she said first. Then: "This is Gerry's, and this is James's."

"Look at the last page. Whose writing is that?"

"Catherine's."

I sat back in my chair. "Why are you afraid?"

"Everyone's dead, except me. And Catherine. I don't want to die." She stopped. "And I want him to keep his promise. He says the experiment is over."

NINE

WE LEFT right after the funeral. The mourners were few. I looked for the man from the service station, and didn't see him. Cosmo Ender was a no-show, too.

After considering several options – bodyguards, police protection, new live-in help – we finally decided to take Virginia with us. She didn't know the whole story, but she might know enough to be a target. Cat wouldn't have to choose between her mother and Teddy.

We made the trip to New Hope in silence. Virginia was exhausted, and Alex was in a funk, the first I'd seen since she left Steiner's clinic. My attempts at conversation went unacknowledged.

The stakes were higher now. Samantha's death, a potential murder only I suspected, had been my motivation up to now. When Helen was arrested for Vera Carr's murder, I signed on to prove her innocent. The identity of Vera's real killer was not my concern, but the note to Jeff Farnham and the one in Anita's room had been written by the same person, and Samantha's story was the reason Anita was dead.

Was it my job to find the killer? I'd advised the Twin Rivers authorities to get in touch with Jeff Farnham and, between them, maybe they would solve the two killings they considered crimes, but Samantha was still a suicide. The personal stakes were higher, too. If the three dead women were linked, someone had gone to extraordinary lengths to keep them quiet. One more death – mine – wouldn't matter.

I pondered the notion that the experiment was "over." Why now? Was it because Teddy had proved so successful on the football field? It didn't seem likely. Teddy was "super" in comparison to his opponents and teammates, but the genetic superman was superior in all respects, a breed apart physically and intellectually.

There were people who matched Teddy in size and speed and strength, though perhaps not in a single package, and he'd been admitted to the College as a "challenged" student. He may have been better than others who played his games, and he played the piano like an angel, but it was incremental – a large increment, to be sure, but still within reach. He was not the ultimate man predicted by Cosmo Ender and feared by Wes Vaughn.

Then why was it over? It was certainly possible that the experiments with Teddy had contributed to Steiner's research on genetic diseases, and I had no doubt he could cleanse Virginia of her illness if he wanted to. Alex was proof of that. Was he finished? Was disease vanquished and death fought to a standstill? A thought, nagging for weeks, re-surfaced: Who was I in this brave new world?

ABBY WAS bent, locking the door, as I crossed High Street. "Hey," I called.

She looked over her shoulder, then turned the lock again and pushed the door open. The twins she carried were beginning to show. "I didn't know you were back," she said.

"Leaving a little early, are we?"

She laughed. "I'm getting an injection at the clinic this morning. I'll be back in an hour."

Steiner and "injections" had become a couplet with ambiguous connotations. There was Alex on the one hand, and Teddy on the other. "What's it for?"

She shook her head. "Something about making sure the babies get enough nutrients from me. It's supposed to be the last one." She stepped down from the porch. "I'll see you in a few minutes."

Inside, I opened a drawer and scoured the consent forms the Spillers had signed. There was nothing about injections. Had the procedure changed, or was it something else? Or, was paranoia setting in? As far as I knew, everything Steiner had done was good. Alex was cancer-free, and the Project Sickle Cell patients were cured. Ninety-nine percent of the babies created in his clinic were alive and well. The Teddy Black experiment seemed dubious, but I really knew nothing about it. Alex had been kept secret for good reason – maybe Teddy was, too.

On the other hand, three women were dead. Two of them knew about Teddy, and the person who killed Anita Moore had murdered Vera Carr as well. Virginia Edwards, also in on the Teddy Black experiment, feared for her life. If Steiner or Ender were responsible for all the death, Alex and I might be on the list as well.

There was a surprise in the mail. Rather than months, the state Supreme Court had taken just more than a week to deny our request that it consider the fingerprinting appeal. Steiner would not be a happy camper. I reached for the phone, but it rang before I lifted the receiver. "Harry Monmouth."

"Jeff Farnham, Harry. Calling about the fingerprint analysis you asked for."

"What did you find?"

"Nothing. We raised all the prints on the paper, eliminated yours and Abby's, and sent them to Washington and Lyon. There was no record in either place."

It was another blow to the conspiracy that had been forming in my head. Steiner was a law-abiding citizen who had avoided fingerprinting for more than 60 years. "What about the forensics exam?"

There was a pause. "You were right. They found Vera Carr's blood and hair on the edge of the hearth."

"Great. Will you let Helen out of jail now?"

"We've talked about it, Harry. I don't know. She still could've killed her."

"And left the bloody rug there for you to find? And hauled the body a quarter of a mile?"

"Yeah – well –"

"Have you talked to the Raven County Sheriff?"

"Yes."

"Don't you think that makes your note a little suspicious?"

"Well –"

"Bobby Hood will. I'll wait two days to file my bail petition. Tell the County Attorney he's going to look silly if he doesn't let her go before then."

I pushed the button down and called the Head Matron at the Women's Institute. After leaving a message for Helen, I dialed another number. Missy wasn't in, so I left word again. Abby leaned in the door. "I'm back," she said.

She looked tired. The first frenzy of excitement was long over, and the responsibility that comes with children – even before they're born – had begun to set in. "Everything okay?"

She took a deep breath. "Yes. We're all fine."

"Are you sure?"

"Yes."

"Good. Would you get Frank Steiner on the phone for me, please?"

She shook her head. "He's gone. One of his assistants did the injection."

"Where to?"

"London."

"How long's he going to be away?"

"I don't know."

The phone rang again. Abby answered. "It's Missy Farrell," she said.

I took the receiver. "I guess you've seen the mail this morning?" Missy said.

"Yes."

"When can you deliver your client to the Sheriff's Office?"

I laughed. "I don't know."

"Why not?" she said, outrage poised.

"He's out of the country. What can I do?"

"That sonofabitch. He'll do –"

"He doesn't even know about the order. And I told him not to expect it for another two months."

I paused. "The Sheriff already has a set of his prints. Why don't –?"

"Why?"

"It doesn't matter. Check 'em out."

"Well –"

"Jeff might tell you there's no record of the prints, but don't take his word for it. Or mine. Satisfy yourself."

HELEN DIDN'T wait to hear what I had to say. There was something on her mind. "I killed her, Harry," she said in a soft voice.

I was startled. "Who?"

"Samantha. I killed her. Like I stuck the needle in her arm myself."

It was hard keeping it all straight. I rearranged my thoughts. "How?"

"I betrayed her. More – more than once. She finally had enough."

The change in demeanor was welcome and troubling at the same time. The twisted features in the courtroom had become resigned. I probed. "So – Samantha committed suicide because of you?"

"Yes. She'd threatened it before. I didn't believe her, but this time she meant it."

"Why?"

"Because I'm a pig. I cheated on her over and over until I was so sick of myself I finally ran away. She followed me to New Hope. She said she'd give up the dope, and we decided to try again. But there was Vera and – and others." She stopped. "She caught me with Vera that night. There was a – an argument, and Vera fell and hurt her head. Samantha was out of her mind. She said she'd kill us."

"You didn't take that seriously, did you?"

"I didn't know. That was the worst I'd ever seen her. And when Vera was murdered, I didn't know what to think." The tawny eyes stared into mine. "I've made my peace with it, Harry. I wanted someone to know."

I didn't like the sound of that. "What happened the night Samantha died?"

"We talked. The same words we'd said a dozen times. I think she realized who I was at last, that I couldn't truly love her the way she loved me." She closed her eyes. "She gave up."

It was another revelation. The picture should have provided a clue. I knew that Helen and Samantha were capable of jealousy and rage – just like me – but my personal link to both of them got in the way. "There was a picture on the piano –"

"I took it when I left," she said. "I didn't know what would happen." She blinked for a few seconds. "I didn't want anyone to know about – us."

I nodded. "What about her wallet? And the laptop?" She shook her head. I debated the next question. "Did Samantha ever mention her will? Who would get her – things when she died?"

I watched her carefully. "No," she said.

We sat quietly for a minute or two. "I think they'll let you out of here pretty soon," I said. I explained the new evidence. She heard me, but I don't think she was listening.

I rose to leave. She reached for my hand. "Pray for me, Harry." I checked the visitor's log on my way out. Her parents had come to see her, and I'd just missed the priest from St. Thomas More. Cat Edwards had been there every day.

I stopped by the Matron's office, but she wasn't there. After leaving a note, I passed through the gate to the parking lot. Suicide was back in the mix – resurrected by that hoary staple of human suffering, unrequited love – but questions remained. Helen had surrendered in the battle with herself. I said a rusty prayer.

"**YOU HAVE** a visitor," Abby said, as I passed through the door. I raised my brows. "Cosmo Ender."

I looked through the doorway into my office. He was standing by the window, staring out at the parking lot. I crossed the threshold. "Doctor Ender?" He turned. The carnation was white this time. "Have a seat."

"I can't stay, Harry." He remained standing. "I understand that Virginia Edwards is visiting you?"

"Yes."

"I'd like to see her."

"Okay."

"Good. I'll call tomorrow. Thanks."

He turned for the door. "Cosmo?"

He looked back, smiling. "Yes."

"Can we talk for a minute?" He hesitated, then sat in the chair in front of my desk. "Virginia's afraid of something."

"She is? Of what?"

"I don't know exactly. You, maybe."

The blood rose in his face. "That's ridiculous. She's not afraid of me. I – love her. She knows that."

"Did you know her maid was killed the other day?"

"I know she drowned."

"And the Blacks, not so long ago. Her husband." He was silent, his face frozen. "They all had something in common – Teddy Black." There was still no response. "I know who Teddy is, Cosmo."

"I know. Virginia told me."

"What do you know about how his parents died?"

He rose. "Nothing."

"What about Steiner?"

"What about him?"

I hesitated. "Has he been to Twin Rivers recently?" He laughed. "You told Virginia the experiment was over. What does that mean?"

"Just what I said. It's over."

"Are you talking about Teddy?"

He turned away. At the door, he looked back. "If I were you, Harry, I'd quit worrying about Virginia Edwards and Teddy Black. Stay closer to home." He disappeared through the doorway.

I considered the threat. Was it lethal? The idea that I knew about Teddy had barely registered. Would Steiner stop Alex's treatment if I didn't back off? Our new life was precious. The notion that it might be taken from us was chilling. One way or another, Steiner *was* playing God – what was given could be taken away.

And what did I care, really, about Teddy Black and Virginia Edwards? It was just an adventure, a game to take my mind off my troubles. Those troubles were gone now, relieved by a magician named Frank Steiner. There was no reason why I should continue trying to piece the puzzle together.

ALEX DREW the nightgown over her head and stood before the full-length mirror. I watched as she turned, first one way and then the other, then stepped closer to examine the details of her face. Backing up, she weighed her breasts in her hands and let the fingers slide down her torso to her hips. Provoked by the unknowing eroticism, I pressed against her from behind. "Taking inventory?" I said. She pushed back, and we fell into bed.

An hour later, she rolled over and switched on a lamp. After a moment, she rose and returned to the mirror. I propped my head on my hand to watch. She turned toward me. "Something's wrong," she said.

I smiled. "Not that I can tell. You look perfect to me."

"That's what's wrong."

"What do you mean?"

She sat down on the bed, and leaned toward me. "Look at my hair. The gray's all gone."

"A by-product of your treatment, I imagine."

She thrust out her hands. "I've had spots on my hands for 10 years. They're gone, too." She cupped her breasts. "I haven't been this – firm since the baby was born. That's 30 years ago."

"Are you complaining?" There was no response. I wasn't quite ready to say what I believed. "My theory is that Steiner's treatment cleaned up miscellaneous bad cells while it was getting rid of the cancer."

She shook her head. "*Age* causes gray hair and liver spots, Harry."

So much for theories. "What are you saying?"

"I'm – not sure. All I know is my defects seem to be disappearing. Even my eyes."

"What about your eyes?"

"I've worn reading glasses since I was a child. I don't need them anymore. My vision's perfect."

Alex had been outspoken about genetic engineering. She didn't want to become a machine serviced by Steiner in his laboratory. Now the very thing she feared had come to pass, something we still couldn't put into words, and her reaction wasn't rage but wonder.

I finally had to face it. I was afraid, not for Alex, nor for a world overpopulated by Methuselahs, but for me. I looked at the spots on my own hands. A few short weeks ago, Alex was old beyond her years, near death, and I was planning a life without her. Now I was closer to the grave than she. Maybe God and genetics could coexist after all.

TEN

THE CONFERENCE championship was played before a nationwide television audience on a Thursday night in early December. The opponent was the College's most hated rival, the private school down the road in Five Points. Seven minutes into the second quarter, the score was 45-0 and, despite the boos and catcalls directed at the coaching staff, Teddy spent the rest of the evening on the bench. His statistics were so overwhelming there was no need to risk injury to pad them.

The play-by-play announcer was especially upset at Teddy's departure. Teddy and the coaches and the College "owed" the country a longer look, not least because the network's second half sponsors would suffer, though he didn't mention that. Sure enough, the next day the ratings services reported a sharp drop in viewers for the second half. It was another demonstration, if one were needed, of the solid gold status of Teddy Black.

As expected, the media had found its way to Twin Rivers. The story of the foundling from Cedar Grove Cemetery was chewed over for weeks, but so far the trail grew cold with the deaths of Paul and Sylvia Black. Cat was coming under increasing scrutiny. Dubbed "the girl next door," the speculation ranged from childhood sweetheart to ruthless Svengali, tropes that required no effort and little imagination. The sports networks had established outposts in New Hope for the duration of the season, and the College had supplemented its security details with off-duty policemen and state troopers. It was the gaudiest circus yet, and Teddy the gladiator nonpareil.

Vera Carr's murder was important again. Why was she dead? Whatever threat Samantha had made, and despite Helen's fears, Samantha wasn't Vera's killer. Samantha was left-handed. According to the coroner, the blow that killed Vera was struck with a right hand.

I had reluctantly concluded that Jack Peeler was my prime suspect. His football team was on the verge of a championship that would set him up for life. Samantha had confided something that might end the dream. Plus, Jack lived in Samantha's building. It would be a simple matter to climb the stairs from the fourth floor, or take the elevator, and talk his way into her apartment. A suggestion that he was reconsidering the interview request would probably do it.

Unfortunately, all of that was deemed "circumstantial" by the law, and there was a big flaw. My motive for Vera's death was her notion that the players couldn't read, and couldn't possibly be eligible to play football, but I only had her word for that. I reflected again on the seeming absurdity of the charge. More would be needed to make it the reason for her murder. And I needed "direct" evidence that Jack was responsible for at least one death. I had conceived a way to get at it, but required cooperation from an unlikely quarter.

I passed Abby at her desk. "I'm going to get some lunch," I said. "I'll be back in an hour or so."

Missy Farrell was standing on the brick walkway. "I was just coming to see you," she called. Small and slim as a boy, the huge green eyes watched me approach. Her chestnut hair was a helmet that encased prominent cheekbones, a full mouth and Roman nose. The business-like expression grudgingly gave way to her usual smile.

"Have lunch with me," I said.

"Okay."

"Franky's?"

"Fine."

A few minutes later we were seated at the table in the window. She removed two sheets of paper from her purse and handed me one. "That's from the FBI," she said. "No matches." I grinned. She gave me the other sheet. "From Interpol. The prints belong to someone named Wilhelm Egger."

"But – they had nothing the first time."

"My search had no time limits. The Interpol prints were taken in Berlin in 1930. Egger worked at the Kaiser Wilhelm Institute. He was 26 years old at the time."

"But –"

"Steiner swears he was born in 1943. The prints on the paper you gave Jeff Farnham were made by a man who was 39 in 1943." She paused. "He's 106 now."

It seemed impossible, but I knew it wasn't. Steiner – Egger – had experimented on himself. At some point in the past, he had "reduced" his age just as he'd done for Alex. But I wasn't ready to deal with it yet. I needed to talk to Ender. "It's obviously a mistake," I said.

She stared at me. "Maybe. I have a call in to Lyon. I'll let you know."

THE TELEPHONE was ringing. I heard Alex answer it. "It's for you," she called up the stairs. "Jeff Farnham."

I stepped into the hallway and picked up the receiver. "Hello?"

"Harry, I have bad news." He paused. "Helen Tanner's dead. She hanged herself in the shower this morning."

The shock I didn't feel condemned me. My note to the Matron had suggested that Helen be "supervised" more closely than usual, and maybe she was, but it wasn't enough. Someone bent on death was hard to deter.

Helen was a bomb at the end of a long fuse. Lit years before when she realized she was not who she was supposed to be, it grew precariously shorter when everyone else knew it, too. The last shred of fuse burned away when she assumed responsibility for Samantha's death, and the bomb exploded. I had added to her despair and I owed her more than a note to the Matron, but the truth was I didn't really believe she'd do it. In love with life again, a desire for death was inconceivable to me.

The idea that she had actually killed Samantha was still alive, barely. It was possible she'd done it for the money, and hanged herself when the money wasn't forthcoming, but I didn't believe it. "Have you called her parents?" I said.

"Yes. The coroner has the body."

"I want the charges against her dropped."

"Well, obviously we can't —"

"No. I don't want her to be an accused murderer when she goes to her grave. I'll file a motion if I have to, and I'll make it as nasty as I can."

"I'll – look into it."

"Thanks." Alex was standing in the foyer be-low me. I leaned over the banister. "Helen's killed herself."

"Oh, God." After a moment, she said, "Why?"

I couldn't share her troubles with anyone, not even Alex. "I don't know."

ABBY KNOCKED on the door and pushed it open. "Ms. Wells is here," she said.

I rose. Some routine business had piled up. Samantha's estate still required my attention, and a complete evaluation of her property was at the top of the list. Wendy Wells was an old friend who had taken over her father's very successful real es-tate business a few years earlier. Her office was just down the street. After the preliminary pleas-antries, I said, "I need an appraisal of one of the penthouses at The High. Is that within your area of expertise?"

She laughed. "Absolutely. You're talking about Samantha Clarke's place?" I nodded. "An appraisal's no problem, but – would you be inter-ested in selling it?"

"Sure, if the price is right."

"What about the furniture? Would you sell the place furnished?"

"Same answer. Why?"

"I showed the other one – the empty one – to a client several months ago. He liked it, but the idea of paint and wallpaper and furniture was too much."

"Who was it?"

"Win Honeyman. He's going to retire pretty soon. He'll need a place to live."

I nodded again. "I'll still have to have it all appraised, but I if you bring me a price for the whole thing I'll consider it."

"Okay. Thanks."

I looked out the window and pointed. "I have a red Porsche, too. Do you think the Chancellor would buy it?" She laughed again.

An hour later, I turned onto High Street and drove west. It was time to return the Porsche to its garage, and while I was there I could make a list of the truly personal things that would be excluded if the Chancellor bought the condominium furnished. I wasn't sure who might want them, but couldn't bear the thought they might simply be discarded.

The entrance to the garage was from West Second Street. I stopped at the striped barrier and inserted a key. The bar lifted. I unlocked the door to the mailroom and used the same key to call the garage elevator and select my floor, and to open the door to Samantha's apartment.

There wasn't much – her clothes, of course, the statue next to the bed, a silver comb-and-brush set in the bathroom. I picked up the brush. A few strands of blonde hair wound through the bristles, a tiny bit of her left behind. After tucking the Twin Rivers yearbook under my arm, I paused in the vestibule to lock the door. The entrance to the other apartment was directly across the hall. I hesitated, then tried the door. It was locked.

Back in the office, I turned the pages of the yearbook idly, my mind elsewhere. Helen had removed the picture and stuffed the frame in the piano bench, but the wallet and laptop were still unaccounted for. Despite what Helen had said, and done, I refused to believe Samantha had killed herself.

I heard someone enter the outer office. Abby was at lunch, so I walked to the door. "Hey, Harry," Wes Vaughn said. "Do you have a few minutes?"

"Sure."

He followed me into my office. "I know you're not part of the sickle cell litigation," he said, "but we need your help. And your client's."

"I'll do what I can. I can't speak for Steiner."

He nodded. "Everybody in Project Sickle Cell is turning white."

I laughed. "What?"

"It's not funny, Harry. It starts about three months after the treatment. Of the 410 patients, 301 of them are partially white. Or pink. Like you." He stopped. "And it's progressive. It begins with an arm or a face and goes from there. The first few patients are about 80 percent white. It's not just skin color. Hair is changing. Eyes, too. Half of them have blue eyes now." He stopped again. "We want Steiner to fix it."

I recalled Steiner's contempt for the sickle cell patients and the people who forced him to start the program. Was this a side effect that would've been eliminated during the clinical trial he wanted? Or was it intentional, arbitrary payback? Was Steiner turning black people white just because he could? Another thought occurred to me, and I set it aside. "Steiner's out of the country," I said. "I don't know when he's coming back." I considered. "I'll talk to your friend Ender. Maybe he can help."

ENDER AND Virginia were in the living room. "How long's he been here?" I said.

"About an hour," Alex said.

"Any fireworks?" She shook her head. As I watched, Ender rose and bent to kiss Virginia. On his way out, he nodded to me, and opened the front door. "Do you have a second?" I said. He stopped and turned around. "I know you're close to Frank Steiner. What – what's the plan?"

"What do you mean?"

"He's cured Alex of cancer and apparently made her – younger. He – and you – have made Teddy a sort of superman. You've promised to make Virginia walk again. What's next?"

"You should ask him."

"He's not here."

"Ask him when he comes back. If he comes back." He turned away.

"Wait. He's not coming back?"

"I don't know. It depends on you."

"Me?"

He hesitated. "I have a proposition for you, Harry, but I'm not quite ready to make it. I'm leaving town myself for a few days. When I get back, I'll be in touch. Please don't do anything rash in the meantime." We'd reached his car. "I'll see you." He opened the door.

"Can I ask you something else?" He waited. "The Project Sickle Cell patients are turning white." He smiled. "Do you know why?"

"No, but I can guess."

"What is it?"

"It's like everything else. Skin is an organ. Skin color is determined by our genes. People of European descent have white genes, and people from Africa have black genes." He climbed into the car.

"And it can be altered?"

"Yes, easily. The black gene is actually the norm. The white gene is a mutant."

I stood there until he was out of sight. Ender or Steiner, or both, wanted to make a deal, presumably to ensure my silence concerning Teddy Black. If I didn't agree, Steiner might not return from Europe. Something might happen to me.

It seemed silly in a way. His methods – performing clandestine experiments on an abandoned child – could certainly be criticized. There might even be laws against it, which would explain his journey overseas. But his success was beyond question. Beauty, strength, endurance, had all been bestowed on that child. Steiner had even installed a "creative" gene for music. Teddy was a big step toward the superior being at the end of the rainbow. Inevitably, ethics would give way to the acclaim of "science," and the people would go along.

Tampering with Project Sickle Cell, on the other hand, would enrage an influential segment of the populace, but Steiner could call the "white" skin a side effect and offer to fix it. It was an option that would surely roil the black community. Skin had served as the great divide for centuries – it was arguably more profound than gender. The notion that someone could *choose* his color raised all kinds of possibilities.

The idea that had been festering since Wes Vaughn's visit returned. I leaned in the door. "I need to check something at the office," I called. "I'll be back in a few minutes." I walked down the hill and crossed the street. Seated behind my desk, I unlocked a drawer and withdrew the scotch and the red leather binder. I poured the scotch, and turned to the tab marked "Skin."

HELEN'S PEOPLE were originally from New Hope, and the family plot was in the Old New Hope Cemetery. The crowd stood five deep around her bier and the pavilion erected for the family. Maybe she wasn't as alone as she thought.

The priest was nearly finished. I usually ignored the preaching aimed at a captive funeral audience, but this time it made me angry. Her religion no longer slaughtered those who disagreed with them – its own adherents were the victims now. Helen and countless others had succumbed because they couldn't force themselves into the mold created by the priests. Dogma designed to preserve power and wealth made them heretics, forever denied the redemption they were taught to seek.

But rituals were for the living. I found Helen's parents and identified myself, and introduced Alex. Mrs. Cheek cried when I told them the murder charge had been dismissed. Mr. Cheek limited himself to a still firm handshake and a nod. I let Alex go home, and remained behind to commune with the ghosts.

Climbing to the highest ground in the cemetery, I sat on a marble bench next to the stone with my grandfather's name on it. He'd been at the center of a scandal that convinced Alex and me to move our burial ground to a less ostentatious location 50 yards away. Samantha's grave, not yet healed, was on the other side of the bench.

"Harry?"

I turned my head. "Hi, Cat."

"Can I join you?"

"Sure."

I made room on the bench and she sat down. We gazed across the walls and the stones and the grass, much as we'd watched Teddy and his team-mates at practice three months earlier. "She was my friend," Cat said. I nodded. "I'm not ashamed of it."

"Good." We sat quietly. "Ready for the big game?"

She sighed. "I guess so."

"Teddy's due for another injection pretty soon, isn't he?" She stared at me. "According to your note in the red binder, the last one was on June 20. Right?"

She hesitated. "Yes."

"Do you do it?" She nodded. "What does he think about it, Cat? It can't be very – satisfying."

"He doesn't know."

"What?"

"He doesn't know. He forgets it as soon as I've finished. Just like he's forgotten everything else."

"You mean – he doesn't remember anything that's happened to him?"

"It's part of the treatment."

"Not even that bed?"

"It hasn't been used for years. If he ever knew about it, he doesn't remember it now."

I nodded again. That was probably in the details behind the "Brain" tab. "Why do you do it?"

"For my mother. And for him. I'm – We're responsible for who he is. I feel sorry for him." She looked at me. "What would happen to him if I didn't?"

"It won't be a secret forever. Believe me. What'll happen to him then?" She didn't answer. "What does he think when you're brandishing the needle?"

"He thinks it's for his asthma." I lifted a brow. "He has asthma. The injection takes care of that, too."

We were silent again. "How's the investigation going?" she said.

"It's not. The Chancellor put the quash on it."

"Why?"

"Because he didn't want Vera Carr's murder to taint the football team."

"Did you know she took her story to Jack Peeler?"

"Vera?"

"Yes. She told him the players can't read."

"When?"

"Right after she had lunch with you."

"Did she tell you that?"

She shook her head. "She told Helen. Helen told me."

I turned to face her. "Is that what you were talking about that day at practice? That the football team can't read?"

"No."

"You said there were two sets of rules. What did you mean?"

She hesitated. "Most of us play by the College's rules. The football players play by the Organization's rules. They aren't the same thing."

ELEVEN

THE CLASS was called "The Importance of Being You," and it was worth three credit hours a semester. Every desk was occupied, so I had to move a chair from the room next door. I knew none of the faces, and I hoped no one recognized me.

There were several football players present, discernible by their bulk, but there were many obvious non-athletes as well. That was reassuring – it would be impossible to conduct such a class without exposing the students who couldn't read. Some of them were nodding – induced by the soporific lecture on the evils of "judgmentalism" – but I ignored that. I'd slept through lots of classes in college and law school.

There was no class participation. The instructor spoke and the students, most of them, listened. I looked around the room. No one had a book open, and no one was taking notes – understandable in the case of football players who just wanted to get by – but, again, the 80 percent who weren't football players didn't have books or notes, either. They just listened as if expecting to absorb the material by osmosis.

After class, in my guise as field man for one of the accrediting organizations, I remained behind to talk to the professor. "This is primarily a lecture course, I guess?" I said.

"Yes."

"Is there a textbook?"

"No. There's other required reading – Internet, newspapers, that type of thing."

I nodded. "I noticed no one was taking notes. Is there a final exam?"

He shook his head. "There's a colloquy."

"A what?"

"A colloquy. Each student derives an argument from the class syllabus and what he's read during the semester, and defends it."

"Verbally? With you?"

"Yes. Like defending a dissertation." He paused. "My lectures give them a frame of reference."

"Meaning what, exactly?"

He stared at me. "They learn the parameters of acceptable ideas from me. Information from other sources is draped on that framework."

"I see." I hesitated. "Do any of your students have trouble reading the materials?"

His gaze grew more intense. "Of course not. They're in college, aren't they?"

I had 20 minutes to make my next class. The belief that a kid could read just because he was in college was universal – I shared it myself. But that assumption was grounded in the notion that teachers taught and students learned, a paradigm Helen claimed was no longer operative. Certainly, there was nothing in "The Importance of Being You" that guaranteed a literate pupil.

The next two classes were identical to the first in structure and rigor. The football players were again far outnumbered by ordinary students. Walking back to the office, I kicked around the idea that this was what higher education had become, and rejected it because I knew there were still math and physics and chemistry departments at the College. Surely they required more than a "colloquy" to advance.

I stopped at the Registrar's Office, and picked up a catalogue of all the courses offered on campus. Undergraduates were 60 percent of the students, the overwhelming majority enrolled in the School of Arts and Sciences. I confirmed that the "Sciences" classes required the usual labs, textbooks, papers and final exams.

Most of those in the "Arts" did, too, but there were about 40 – one or two in almost every department – where the course descriptions were identical to those I had attended today: "Seminar combined with independent study. One-on-one with instructor." About half had a further notation: "Upper Level." The classes were taught by 12 different professors.

I studied the class schedules I'd received from Helen's office. Of the 24 freshman football players, all were attending at least two of the 40 "seminars" except one – Teddy Black. He was a music major, and none of the doubtful courses were conducted by the music department. Nineteen of the players were enrolled only in the "seminar" classes.

There were probably 800 students in those 40 classes. Of those, no more than 100 were football players. There was no requirement that they do anything except perhaps argue with their instructors at the end of the semester. Reading and writing were unnecessary, and grades would be

whatever the teachers wanted them to be. I sus-
pected the grades were pretty good.

It wasn't coincidence. The players had been
directed to those courses, undoubtedly by "counse-
lors" paid by the Athletic Department. It would be
hard for Jack Peeler not to know about it. But
what, exactly, could he do? He wasn't responsible
for the curriculum at the College, or the 700 stu-
dents who weren't football players. I decided to go
over Jack's head.

I turned to another issue. Cosmo Ender had
made an appointment for 10:00 A.M. Wednesday,
two days hence. I had examined the Teddy Black
affair from every angle. In the broadest sense, of
course, it was unfair. That a creature of science
would prevail over "ordinary" boys wasn't right.
But the titans of college football, all of them, were
always looking for an edge. Fancy nutrition,
weight training, psychology – not to mention facili-
ties that drew the finest of those ordinary players –
were only the latest innovations. Who among them
would turn away a Teddy Black, whether they
knew of his advanced genetics or not?

The Organization had rules against "perfor-
mance enhancing" drugs. They had detected none
in Teddy because he was who he was – a man
whose very being had been altered, whose genetic
makeup was superior to that of everyone else.
Theoretically, there were more to come. Perhaps
they were already among us, and someday all the
players might be supermen. Should Teddy be con-
demned because he was the first, a state of affairs
he neither asked for nor knew about?

He was a godsend for fans and media, and a
topic of conversation for the whole country. A ce-

lebrity who refused to join in the celebration, he was the object of unending fascination, and the dollars he generated for untold endeavors were immense. Jack had warned me of the perils of messing with Teddy Black. Was I ready to kill the golden goose?

And maybe Teddy was the real victim. He performed without the burden of knowing the source of his talent, and would undoubtedly go on to great fame and fortune, but his life had been confiscated. What would that life have been? I thought I knew but, again, someone else would have to help.

I was left with the idea that Steiner feared the law. It seemed ludicrous. He was above the petty regulations that governed the rest of us. What would Ender offer for my silence? Why did he care? If I was right, that Steiner would ultimately be hailed as a god, Ender would share in the homage. What was the downside for him?

Interpol stood by its report that the fingerprints belonged to a very old man named Wilhelm Egger. I continued to scoff, and insisted that Steiner would provide his real prints when he returned. Missy didn't buy it, but agreed to await the inevitable.

THE CHANCELLOR'S House was a yellow frame mansion on the corner of Capital and High Streets. The oaks and poplars were bare, the lilacs and azaleas ragged. Only the ancient magnolias provided shade from the setting winter sun. I climbed to the entrance portico, passed between twin triangles of Corinthian columns, and knocked on the door.

The Chancellor himself greeted me. "Harry. Come in." I stepped into the high foyer and followed him to a warm, book-lined room with a fireplace that occupied half the outside wall. The logs were piled high, and the crackling flames provided a welcome antidote to the cold outside. "Let me have your coat," he said. He gestured to a compact, leather-covered bar in the corner. "Fix yourself a drink."

The liquor was all in crystal decanters with silver labels draped over the necks. I filled a glass with ice, picked up the jug marked "Scotch," and poured. Winfred Honeyman sat in the wingback chair next to the hearth, and I lowered myself onto the leather sofa opposite him. There was something different about him. Maybe it was the missing tie.

I told him my story. When I was finished, the Chancellor said, "Are you telling me we have crip courses on campus? We've always had them. Every school does." He smiled. "'Football Physics.' 'Home Ec for Husbands.' I took one myself. In summer school." He smiled again. "I got an A."

"There are at least 40 of these classes, Win. They've been offered every semester for 15 years, and 820 kids are enrolled now. The average grade last semester was B. There were no D's or F's."

"A lot of our kids carry heavy academic loads. What's wrong with them taking on something a little easier?"

"These are the only courses our football players are taking."

He glared at me. "Why have you interested yourself in this? I thought you agreed to quit prying into the football team."

I chose not to challenge his recollection of my earlier errand. "The players aren't learning anything here. This – arrangement has to be a violation of the Organization's rules."

"Not if you keep your mouth shut." Then, recovering himself, he said, "The Organization doesn't require that the players learn anything. All they have to do is maintain a certain grade point average."

"But the College –"

"We do what we can. These kids are completely unprepared when they get here. You can't expect us to turn them into Shakespeare scholars overnight."

"So they shouldn't be here at all?" He didn't respond. "What about the others, the ones with the grades and the test scores? Why allow them to take these classes?"

"We need them."

"What?"

"We –" He rose. "It's been a long day, Harry. Thanks for dropping by."

I stood there for a moment, then found my coat and went to the door alone. It was dark, and the moon only a sliver in the southern sky. Home was just a block east, but I chose the office instead. I sat down and lifted my legs to the ottoman, and stared into the darkness.

I had labored under the impression that the corruption, great and small, was limited to the football team. The terrible imperative to win, the ambitions of players and coaches, the pressure from fans and media, sometimes led to behavior the College and its peers chose to prohibit. The Organization enforced those rules but, beyond requiring that its members maintain players' "grades" at a certain level, it had nothing to do with the academic side of things.

Many of the football players at the College lacked the skills to succeed there. Rather than forego the services of those players and the cash they generated, the College had created – by design or practice – an academic gulag where they could toil at nothing until their eligibility expired. There would have been criticism had this wasteland been limited to football players, so the bogus classes were open to everyone, ensuring that a wide swath of the student body wasted its time as well. None of it was a surprise to the Chancellor.

The tutors were an expensive sham created to obscure the fact that the players weren't learning anything. It was an unacknowledged kabuki in which everyone – coaches, administrators, faculty – participated. The players were the only losers.

The benefits of the education they were promised were illusory. The stars played pro football. The others, the vast majority, graduated with worthless degrees into a world that had no place for them. The cruelty was hard to accept, but it wasn't the reason Vera Carr was murdered. It wasn't against the rules, and it had been going on for a long time. A team that couldn't read, on the other hand, would be harder to overlook.

I WANTED information before entertaining his proposal. "I have some questions," I said.

Ender smiled. "All right. It'll be public pretty soon anyway."

That stopped me for a minute. If the secret was to be revealed, what did he want from me? "Who's Wilhelm Egger?"

"He's my father."

I nodded. "And who's Frank Steiner?"

"He's my father, too. They're the same man."

I should've been shocked, but I wasn't. "He's made himself younger?"

"Yes. He's been working on it most of his life."

"But how? How can somebody do that? Wasn't it apparent to the people around him?"

"He was blessed with a lot of turmoil." Ender paused. "My father worked for a man named Fritz Astel back in the '30s and '40s. Astel developed the rudiments of the procedure. He wanted to test it on the Jews. His superiors refused – long life for Jews wasn't what they had in mind." He stopped again. "My father was his guinea pig. He was Jewish, too, but Astel didn't know it."

"Why did he change his name?"

"He changed his identity altogether when Astel died. He moved all over Europe, taking the opportunity to become younger each time. It was easy in those days. The continent was in ruins, records destroyed, all that."

"How could it happen 70 years ago? I mean – the genetics business had just started."

"Astel was ahead of his time. It was primitive, of course. Father injected himself after Astel died, and he's spent his life perfecting it."

"Why isn't he younger?"

Ender laughed. "When he came to the U.S. he was in the public eye, so he let himself age, knowing he could reverse it when he was ready."

"Is he ready?"

"Yes."

"Why?"

"Long life – youth – is worth less if we're still subject to disease and malfunction. Cancer and near-sightedness, for example. It's taken years to eliminate them."

"And he's done it?"

"Yes. It's all part of the package now."

"So that – experiment is over?"

"Yes."

"And Alex was the last mouse."

He nodded. "Mrs. Monmouth is as genetically perfect as we can make an otherwise ordinary woman. She's in her mid-20s now. The rest of her life will be free of problems associated with aging." He paused. "She's the template for all who come after her."

"Will she get old again?"

"Yes, but much slower than usual. And she can do it again if she wants to."

"Is it reversible?"

"Certainly."

That was laughable, of course. Why would Alex return the years Steiner had given her? "How does he do it?"

"As we grow older, most of our cells are subject to disease and death. They're designed that way. Only the immune cells are immortal."

"How come?"

"They have an enzyme that stops cell death. Our other cells reject the enzyme. Father found a way to make the mortal cells accept it, and added new cells to replace the dead ones. It's the proverbial fountain of youth."

"Are other people working on it?"

"Yes. His work will short-circuit all that. He's generations ahead of them." He paused. "He had a big head start."

"Was Teddy Black part of the experiment?"

He nodded. "He was essential to the disease therapy." He leaned back. "There was more to Teddy, of course. We gave him some of the less subtle human characteristics – size, muscle, bone structure."

"Skin color?"

"Yes."

I hesitated. "No one's buried under that pink stone in Greenwood Cemetery, are they?"

"No."

"Anita knew about it?"

He nodded. "Jim Edwards made her a proposal, and she leaped at it."

"Why?"

"She wanted something better for her son." He straightened in his chair. "She insisted on the music gene."

We were quiet. "So Steiner's work is done?"

"Not quite."

"Why not?"

"Your wife was a fully-developed human being when her genes were altered. Teddy was four years old. They still have most of their original genes which might cause trouble we can't predict. The injections are designed to detect that."

"And?"

He rose and crossed the room to the window. "I was one of his experiments. My mother was three months pregnant with me when he sent her over here. He wanted to know if the changes he'd made to his body were passed on to me." He turned his head. "They weren't. So he branched out."

"To what?"

He leaned over the desk. "I can't say. It's not finished." He paused. "There'll be a press conference in London on Friday. There will be no names mentioned. Just the procedures and the results. It'll be highly technical, and it will take months for it to sift down to the general public."

"He's not going to mention Alex or Teddy?"

"That's right. And we ask that you do the same for the time being, say, six months. Just keep quiet. The world will have had a chance to absorb it by then. The individuals involved won't be so – immediate." What he meant was that Steiner's deification would be in full swing in six months, and Alex and Teddy wouldn't matter. "In return –"

"When's he coming back?" I said.

"Next Wednesday." He resumed his seat. "In return, he'll make you the same age as your wife."

Greedy for life I wasn't entitled to, and cowed by death inevitable till now, I coveted immortality, a preposterous notion only weeks ago. Before Steiner, death was implacable, but it was one thing if everyone died, quite another if some did not. I would do what he demanded, and join my bride in her brave new world, secure that we would live together for a very long time. "What about Virginia?"

"She'll begin her treatment as soon as he comes back." He smiled. "Everything I've done has gone into his research. I, too, shall be retrofitted."

"And the sickle cell people?"

"He'll fix those who want to be fixed."

It was all very neat, but the joy was becoming uncertain. I felt like a minor god bargaining with Zeus's emissary. I decided to try for more. "All right, but I need a favor. From you."

He blinked randomly, in the same fashion as his father. I drew a hairbrush from the drawer and handed it to him.

TWELVE

THE BALL stopped on the edge of the green and then, ever so slowly, began to roll back to the hole. Gathering speed, it struck the pin, backed up six inches and rolled into the cup. I raised my arms like the pros do on TV. Jack presented his knuckles, and I bumped them with mine.

"That'll be hard to beat," he said. Measuring his shot more carefully than usual, he struck his ball with a six-iron – I used a three-wood – and watched as it missed the hole by a foot and rolled five feet past. "That's it. You've got two strokes here." He pulled the scorecard from his pocket. "It's a push."

We retired to the bar. My game was a little better, his a little worse, but the fact was I'd negotiated a few more strokes on the first tee. We were approaching an equilibrium that might earn me a dollar or two in the future, assuming our game continued. Was he a killer or not? "Did you know Vera Carr?" I said. He shook his head. "Ever meet her?"

He hesitated. "Yes."

"When?"

"A day or two before she died."

"What was the occasion?"

"She came to my office to tell me – something about the tutor program."

"That her players couldn't read or write?"

He paused again. "Yes."

"Was that news to you?"

"Not really. Lots of people know it, or sus-pect it. They just don't know what to do about it."

"You could start by not taking advantage of those kids."

Pain crossed his face. "Is that what we're do-ing?"

"Well –"

"If they didn't come here to play football, and get a diploma, what would they do? Their – litera-cy wouldn't change. They're supposed to know how to read and write before then. It's not our fault they don't." He grimaced. "We can't go back, Har-ry. And some of them do okay."

"What do the other schools do? Are their re-cruits any better off than ours?" He shook his head. "They could go to trade school. Or junior col-lege. Or take remedial classes here."

"Or they could learn to read and write before they come." He stopped. "They do take remedial classes here. Some of them. Most aren't interest-ed."

"Why not?"

"Because they haven't been taught that, ei-ther. It's not cool." He ordered another drink. "And it's not cool to go to trade school. They're bet-ter off here than in junior college."

"Your counselors send them to phony clas-ses."

His lips pressed together. "I don't like it any better than you do, but I suspect it's a mutual choice. They don't come here to go to college – they come here to play football. The guys who don't want those classes don't pick them."

"We kid them about pro football. They kid themselves."

"That's hindsight. Everybody's not a Teddy Black in high school. How many times have you seen some kid who was barely recruited make it big in the NFL?"

Everything he said was true, but that didn't make it any better. The spectacle diverted attention from the failure of those in charge, and the people in the stands – including me – were only too willing to participate. "Speaking of Teddy Black, Samantha told you about him, didn't she?"

"What do you mean?"

"That he's been, uh, altered."

He laughed. "You mean that he was assembled in a laboratory? Like Frankenstein?" I nodded. "I didn't pay any attention to that." He laughed again. "I thought she was drunk. She sounded like it."

It took me a second to realize that, unlike me, Jack didn't live in Frank Steiner's world. What was growing commonplace to me was fantastic to him and probably everyone else. "Did you tell anybody what she said?"

"Of course not. It was crazy."

"What about Vera Carr's story?"

"I called the Chancellor because of the Organization's hot line. It wasn't necessary. He's well aware of our academic deficiencies."

MY FRIEND at the *Chronicle* had arranged a computer and monitor on Samantha's desk. "It'll start any minute now," he said. Steiner's press conference was being streamed live on a website called *Genes R You.* I took a pen and yellow pad from my briefcase and sat down to watch. Wes pulled up a chair beside me.

The podium was empty for the first minute or two, and then a man who identified himself as President of the American Pharmaceutical Association appeared. After fussing with a balky microphone, he launched into a tedious recitation of his organization's high-minded goals followed by a truncated version of Steiner's résumé. It was unremarkable until the last few lines. "The man you are about to meet was born in 1904. You won't believe that, but hear him out. He will change the world."

Steiner parted a curtain, shook hands with the man who introduced him and stood facing his audience. I was stunned. The very fit 65-year old I had last seen a few weeks earlier was now in his 30s. He no longer wore his glasses. The experiment was over, and he had shed his disguise.

I could almost feel the skepticism in the room. He went through a brief history of his self-treatment, and a technical description of what he'd achieved – a combination of Alex and Teddy Black. Besides himself, though, no human subjects were mentioned. I found what he said hard to believe, and I knew it was true. Wes stared at the screen, his expression troubled.

There were two categories of news people at the press conference. The majority came from medical publications of one sort or another – magazines, journals, websites – and the others represented general interest outlets like newspapers, networks and cable. The former, mindful of Steiner's reputation in the genetics community, were dubious, but treated him gently. The latter produced a loud, collective horse laugh.

I took a few notes. One exchange, with one of the medical types, caught my attention. "Doctor Steiner, would you explain again the need for the post-treatment injections?"

"Yes. So far, we only treat body cells in existing human beings. We can't deal with all of them – there are far too many. We don't know what impact those untreated cells will have on the subject. The injection, followed by a blood test, is intended to highlight potential problems."

"So – it's a lifelong thing?"

Steiner shook his head. "It doesn't have to be done at all. It's just a screen. If the subject doesn't care about that, he can forego the injections altogether."

I was relieved to know that Alex and I could live our lives without visiting Steiner once a month. The discussion continued: "Is that a flaw in your process?" the reporter said.

Steiner frowned. "I wouldn't call it a flaw, but old genes are a problem I hope to address."

"How?"

"Germ cells – sex cells – are far fewer, and they are more easily manipulated. Early embryos are easier still." He smiled. "We might cleanse the old genes before they really get started."

The medical segment of the audience stirred. "Are you suggesting that this treatment be extended to unborn children? And their children?" said another reporter.

"I am. When the public's ready for it, of course." His eyes started to blink. "The procedure would be slightly altered. Instead of reversing cell aging, we could just slow it down. Or maybe elimi-nate it."

Wes looked at me and nodded. I recalled Ender's words two days earlier. Steiner had "branched out" after failing to pass his altered genes on to his son. Was this the business that re-mained?

A bombshell of a different sort was dropped near the end. One of the "big media" guys, with a broad smile on his face, said, "Assuming all this pans out, Doctor Steiner, have you thought about the economic impact of these – discoveries?"

Steiner smiled, too. "You mean how much money will be made?"

"Yes."

"The disease therapy research was done un-der the auspices of the American Pharmaceutical Association. I'm sure they'll make a profit some-how." Everyone, including the Association's man, laughed. "As for the rest of it – the age reversion, the physical and creative enhancements – they're mine." He paused. "And I plan to give them away."

The room was silent. "For nothing?" said an-other reporter.

"Yes. I'm only a few months from devising the means of gene transfer by mouth or nose. A pill or an inhaler, whichever is easier. When it's ready, I'll make it available to anyone who wants it."

Wes sat open-mouthed as Steiner wrapped up the proceedings. He was returning to New Hope, he said, where he planned a further an-nouncement on the prospects for mass distribution of his "product."

"You're going to have to revise your talking points," I said to Wes.

"I'll believe it when I see it," he said. "Nobody would give those things away." He turned his head toward me. "And people won't like it."

"Are you nuts? The people will love it."

"Not the people I'm talking about."

Moments later, we stepped outside. Wes turned in the direction of the West End Mosque, and I headed east. The coroner was behind his desk at the courthouse. "Do you still have the reports Steiner sent you?"

"Yes."

"Can you make me copies?"

He frowned. "They're all at least 50 pages."

"Let me borrow the originals then."

He hesitated. "Okay. I keep them in a binder."

"Great."

Outside again, I turned toward the office. Classes were almost over and there was no game this week, but the Greek houses were decorated in New Orleans themes, and the weekend kegs had already been tapped.

Steiner's reports were kept in chronological order. The first couple of pages provided personal information about the parents, followed by copies of the consent forms they had signed and transcripts of their interviews with him. Next came pages and pages of what appeared to be computer code, formulae and calculations. The last section of each was text interspersed with charts and diagrams.

The parents were almost all people of limited means without children and, unlike Abigail Sloan, at the end of their child-bearing years. They had exhausted themselves and their resources trying to have kids, and in every case Steiner's fee was waived. The interviews were tough to read – hard, technical jargon on one side, sad, sometimes desperate pleas on the other.

The computer code, of course, was meaningless, but I turned the pages anyway. It was all 1s and 0s – the first line of the first report began "10 101010 00100 10101 11011," and continued in a similar vein for 22 pages. The only different number in the whole thing was the last one – "9." The first number on the next report was "9," and the last was "8." That sequence continued in the others. The first number on the most recent report – the Spiller boy – was "2," and the last was "1."

The pages of text were typed on a form entitled "NECROPSY." The first report was for "Subject No. 10," who was implanted in her mother's body on January 2, 2002. She was born September 12, 2002 and died three months later. Subject No. 9 was conceived in Steiner's clinic in February of 2002 – he also died at three months. Six more began as embryos at the clinic – one a month from March to August, 2002 – and died as infants or small children. Subject No. 3, a little girl, was just past her second birthday when she died in early April, 2005.

The Spillers' son was Subject No. 2. He was conceived on April 10, 2005, and died in August of 2010. I tried to sift the verbiage and couldn't translate it. There was a lot of talk about vectors and chromosomes and genes that meant nothing to me. I skipped the formulae and calculations and tried to parse the diagrams.

One in particular, a page appended to the end of all nine reports, caught my eye. It was composed of circles numbered 1 to 22, and one more labeled "X/Y." Inside each circle except "X/Y" were two roughly identical elongated "worms" or cylinders. The "X/Y" worms didn't resemble each other. I recognized it all as a representation of the chromosomes and DNA found in the human body. Beneath that was a larger circle labeled "cell," with all 23 pairs of chromosomes inside.

The first eight reports depicted the strands of DNA with colored bands that changed from page to page, and the cell was punctured by "arrows," some red and some green, called "vectors." The Spiller child's report was the same except for one thing: Instead of 23 pairs of chromosomes, there were 24. If the scientists said we had only 23, and the Spiller boy was assembled in Steiner's lab with 24, something was wrong. And why were the subjects numbered from 10 to 2 instead of the other way around? Who was Subject No. 1?

I called out. "Abby."

She stuck her head in the door. "Yes, sir?"

"What day was it you – became pregnant?"

She smiled and stepped into the room. "The date?"

"Yes."

"August 31. Why?"

"What day of the week was that?"

"Tuesday."

"So that makes you what? Four months?"

"Yes, sir. A little less."

I cleared my throat. "I'm applying for the job of godfather. I hope you'll give it serious consideration."

She bent to kiss me on the cheek. "No further applications will be accepted."

"Great. Thanks."

She smiled again, and returned to her desk. I looked back at the report. The Spillers' son died on August 21. The body was delivered to Steiner one day before Abby's early embryo – one not yet divided into body and sex cells – was implanted in her womb. The whole thing – nine sets of parents destroyed by the calculated destruction of their helpless children – was sickening. What were the prospects for Subject – Subjects – No. 1?

The report for Subject No. 2 was not among the papers that Steiner had turned over to Missy. I removed it from the binder and walked into the outer office. "Would you make a copy of this, please," I said. "Have it delivered to Missy Farrell."

Abby's phone rang. "Mr. Monmouth's office," she said. "Yes, sir." She looked at me. "Cosmo Ender."

I returned to my office, and picked up the re-ceiver. "Yes?"

"We have processed the strands of hair," he said. "In terms of her life, where do you wish to go?"

"The end. The very end."

Teddy Black had not yet been identified, but the secrets of Teddy Black had been revealed, and Alex's anonymous rejuvenation was now part of the scientific discourse. But three women were dead – four if you counted Helen as an unintended conse-quence – and the search for their killer was tepid at best. Cosmo Ender had agreed to help.

THIRTEEN

ENDER HAD seriously underestimated the public's response to Steiner's press conference. Most of the regular media treated it as a curiosity, something on which their "experts" could opine, and most of those were skeptical. The social media, however – the bloggers, the tweeters, the ordinary people who now had an audience – were already lining up to become young again. Excursions to New Hope, thousands of them, were planned for his next appearance on Wednesday night.

The country's "newspaper of record" and one of the network news programs had a different take. They wondered editorially if "ordinary" people were ready for the responsibilities imposed by superior genes and long life. Current resources were finite – perhaps only a few proven leaders in various fields should be allowed the treatment at first. If Steiner's process was real, regulation was necessary. Government should step in.

The most startling aspect of the public reaction was the utter absence of fear. Even the few naysayers couched their objections in philosophical or religious terms. Some worried what God would say, but no one questioned what Man might do. When the piper called the tune, the children would follow, regardless of where his path might lead.

So far, the connection between Steiner and Teddy Black had not been made, but the comparison of Teddy to Steiner's "superman" was just a matter of time. Two big stories – the national championship game and Steiner's treatment – were all over the Internet. Teddy resided at Spencer Hall, two miles from the temple on the hill. The local media had remained studiously silent.

Alex and I stepped onto the elevator. "Are you sure you want to go through with this?" she said.

"Sure. Why not?"

"It's still experimental, isn't it?"

"They've done it before. Ender said it was like being there." The elevator stopped. We turned left, away from Steiner's office.

"But, still –"

"I'm only going to be here an hour or so." I smiled. "And you'll be watching over me."

Ender met us at the door to his office. "Are you sure you want to do this?" he said. "It's still experimental." I laughed out loud and so did Alex. "Really," he said. "Something might go wrong."

"I'll chance it."

"Our Memories Lab is across the hall."

It wasn't really a laboratory at all. The room was round and without windows. The wall and ceiling were white, and a thick white carpet covered the floor. The only furniture was a sleek leather chair, much like a first class seat on an old 747, which could be adjusted to several positions. A stiff, leather cap was attached to the top.

"Sit down," Ender said. "Get as comfortable as you can." I complied. He stared at me. "You will find this – unsettling because nothing in your experience has prepared you for it." He paused. "This is Ms. Clarke's memory. For all intents and purposes you will be her."

"Meaning?"

"Conjure up a memory of your own and try to imagine someone else remembering it. It's disturbing. Even more so because she was a woman."

"Why's that?" Alex said.

"We all have implicit, or reflexive, memories we carry with us. Emotions, things we know by rote, the routines of life. They can't be separated from the specific episode Harry will experience because they are part of that memory. Men and women live very different lives." He looked at me. "And you're making a memory of your own at the same time. It's jarring, to say the least."

"Will it interfere with what I want to see?" I said.

"It shouldn't. These are the last memories of her life, maybe the most potent she ever collected. It should be very vivid. And remember: Whatever period of time was actually involved, the memory will be short. We've enhanced it, but you won't experience the actual event. Only her recollection of it."

"Okay."

"One other thing. You may lose consciousness at some point."

"Why?"

"We don't know. Maybe to keep your brain from overcooking. You'll have a large portion of her life in your head."

"Does it go away?"

"We don't know that either. It seems to fade in and out." He gestured toward the chair. "The

cap and chair have sensors." Pointing to a translucent panel on the other side of the room, he said,
"We'll be in there monitoring your neurons." He
drew an inhaler from his coat pocket, and held it
up. "These cells are empty except for her memory
genes. Hold it over your mouth and nose, squeeze
and inhale."

I watched them disappear behind the panel.
It seemed like only yesterday Alex and I were arguing about the morality of all this. We'd come a long
way since without further debate. I slipped on the
cap and raised the inhaler to my face.

*Moonlight streamed through the windows into the darkened room, pale illumination that contrasted with the bright, dense glow of the fire. The
only sound was the crackle of the flames, the only
scent the burning oak. Despite the fire, the carefully prepared chamber was cold. The clock chimed 10
times.*

*I stumbled to the window, and closed the
drapes. Behind me, a million miles away, I heard
the door open and close. Tears, unnoticed before,
wet my face. The love was almost hate, but nirvana – fleeting, urgent – was close at hand. I drew a
box from the bedside table, and found the instruments of my salvation.*

*The needle pierced the bulging blue vein. In
seconds that seemed like hours, the poison made its
way across the blood-brain barrier, and the pain
began to recede. The hurtful words and scalding
emotions faded, replaced by the false serenity I
needed so badly. My lids grew heavy and my head
nodded. Somewhere in the distance, I heard footsteps. I tried to open my eyes.*

A man stood in the doorway. I knew him, but why was he here? How did he get in? I tried to speak and couldn't.

He was standing beside me. I lifted a hand, but he pushed it away. He opened my robe and touched me. The cold fingers squeezed and probed and stroked. I couldn't move. Helpless, I closed my eyes and endured it.

The caresses stopped. His voice came from far away: "I think you need a boost, Samantha." I forced my eyes open. He held the syringe, wrapped now in a handkerchief, close to my face. "I believe this will do." He plunged the needle into my arm. Another burst of pleasure, agreeable and agonizing at the same time, swept over me . . .

I OPENED my eyes. I felt again his hands on my body – her body – and shuddered. The last, calamitous seconds in her brain, followed immediately by a near-cataclysm in mine, had left me insensible. I became aware of someone standing over me, and lifted my head.

"Harry?" Alex said. I straightened in the chair, and tried to smile. "Thank God. I thought you were dead."

"I think I was. For a second."

"What was it like?" said Ender.

"Like nothing I ever want to do again."

"Did you get what you were looking for?" he said.

"Part of it." My journey into Samantha's memory had revealed the killer's identity, but the evidence I hoped to find was missing. My account of her last few minutes would never be allowed in court. I needed something else.

"Are you sure you're okay?" Alex said. I nodded. Her cellphone rang. "Hello?" A pause. "He's with me, but he can't talk right now." She listened again.

"Who is it?" I said.

"Abby. She says Missy's been calling all morning."

"Let me have it." I spoke into the phone. "Did she say what she wanted?"

"No," Abby said. "She just needs to speak to you as soon as possible."

"Tell her I'll drop by her office." I looked at my watch. "In about half an hour."

Alex was shaking her head. "I think you need some rest. Why don't you come home with me? You can call Missy later."

The irony was depressing. "No, thanks. I can drag these old bones around town a little while longer."

"Come home when you're through," she said. "Okay?"

"Okay." I hesitated. "I have something I want to run by Cosmo. I'll see you in an hour or two."

She left us in the hallway. Ender and I sat down in his office. "You watched that press conference, I suppose?" He nodded. "What about this germ cell business?" His face went blank. "Do you know about his – experiments? Who's Subject No. 1?" There was no answer. I leaned toward him. In my mind I told him that if something happened to Abby or her children, I would raise heaven and hell to see Steiner prosecuted for something. What I actually said, with as much menace as I could muster, was, "I hope nothing goes wrong."

He was unimpressed. "I'll pass it along."

Moments later, I climbed the hill to High Street. The bars and restaurants were nearly deserted, buttoned up against the cold. The few students shuffling up and down the street were dressed like it was still August, and trash from a street party – staged to send the football team off to New Orleans – whirled in the wind like confetti. I'd never seen New Hope so ugly.

I pushed through a door on the south side of High, and climbed familiar stairs. Missy's office had once been the den of a man close to me, closer than anyone knew. The burial plots at the cemetery had been chosen because of him. He was a man of integrity, and I hoped he wasn't watching.

The décor had changed. Instead of the unadorned chaos – hardwood floors and bare walls with files and drawings and stacks of loose paper everywhere – there was calm. It was soft carpet and fabrics, wallpaper with a tasteful legal motif, and not a scrap of paper anywhere except a short pile I recognized as Steiner's report on Subject No. 2. I looked around the room. "I can still smell his cigar."

Missy smiled. "I know. I've stopped trying to get rid of it." She picked up the report. "This is criminal."

"Maybe."

"What do you mean, 'maybe'? He was experimenting on the child. It's monstrous."

"Have you read the forms your clients signed?" She nodded. "Would you agree that the word 'experimental' shows up in practically every paragraph?"

"Yes, but –"

"Do you think the Sheriff or the County At-torney would charge Steiner in the face of that agreement? That they could ever prove what he did was criminal? Or even negligent?" She didn't answer. "Have you heard about this age reversion thing he plans to give away? And the other stuff?" She nodded again. "Who's going to get in the way of that?"

She fell back in her chair. "It's not right, Harry. You know it's not right."

I knew it better than she. I knew that eight more children had been "experiments," but I wasn't going to do anything about it. I needed Steiner. "Maybe not. But life gets cheaper all the time." I rose and turned for the door.

"Harry?" I looked back. "I sent Joe Spiller a copy of this report. He'll be very unhappy."

"He won't know what it means."

She shook her head. "He'll know enough."

I stopped by the office on the way home. "A woman named Catherine Edwards called," Abby said, handing me the message slip. "She wants you to call her."

Cat answered after the first ring. "Where are you?" I said.

"New Orleans. Have you heard about your friend Steiner?"

"Yes. Has Teddy?"

"I don't think so. Not yet. A reporter stopped me in the lobby a few minutes ago." She paused. "I'm going to tell him, Harry."

"Who? Teddy?"

"Yes. I don't want him to see it in some newspaper."

"Well, that's probably —"

"I wanted you to know in case something happened. How's Mother?"

"She's fine. Her treatment starts Thursday." I waited for a response and received none. "Cat?"

"I'm glad for her, Harry, but – I don't think it's worth it."

It began to snow as I trudged up the hill. I, too, questioned my bargain with Missy's devil. I had once viewed Steiner and his ilk as "mad scientists" bent on unleashing unfathomable misery on the rest of humanity, but he and his colleagues were actually just businessmen filing patent applications and selling drugs, commerce that would have been banal had it not been so consequential. The prospective pot of gold was incalculable – the profits that might flow, after the philosophers gave way, were beyond anything that had gone before. But Steiner wasn't interested in gold. He was after something else.

In the beginning I just wanted Alex to get well, consequences be damned, but Steiner had gone beyond that. Rather than object to his meddling, we embraced it, and now I was in the balance. Any apostasy on my part and the years I'd been promised – the ones Alex and I would share – would be withdrawn.

And what was true for me was true for everyone. Yes, he said he would give the years to whoever wanted them, and he probably would, but at what price? He didn't want money, he wanted souls. Lucifer was once an angel. If he didn't play God, who would?

Resistance was unlikely. Even now, after divining the cost, the notion of forfeiting those years was unthinkable. Alex was right. My life belonged to Steiner now.

An incidental side effect of the Teddy Black experiment was the death of three women – Samantha, Helen and Anita. Steiner's creature had stirred passions in ordinary men, and the threat of exposure that might destroy Teddy was intolerable.

But it was a fourth woman, Vera Carr, who was the key. Her death had nothing to do with Teddy, but her killer's motivation was the same. I'd seen him in Samantha's mind, but evidence was still necessary.

FOURTEEN

I **LIFTED** the half-eaten plate of food and carried it to the sink. After pouring a glass of brandy, I returned to the dining room table and watched Alex finish her dinner. She had regained her appetite along with everything else. Her sleep was sound, and she woke refreshed. Her steps were no longer tentative, her voice no longer weak. "Let's talk about the future," I said.

She paused, fork in mid-air, and laid it down. "All right."

We had avoided the future because it required that we face some unpleasant truths. Alex would have to acknowledge, to herself at least, that engineered genes weren't so bad after all, and she had no intention of going back. That, in turn, would force her to confront what I already understood: I was less than she, and undeserving of her.

It wasn't just that she was younger than me – there were plenty of May-December marriages around town. She also had the benefits of age – knowledge, judgment, memories – and the vigor to take advantage of them. Without Steiner's magic, my contributions to our life together would be redundant first, then obsolete. Alex would abide with me, but she would chafe at the limitations.

I hadn't mentioned Steiner's grant of years, and I didn't know why. She'd been silent in the face of his announcement. "Ender says Steiner will make me young," I said. "What do you think?"

She hesitated. "I've loved you for 30 years, Harry. I still love you. Nothing will change that."

"Till death do us part?"

She smiled. "Yes."

"But you have no preference as to how soon that might be?"

She paused again. "I'm afraid."

"Why?"

"I'm a freak. I'm younger than my children, and all my friends are older than me." She looked away. "And so are you."

"Steiner says he's going to fix all that."

"Yes, but what if he doesn't? Or what if he does? Will we pop a pill every few years to stay alive forever? Vampires stumbling about in the daylight?"

"I'm sure we'll have to adjust."

She nodded. "I'm adjusting already. I've counted on death all my life, and now it doesn't matter. I have all the time in the world. More, maybe." She paused. "What am I going to do with it? There's no need to plan for tomorrow. There's no *need* to do anything." She rose and pushed in her chair. "And if there's something beyond death, I'll never know it."

"So – you'd reverse the years if you could?"

She shook her head. "I didn't say that. I may be one of the vampires. That's why I'm afraid."

THE STREETS were packed, and the people were still pouring into town. It was a pilgrimage, and Steiner was the Messiah. A perimeter of saw-horses and yellow tape, supplemented by armed policemen posted at intervals, had been established around his temple, and the humanity that radiated from it numbered in the tens of thousands. Television cameras, including one operated from a blimp overhead, recorded the scene for those who couldn't be there.

New Hope's reaction was mixed. The College was playing for the national championship in three days, and it seemed to some that should be the focus of attention. But New Orleans was 900 miles away, and a crowd larger than the one that would gather in the dome was right here. The outcome was a foregone conclusion anyway – the College was favored by five touchdowns.

I switched off the TV, and debated whether or not to brave the masses. The spectacle won out, and I walked down the hill. At the office, I leaned in the door to see if Abby wanted to join me. "Someone's waiting to see you," she said in a hushed voice.

Frank Steiner was sitting behind my desk. He rose as I entered the room. "We have business, Harry."

He sat down again, and I took a chair across from him. "Business?"

He nodded. "We have patents to file. Ten of them. No, eleven."

"I'm not a patent lawyer, Frank."

"But you know one?"

I considered. "Yes. A guy I went to school with is the best in the business."

"Trustworthy?" I nodded. "Good." He pushed a leather briefcase toward me. "It's all in there." He stood up. "Take care of it. It's the only written record there is." I lifted my brows. He pointed to the side of his head. "I keep it here, too. The important parts."

"What do you want patents for? I thought you were giving all this away?"

"I am, but I'm going to do it my way. I don't want any interference."

He crossed to the door. "Frank?"

"Yes?"

"We need to discuss a few things. Do you mind?"

He hesitated, then returned to his chair. "Well?"

I lined them up in order of moment. "Why Alex?"

"I was finally ready to do the cancer therapy. She's a strong woman, and she had – beliefs. And she resisted."

"So?"

"She knew the treatment was more than a cure for her cancer. I could see it in her eyes when she came for her first injection." He stopped. "But she didn't mention it. I gave her every opportunity to say something." He smiled. "She didn't."

I nodded. "The white people in Project Sickle Cell. Did you do it on purpose?"

"Yes."

"Why?"

"They called me a racist. They said white people hate black people. I've given them a chance to find out if it's true."

"Can you fix it?"

He nodded. "If that's what they want." He leaned forward. "I'm guessing there'll be no takers.

It's they who hate the color of their skin, not me. They have a choice now."

We were quiet. He pushed up from the chair, and I waved him down. "Samantha Clarke called you right before she died, didn't she?"

"Yes."

"And she told you she knew all about Teddy Black?"

"Yes."

"And you called the Chancellor?" He nodded again. "Why?"

"I thought he should know."

"He didn't know before?"

"No."

"Didn't it matter to you? It was your secret."

He shook his head. "I'm done with Teddy. He's a relic now. I wanted to wait until Alex – Mrs. Monmouth – was finished to reveal him, but it made little difference to me." He paused. "I knew it would matter to the Chancellor."

"Were you surprised when Samantha died the next day?"

"A dope addict? Certainly not." He glanced at the clock. "Speaking of your wife, I know you're anxious to join her. I can begin your treatment any time you wish. As long as you keep your side of the bargain."

"Six months of silence?"

"Yes."

"Teddy's going to be discovered pretty soon no matter what I do."

"Teddy's not the important part."

He stood up again. "There's one more thing," I said. "I've seen the reports on Subjects 10 through 2. Who's Subject No. 1?"

He smiled. "You're very resourceful, Harry. I'm glad you're my lawyer." He pointed. "Subject No. 1 – two subjects, actually – are in the next room."

"What have you done?"

He resumed his seat once more. "You're familiar with what I've accomplished. The physical enhancements for Teddy, the age reversion for your wife. Disease eradication for both. The twins will have all that and more." He stopped. "But none of it solves the problem of their original genes." He paused again. "It's not the last word."

"What is?"

"A man or a woman whose DNA is perfect. Someone who's without flaw. The epitome of the human race."

"Superman?"

"That term has been discredited, but it's good shorthand."

"And Abby's twins will be the first?" He nodded. "How many will there be?"

"Enough."

"Enough to do what?" He didn't answer. "You've added another pair of chromosomes?"

"Two."

"Two?"

"I designed the 24th pair to cleanse the subject's own genes of defects. The 25th contains all the superman genes."

"Designed?"

"Created."

"From scratch?"

"Yes. The chromosomes are artificial. It's like software design using DNA code." He smiled again. "It's my finest achievement. Pretty soon, I can make anything I like. I won't need real human beings at all." He gestured toward the briefcase. "It's in there, too."

"This artificial DNA was added to Abby's embryo?"

"Yes."

"Meaning it'll be passed on to their children? And so on?" He nodded. "How do you know they'll survive? The other kids didn't."

"I tested billions of combinations on the computer. I was left with ten that required a sequence of live subjects. The twins are the culmination of all that."

"So – you knew the first nine would die?"

"Yes. Eggs to make omelets, you know. I needed their bodies to make the necessary adjustments."

I'd been under the spell of "science" until then, and I fought to conceal the revulsion. What would people designed by Frank Steiner be like? "Is that what the six months is really for?" He nodded. "What if I told Abby?"

He rose once more. "That would be too bad for you. I'm sure Mrs. Monmouth would be disappointed." He reached the door and looked back. "And what would you tell Abby? That in a few months she'll give birth to the two most accomplished beings in the history of mankind?" He laughed. "What would she do? End her pregnancy? Strangle her newborns?" He shook his head. "I don't think so." He pulled the door closed behind him.

I considered the future that Alex refused to contemplate. Was Steiner's world inevitable? Were we capable of rejecting it? And if not, who would be in charge? Would it be better for some faceless bureaucrat, ever more dismissive and corrupt, to decide who would live and how and for how long? Or should the brilliant man responsible for it be allowed to allocate his creations as he saw fit?

Like the Pope, Steiner had no divisions, but he was like the Pope in another sense as well: He promised eternal life, and his adherents, maybe billions of them, would follow him as long as the promise included them. Conflict was likewise assured.

I looked at the briefcase. It was everything Wes Vaughn had predicted. More, actually – Wes believed that science could only manipulate genes created by God, but now Steiner could make them. Eventually there might be more "creators," men or women still imbued with mankind's flaws, and "humans" would be unnecessary. What sort of "people" would they build? How would everyone get along?

I stepped outside. Steiner had filled the last gap in my evidence, but I still needed to figure out how it was done.

MIKE LOOKED up as I crossed the lobby. "Can I see your guest book?" I said. He pushed it toward me. "Thanks."

I looked at the first page. The initial entry was only four weeks earlier. "Do you have the one before this?" He opened a drawer and handed me another book, identical to the first. I found the day I wanted, the day before Samantha died. One name appeared twice. The first visit lasted less than 20 minutes, the second almost an hour. I turned the book around and pointed. "Do you re-member that day?"

He looked at the name. "Yes."

"He was here twice?" He nodded. "And he used your key?"

"Yes."

"Is it a master?" He nodded again. "Tell me what you remember about the second visit."

"He said he wanted to take some measure-ments and stuff. I gave him the key and he went up in the elevator."

"And stayed for an hour?"

He looked at the book. "I guess so. I didn't pay much attention."

"Can I keep this for a while? I'll bring it back."

"Well – okay."

"And – can I borrow your key for a few minutes?"

"Sure."

"Thanks." I checked my watch, then stepped onto the elevator. On the top floor, I used the key to call the garage elevator. At the bottom I emerged from the mailroom, walked through the parking garage, and turned east on Second Street. A cramped little hardware store on the corner of Second and Anderson had weathered the change. I opened the door, causing the bell to jingle, and crossed the threshold. The proprietor, a sour old man I'd known for years, appeared. "Good morn-ing, Mr. Macklin."

"Harry."

I drew the key from my pocket. "Can you make me a copy of this?"

He examined it for a moment and then, without speaking, turned around and fitted it into a machine with wheels and handles and a large gray dial. Next, he opened a drawer and sorted through a collection of blank keys. Choosing one, he slipped it into a slot next to the first one. I looked at my watch again. "How's business?" I said.

He grunted. "Terrible."

"These kids aren't much into nuts and bolts, I suppose?"

"No. They're not."

He made a few adjustments to the machine, and flipped a switch. Bits of metal fell away as it conformed the blank key to the original. After a few seconds, he removed both keys and – pressed together – held them up to the light. Not quite satisfied, he repeated the grinding operation. "Is there much call for keys?" I said.

"No."

"Ever see one like that?"

He didn't answer. Instead, he handed me the keys, opened an ancient account book and wrote out an invoice with my name on the top line. When he was finished, he tore it from the book and gave it to me. "That'll be $9.50," he said.

I reached for my wallet. "Does that book make carbons?" He nodded. "How long do you keep them?"

He stared at me. "Forever. Taxes." I felt his eyes on my back as I passed through the door. Minutes later, I used my new key to enter the mailroom at The High and take the garage elevator to the top floor. Opening Samantha's door, I stepped inside. According to my watch, the whole thing took 55 minutes.

The killer had followed the same path. He had acquired his new key the same way, and returned the original to Mike. The proof was tucked away in Mr. Macklin's account book, and it was likely the old man would recall the visit as well. When the killer was ready, he used the key to take the elevator from the mailroom to Samantha's floor and open the door.

Her memory had ended too soon, but I could imagine the rest. The killer had searched the apartment, coming away with her wallet and keys. He left via the garage elevator and walked the few paces to the *Chronicle,* where it was an easy matter to unlock the door and pilfer her laptop. And, because Anita Moore might reveal what she'd already told Samantha, her life was forfeit as well.

That left Vera. Among all those who knew of the corruption at the College, she was the only one willing to speak out, and she had to be silenced. The scandal of a football team that couldn't read had to be suppressed at all costs. After learning she'd been to see Jack, the killer followed her to Helen's house. He was the man Vera had seen in the window. My evidence, still thin but better than before, was complete.

FIFTEEN

AN IMMENSE moon, low in the winter sky, hung over Steiner's temple but did nothing to relieve the darkness. It was brick-red, and dull, an extraordinary circumstance that – judging from their words and signs – had drawn the prophets of Armageddon to the multitude on the hill. Or perhaps they had planned to attend anyway. A light snow was falling.

There was plenty of man-made illumination. Spotlights hung from the pillars, and floodlights stood at the bottom of the steps. Television cameras, unmanned now, were located just below the middle two columns, aimed at an upright microphone a few feet away.

Local personalities wandered through the throng with their own microphones, broadcasting eager predictions from Steiner's giddy flock. The scent of the humanity was suppressed by heavy clothing worn to ward off the cold, and a cloud of condensation hung over them. Songs and chants I couldn't understand broke out sporadically.

Those who feared the end of the world were far outnumbered by those who expected it to last forever. Surprisingly young, they were orderly but, as the time neared for Steiner to appear, they became increasingly agitated. A few fights were broken up by Jeff Farnham's deputies. The anticipation was palpable.

People fell away as Wes Vaughn – dressed again in robe and sandals – pushed through the crowd. I followed in his wake. We stopped at the perimeter where one of Jeff's men was stationed, 50 feet from the steps leading up to the temple. Suspicious, he stared at Wes, and nodded at me.

A moment later, the Sheriff stood beside us. "Any problems?" I said.

He shook his head. "Not really. It's amazing."

"What's the program?"

"The Chancellor's going to introduce Steiner in about five minutes."

I nodded. "When this is over, I need to speak to you about the Chancellor."

"What about him?"

"Let's wait till this is over."

"Okay." He turned his head. "There he is now." He squinted. "I think." He left us and approached a man who had just ducked under the yellow tape. They spoke to each other, and Jeff backed away. The man, wearing tweeds, a tie and desert boots, crossed the plaza and climbed the steps. When he reached the top, he turned and let his eyes sweep the crowd. Jeff's hesitation was understandable. Even from a distance, I could see that it *was* the Chancellor, perhaps 20 years younger than the last time I'd seen him.

A flurry of activity on the steps signaled the start of the proceedings. A woman adjusted the microphone, the lights were re-trained, and the cameramen moved behind their machines. The great, restive mass of people grew quiet. The snow fell harder.

"Ladies and gentlemen," the Chancellor began, "this is an unparalleled event in the history of the College. We have a man among us, a man without peer, who is single-handedly changing the course of humankind." He paused. "Not only has he devised a method to permit us to live longer, more fruitful lives, he asks for nothing in return."

It was clear from the Chancellor's tone that he found the second proposition more remarkable than the first. He turned and gestured to Steiner's fabulous temple. "I was skeptical when Frank Steiner showed me the plans for this building. The skeptic in me is gone. It's the perfect place for him and his work." He stopped again. "Ladies and gentlemen, I give you Doctor Frank Steiner."

Steiner stepped from the shadows. The absolute, unnatural silence from all those thousands of people seemed the most perfect tribute they could pay. Then it began. From deep within that vortex of humanity − low and high-pitched at the same time, growing always louder − came a primitive roar so intense it seemed to shake the massive temple at his back. No voice, no face, no individual could be distinguished from the great pulsating mob that surrounded him. He stood stiff and straight, and made no effort to stop it.

Finally, he raised a hand and the sound ceased as if turned off by a switch. His voice rang out over the loudspeakers: "We stand on the verge of a golden age. No longer bound by myth and superstition, we look forward to eons of ever-increasing wealth, prosperity and peace. And life." He paused. "Our fate will not be determined by priests or generals or politicians. True giants will walk the earth. Science has triumphed at last."

I felt Wes stir beside me, and moved closer to him. Steiner continued: "We don't just play with life anymore. We create it. New life forms dedicated to serving man are on the horizon." He stopped again, then leaned closer to the microphone. "If there ever was a God," he almost whispered, "He's dead now."

Enraged, Wes shook off my arm and broke through the tape. The debate at the Sunday Convocation flashed through my mind. The new order confronted the old once more, and there was no doubt about the outcome this time – this crowd wasn't here to pray. At the steps, Wes raised his staff and pointed. "You're a liar, Steiner," he shouted. "And a devil. Allah will strike you down." Cops from all sides rushed him as he turned to the crowd. "Don't listen to this man," he cried. "He's evil."

The people, paralyzed, watched in silence. The police seized Wes, and wrestled him to the ground. Out of the corner of my eye, I saw another figure racing across the plaza toward the temple. The dark and the snow made the black-and-white scene flicker and slow like an old newsreel. Steiner, joined by the Chancellor, had descended a couple of steps.

"Steiner," the new man screamed. He dropped an overcoat from his shoulders, revealing a bulky vest around his torso. "It's your turn to die." The twin barrels of a shotgun gleamed in the halo of light. A blast from the gun, followed quickly by another, rent the cold night air. Steiner fell, and the Chancellor dropped beside him. As the police ran toward them, the man climbed the steps and disappeared inside.

Seconds later, a terrible explosion boiled up from the temple and sent flames through the roof. Chunks of marble were hurled into the air and, as the people on the steps retreated, the great columns began to wobble and fall. The pediment fell away and crashed to the ground. A screen of dust and debris rose into the sky and, when it dispersed, only a handful of the pillars – some leaning, others twisted and broken – remained in place.

JOE SPILLER, the man with the gun and the bomb, was dead. Frank Steiner, who took the full force of the first blast in his chest, died instantly. Winfred Honeyman, struck in the throat, succumbed in the Emergency Room. It was unclear if the Chancellor's death was intentional, but he was no less dead for that. Science, Spiller's motive for the slaughter, had failed to save them.

Inexplicably, no one inside the temple – except Joe Spiller – died, though dozens were injured. Steiner's outraged acolytes – deprived, for the time being, of the prize they were promised – had surged over the campus. The shrines to commerce were defaced, the unfinished School of Human Enrichment burned to the ground, and High Street was looted. No one was accountable – Jeff Farnham's small force was helpless and, by the time the National Guard arrived, the mob had done its work and percolated back into the rest of the country. The pilgrims returned to their screens, and began the search anew.

Luminaries from the School of Applied Genetics – heretofore anonymous because of Steiner –

moved to take control of his papers, assuming any could be found amongst the rubble or elsewhere. They were opposed by Cosmo Ender who, represented by Missy Farrell, filed suit the day after Steiner died. Steiner's briefcase rested next to the black leather chair in my office.

I was Steiner now, and no one knew it. The briefcase contained all his secrets, including the "important parts" he'd carried in his head. If Ender was right, it would be generations before those procedures were recreated by someone else, years during which I – and the rest of humanity – would go without the fountain of youth unless Steiner's work was resurrected.

I leaned back in the chair, feet up on the ottoman. Storm clouds were gathering on another front. According to the *Chronicle*, Jack Peeler had notified the Organization of certain "irregularities" in the football team's "academic performance." No details were provided, but speculation was rampant, overshadowing news of the team's preparations for the big game.

There was talk of postponing the game because of the Chancellor's death, but the College and the network agreed he would want it to go on. They decided on a moment of silence instead. The ritual subordination of tragedy to commerce was business as usual, but it was undeniable that the game had been important to Winfred Honeyman. The reading scandal was part of it, but he'd killed three women, and hastened the death of a fourth, so the College could play – and win – tomorrow night.

The telephone rang five times and stopped. Abby had been deeply affected by Steiner's death, even though his part in her struggle for motherhood was over. She had no idea how much he had really altered her life, and it was easier to think about when she wasn't there.

I rose and stacked some wood and kindling in the grate. Seconds later, the well-seasoned oak was aflame. Someone else's memory of a fire – and a man approaching her bed – held me for a moment. Shaking it off, I considered Abby again. Part of me wanted to tell her, to let her decide. Another part said she wouldn't believe it, and still another said she wouldn't *want* to believe it. The least charitable voice – Steiner's echo – claimed that not only would she accept giving birth to supermen, she would welcome it.

Was she up to it? Abby's children would not burst forth from her body fully formed. Despite their unique characteristics, or perhaps because of them, they would need help, and who better than she to provide it? They were first a product of her determination to bring them into the world. If that resolve persisted after they were born, her love and devotion would be unstinting, perhaps a leavening of whatever Steiner had instilled. Maybe I could help.

"Harry?"

Alex stood in the doorway. She wore a thigh-length beaver coat I'd given her for Christmas. Sheer stockings on fine legs, well-turned ankles and black pumps were visible below the coat. She carried a bottle in one gloved hand, and a wicker hamper in the other.

Wes had called Steiner evil, and there were many reasons to think it was so, but I refused to include Alex among them. The last of his immortals, she was the only one who feared it. Despite her unease, she was determined to be the wife and mother she'd always been, albeit in a different – updated – package. The boys would be home in a few days, and we'd decided on the truth. Steiner's magic had been revealed to the world, and Alex was its incarnation.

"Where's Abby?" she said.

"I told her to go home." She set the hamper and bottle on my desk. Removing her gloves, she draped the coat over the chair, revealing a black dress with no back and not much front, and pearls. Her hair was pulled back in an elegant French knot, and she wore diamonds in her ears. I grinned. "What's the occasion?"

She sat in my lap. "Can't I dress up to have lunch with my husband?"

"Of course. Any time you like."

She kicked off her shoes and put her arms around my neck. "Virginia and Gerry left a few minutes ago."

"Good."

"What's going to happen to her now?"

"The disease therapy belongs to the American Pharmaceutical Association. I imagine she'll have to stand in line like everyone else." I paused. "Ender can pull some strings."

"What about the rest of it?"

"I don't know. With Steiner and the Chancellor gone, you're the only one left. What do *you* think?"

"I think – I think it's going to be a disaster."

"Why?"

"We've set ourselves apart from a world we still have to live in. The world will survive. I'm not sure we will." She stopped. "Steiner said he could create life. What comes after that?"

"I don't know." I paused. "Should we try to stop it?"

"How?" I didn't answer. "Nature won't stay the same, either. Viruses, famines, things we don't expect." She paused again. "We'll still have *human* nature, too. As long as we have humans."

"What about immortality?"

"There's only so much room. The babies will be the first to go." She stood up. "It seems counterproductive to me." She crossed to the desk and drew the champagne from its bag. As she removed the foil and wire from the neck, she said, "Species die out all the time, I guess. Only the tiniest brains last very long." She popped the cork. "There's a reason for that."

She found a couple of glasses, poured and handed me one. "Speaking of immortality," she said, "the old-fashioned kind, I have news. I'm pregnant." She reached behind her back and pulled the zipper down. The little black dress fell to the floor, revealing her firm, almost naked body. She took a sip of champagne, and came toward me.

Later, after an old-fashioned celebration, Alex packed the empty bottle in the hamper, and slipped into her coat. "Think of me as your second wife."

"No, thanks. I'm delighted with the first one." She turned for the door. "Alex?"

"Yes?"

"Ender said it could be reversed. Do you think you–?"

"Yes, Harry. If that's what you want." She looked back. "After the baby's born." She disappeared through the door.

I looked out the window. In truth, I didn't want Alex to be old again. I *was* delighted with my first wife. It was just a lame loyalty test, something I'd wrestled with myself, and she passed with flying colors. More serious trials awaited her.

After reviving the fire, I opened Steiner's briefcase. The trouble with men was Man. I couldn't save us from ourselves, but I could buy a little time – it was my turn to play God. Like the atheists at the Post Office, I had little faith in Man or God, but perhaps one of them would step up and we'd back away from the abyss.

I wept as the hungry flames devoured the magic. My young wife would have to look after me in my old age, and Abby's twins would have only each other.

THE QUARTERBACK looked up at the scoreboard as his team broke the huddle. This was the last play of the game, and the College was behind by four points. His voice, a single sharp syllable, was the only sound inside the great dome.

He took the snap at the 50-yard line and dropped five quick steps back, drifting further as he waited for his receivers to run downfield. Three tired defensive linemen made a show of rushing him – everyone else was in the end zone or racing toward it. The crowd rose, and roared as he flung the ball.

Teddy Black and Cat Edwards had vanished. An hour before kickoff, the College's head coach announced that Teddy had disappeared from the locker room, and it was assumed that Cat was with him. An all-points alert was broadcast across the state, and law enforcement of all stripes commissioned to find them, to no avail.

Anguish and consternation issued from New Hope to Las Vegas and beyond. Dark murmurs of kidnapping, and worse, went viral in the media. The game was a second thought when it began but, as it progressed and the College held its own, more attention was paid.

Teddy's back-up had seen a lot of action during the season, and his other teammates – who'd labored in his shadow since August – were determined that his absence not eclipse their effort. They turned the opposition away repeatedly, and managed to be within a single point by the middle of the fourth quarter, whereupon their opponents kept the ball for seven minutes and came away with a field goal.

The College had run a couple of short pass plays, advancing the ball to mid-field, and used up its time-outs. Victory now seemed unlikely. The nascent miracle was about to come up short.

The ball, stark against the white roof of the dome, spiraled through the conditioned air. As it fell, a knot of players leaped and tipped it backwards, toward the goal posts. Two more players, one clad in blue, the other in white, fought for it. The crowd, hushed again, held its breath . . .

THE END

ALAN THOMPSON

Born in Danville, Kentucky, on January 31, 1949, author Alan Thompson grew up in his beloved Chapel Hill, North Carolina. A 1966 graduate of Chapel Hill High School, he received his B.A. from the University of Kentucky in 1970, and his J.D. from the same institution in 1973.

He has practiced law for the past forty years, primarily in Atlanta, Georgia, and now resides in Georgetown, South Carolina.

Alan's civil trial work extended to dozens of jurisdictions throughout the United States, Australia and England, and he contributed to several professional journals and treatises dealing with his particular area of expertise, construction law.

He began writing fiction seriously in 2008, and his first novel, **A Hollow Cup**, was published in 2011. **The Black Owls** was released in 2013, followed by **The Kingfishers** and **Gods and Lesser Men**. He and his wife Barbie have two sons, one a lawyer in Salt Lake City, the other a Navy helicopter pilot currently stationed in Jacksonville Beach, Florida.

You can learn more about Alan and his work at his website, mindsonshelves.com.

Made in the USA
Charleston, SC
04 February 2015